Shakespeare: Text and Performance

SHAKESPEARE 1609
CYMBELINE AND THE
SONNETS

RICHARD DANSON BROWN AND
DAVID JOHNSON

in association with The Open University

This publication forms part of an Open University course: AA306, *Shakespeare: Text and Performance*. Details of this and other Open University courses can be obtained from the Course Reservations Centre, PO Box 724, The Open University, Milton Keynes MK7 6ZS, United Kingdom: tel. +44 (0)1908 653231, e-mail ces-gen@open.ac.uk

Alternatively, you may visit the Open University website at http://www.open.ac.uk where you can learn more about the wide range of courses and packs offered at all levels by the Open University.

To purchase this publication or other components of Open University courses, contact Open University Worldwide Ltd, The Berrill Building, Walton Hall, Milton Keynes MK7 6AA, United Kingdom: tel. +44 (0)1908 858785; fax +44 (0)1908 858787; e-mail ouwenq@open.ac.uk; website http://www.ouw.co.uk

First published in the United Kingdom in 2000 by
Macmillan Press Ltd in association with The Open University

Macmillan Press Ltd
Houndmills, Basingstoke, Hampshire RG21 6XS
and London
Companies and representatives throughout the world

The Open University
Walton Hall, Milton Keynes
MK7 6AA

A catalogue record for this book is available from the British Library

ISBN 0-333-91318-3 (hardback) – ISBN 0-333-91322-1 (paperback)

First published in the United States of America in 2000 by
St. Martin's Press, Scholarly and Reference Division,
175 Fifth Avenue, New York N.Y. 10010

ISBN 0-312-23037-0 (cloth) – ISBN 0-312-23038-9 (paperback)

Library of Congress Cataloging-in-Publication Data

Shakespeare 1609 : Cymbeline and the Sonnets/edited by Richard Danson Brown and David Johnson.
p.cm.
Includes bibliographical references and index.
ISBN 0-312-23037-0 (cloth) – ISBN 0-312-23038-9 (pbk.)
1. Shakespeare, William, 1564-1616. Cymbeline. 2. Shakespeare, William, 1564-1616. Cymbeline – Sources.
3. Shakespeare, William, 1564-1616. Sonnets. 4. Shakespeare, William, 1564-1616. Sonnets – Sources. 5.
Sonnets, English – History and criticism. 6. Britons in literature. 7. Canon (Literature) I. Brown, Richard
Danson. II. Johnson, David, 1962 May 20- III. Title.

PR2806 . S5 2000
822.3'3–dc21

99-055778
CIP

Copyright © 2000 The Open University

This book is printed on paper suitable for recycling and made from fully managed and sustained forest sources.

Edited, designed and typeset by The Open University

Printed and bound in the United Kingdom by The Bath Press, Bath

008678B/aa306b2i1.1

1.1

To the memory of Tony Coulson 1944–2000

CONTENTS

Preface

Shakespeare 1609: 'Cymbeline' and the 'Sonnets' is the second book of a three-volume series designed for the third-level Open University course *Shakespeare: Text and Performance*. This book explores how Shakespeare has been interpreted since his death in 1616 by focusing on two texts first published or performed in about 1609: the play *Cymbeline* and *Shakespeare's Sonnets*. As well as being roughly contemporaneous, these texts have had a more controversial reception than Shakespeare's major plays. *Cymbeline* has been widely neglected, while *Shakespeare's Sonnets* was largely ignored by the seventeenth-century reading public, only to be enthusiastically embraced by more recent generations.

The material in *Shakespeare 1609: 'Cymbeline' and the 'Sonnets'* is divided into two parts:

> critical discussion of *Cymbeline* and *Shakespeare's Sonnets*, which considers their common historical context in 1609; the varied ways in which they have been interpreted by subsequent generations; their generic distinctiveness; and their complex representations of sexuality;

> sources and analogues for both *Cymbeline* and *Shakespeare's Sonnets*, as well as key interpretations of both texts by influential critics.

Shakespeare 1609: 'Cymbeline' and the 'Sonnets' is best read in conjunction with the other two books for the course *Shakespeare: Text and Performance*. The first book, *Shakespeare: Texts and Contexts*, provides critical introductions to nine of Shakespeare's major plays, and the many contexts in which they have been produced. The nine plays are: *A Midsummer Night's Dream, Richard II, Macbeth, Antony and Cleopatra, Hamlet, Twelfth Night, Measure for Measure, King Lear* and *The Tempest*. The third book, *A Shakespeare Reader: Sources and Criticism*, supplements *Shakespeare: Texts and Contexts*, and contains sources and analogues used by Shakespeare for the nine plays, as well as a substantial collection of exemplary Shakespeare criticism from the last 70 years.

Designed both for Open University students doing *Shakespeare: Text and Performance* and the general reader seeking an accessible route into contemporary Shakespeare studies, these three course books are intended to be read together with *The Norton Shakespeare* (edited by S. Greenblatt, W. Cohen, J.E. Howard and K.E. Maus, W.W. Norton, New York and London, 1997). Quotations from Shakespeare's works in the first two books are taken from this edition and the introductions, commentary and supplementary primary material are referred to extensively. Selections of sources and criticism reproduced in this second volume and the Reader consciously avoid repeating material contained in *The Norton Shakespeare*. We have changed or added act/scene/line references from Shakespeare's plays in all the extracts to coincide with *The Norton Shakespeare*, although we have retained the spelling and punctuation of the original. Finally, we have taken the difficult decision to suppress footnotes and references in the extracts. Faced with the choice of either reprinting the footnotes, or being able to include several more critical voices, we opted for the latter in the belief that our primary audience, undergraduate students, would thus be better served.

Open University courses undergo many stages of drafting and review, and thanks are accordingly due to a number of people for their invaluable contributions to the final product: Lizbeth Goodman and Stephen Regan, who chaired the course for much of its development; Robert Doubleday and Roberta Wood, who were the course managers for the duration; Julie Bennett and Gill Marshall, who were the course editors; Robert Gibson, who was the compositor; Tony Coulson, who was the picture researcher; and Pat Phelps, who was the course secretary. Finally, Michael Scott, the course assessor, gave sage guidance at crucial moments in the evolution of the course.

Richard Danson Brown and David Johnson

CRITICAL
DISCUSSION

CYMBELINE

Chapter 1

David Johnson

Aims

Our first aim in studying *Cymbeline* is to understand the textual complexities of the play in relation to its original context in the London of 1609. We shall also trace the reception history of *Cymbeline*, and reflect in some detail on the reasons for its modest position in the Shakespeare canon. The balance of the chapter examines three controversial aspects of *Cymbeline* that have divided critics and theatre practitioners since its first performance: its generic classification; its representation of differences in gender and sexuality; and its representation of British national identity.

Introduction

In the twentieth century, *Cymbeline* has been performed infrequently, and it has only on rare occasions been included in school literature syllabuses. Compared to the familiar greats in the Shakespeare canon – *Hamlet, King Lear, Macbeth* – it has been sorely neglected, and only determined Shakespeare enthusiasts are familiar with the play. Whereas characters, scenes and lines from many of Shakespeare's works have entered popular culture, we are unlikely to see knowing beer advertisements borrowing lines from *Cymbeline*, or a Holywood film weaving a storyline through the complicated fabric of *Cymbeline*'s plot. Recent evidence of *Cymbeline*'s absence from popular consciousness is provided in the paperback *Classic FM Favourite Shakespeare* selected by the celebrated actor Derek Jacobi. In 200 pages of quotable passages from Shakespeare, there is no mention of *Cymbeline*. The play's fate at the hands of academics has been little better. The *Modern Languages Association Citation Index*, an annual catalogue of all academic publications, provides the following totals. In the last 15 years, *Hamlet* has been the subject of some 933 publications; *King Lear* follows with 484; the rest of the plays average around 300; and *Cymbeline* trails forlornly with 64. Why has *Cymbeline* suffered such neglect? The causes for its lukewarm reception lie in the nature of the play itself, but also crucially in the critical tastes of generations of Shakespeare audiences. It is with them that we commence our enquiry.

In order to familiarize yourself with the characters and main plot of *Cymbeline*, read quickly through the play now. Detailed close analysis of the text is unnecessary at this stage, as our first concern is to establish how audiences and critics have responded to *Cymbeline* since its first performance. **As you read through the history of *Cymbeline*'s reception that follows, note down both what aspects of the play critics have praised and what they have disliked about it.**

Reception history

A precise dating of the first ever performance of *Cymbeline* has proved difficult, but most editors of the text now agree that it is likely to have been premièred at some time between the autumn of 1609, when the theatres reopened after an outbreak of the plague, and the summer of 1610. Some indication of how *Cymbeline* was received by its first audiences is provided by the astrologer Simon Forman, who kept a private memorandum book, where he set down his impressions of a number of Shakespeare's plays. Although he does not specify when and where he saw the performance of *Cymbeline*, scholars agree that he would most probably have seen it at the Blackfriars playhouse in April or May 1611. (Forman's account is reprinted on page 3337 of *The Norton Shakespeare* (Greenblatt *et al.*, 1997).) Forman does not say whether he likes the play or not, instead providing a detailed summary of the plot. Judging from the sequence of his summary, and the amount of detail allocated to the different aspects of the plot, however, what appears to have captured Forman's attention most firmly is the political theme relating to Cymbeline's refusal to pay the tribute to Rome. The only other comment on an early performance of *Cymbeline* we have is that of King Charles I, who saw the play performed at court on 1 January 1634. According to the Master of the Revels, it was 'well liked by the King' (Warren, 1998, p.6).

After a promising start, *Cymbeline* suffered what was to become a protracted if uneven decline, beginning in the latter half of the seventeenth century. At the time of the Restoration in 1660, Shakespeare's standing as a playwright was modest. A new theatre company based at the open-air Red Bull Theatre included only four of his plays in its repertoire of 20 in 1660, and another smaller company based at the Phoenix Theatre in Drury Lane performed only one, *Pericles*. In the next 40 years, there was some improvement in Shakespeare's popularity, although he continued to be eclipsed by his competitors. John Dryden's remarks in *Of Dramatic Poesy: An Essay* (1668) illustrate the characteristic preferences of Restoration audiences. He concedes that of his contemporaries Shakespeare had 'the largest and most comprehensive soul', but goes on to complain that 'He is many times flat, insipid; his comic wit degenerating into clenches, his serious swelling into bombast' (Kirsch, 1966, p.47). Dryden writes that, by contrast, the dramatists Francis Beaumont and John Fletcher

> had, with the advantage of Shakespeare's wit, which was their
> precedent, great natural gifts improved by study ... Their plots were
> generally more regular than Shakespeare's ... and they understood and
> imitated the conversation of gentleman much better ... Their plays are
> now the most pleasant and frequent entertainments of the stage; two of
> theirs being acted through the year for one of Shakespeare's or Jonson's:
> the reason is because there is a certain gaiety in their comedies, and
> pathos in their more serious plays, which suits generally with all men's
> humours.

> (Kirsch, 1966, p.48)

When he moves on to compare Shakespeare to Ben Jonson, Dryden declares the latter to be 'the most learned and judicious writer which any theatre ever had' (Kirsch, 1966, p.48), but concludes with more even-handed praise: 'I must acknowledge [Jonson] the more correct poet, but Shakespeare the greater wit.

Shakespeare was the Homer, or father of our dramatic poets; Jonson was the Virgil, the pattern of elaborate writing; I admire him, but I love Shakespeare' (Kirsch, 1966, p.49).

The reasons for Shakespeare's muted acclaim were therefore twofold. On the one hand, there were those who agreed with Thomas Rymer, who attacked Shakespeare in *A Short View of Tragedy* (1693) for failing to curb his linguistic extravagance, and to satisfy the aesthetic requirements of neo-classicism. On the other hand, the taste of Restoration audiences was for plays of elaborate courtly intrigue, both sexual and political. Performed before aristocratic audiences, the most popular plays were those involving cavalier male figures of dubious intent and resourceful women characters embroiled in sexually charged plots. As Dryden suggests, Shakespeare's plays were comparatively limited in this respect, and the works of Beaumont and Fletcher, and of Restoration playwrights like Aphra Behn and William Wycherley, accordingly enjoyed greater favour.

An adaptation of *Cymbeline* in 1682 by Thomas Durfey sub-titled *The Injured Princess: or The Fatal Wager* shows how Shakespeare's perceived inadequacies were 'corrected' to suit Restoration tastes. In 1681, Nahum Tate had revised *King Lear* to pander to the anxieties of Charles II, with Lear at the end going into peaceful retirement, and Edgar and Cordelia marrying and ruling Britain. For Durfey, also a devout Royalist, *Cymbeline* did not require quite such drastic revision: the play already had a monarch restored to power, and an attractive princess happily married off in the final act. Durfey's changes to *Cymbeline* were therefore directed principally to the characterization: Posthumus becomes Ursaces, a worthy but dull hero; Innogen becomes Eugenia, a long-suffering heroine; Cloten retains his name, but is transformed into an 'over-the-top' Restoration bully; and Giacomo becomes Shattillion, a cynical libertine rake. Catering to the Restoration love of sexual intrigue, *The Injured Princess* downplays the political themes in *Cymbeline*, and Posthumus/Ursaces's final speech celebrates a retreat into a romanticized private realm:

> So Love, the bless'd Physician of the Mind,
> Heals all my Griefs, immortal Joys I find,
> And Heaven on Earth, whilst my *Eugenia*'s kind.

> (Dobson, 1992, p.90)

The eighteenth century saw a marked improvement in Shakespeare's fortunes, as Gary Taylor wryly notes:

> Everyone agrees that, after a slow but steady upward climb,
> Shakespeare's coronation as the King of English Poets finally occurred in
> the middle of the eighteenth century, at some time between the death of
> Alexander Pope (1744) and the birth of William Wordsworth (1770); or,
> to put it another way, between the second Jacobite rebellion (1745) and
> the first year of Lord North's ministry (1770), which would precipitate
> and then lose the war in America.

> (1989, p.114)

Taylor's yoking together of dates of literary and political import for Britain is significant because Shakespeare's works, and *Cymbeline* in particular, were much preoccupied in this period with British national interests. Charles Marsh's and

William Hawkins's versions of *Cymbeline* in 1759, written during the Seven Years' War with France, responded to the upsurge in nationalist sentiment, although they were mindful of Rymer's insistence on the need for obedience to the principles of classical aesthetics. Critics of *Cymbeline* continued to draw attention to the play's failings in this regard. Writing in 1753, Samuel Johnson's friend Charlotte Lennox complained: 'The whole conduct of the Play is absurd and ridiculous to the last Degree, and with all the Liberties *Shakespeare* has taken with Time, Place and Action the Story, as he has managed it, is more improbable than a Fairy Tale' (Vickers, 1976, p.122). Johnson's own assessment of the play published in the following decade was similarly damning. After noting flaws and inconsistencies in the characterization, he concludes:

> To remark the folly of the fiction, the absurdity of the conduct, the confusion of the names and manners of different times and the impossibility of the events in any system of life, were to waste criticism upon unresisting imbecility, upon faults too evident for detecting and too gross for aggravation.
>
> (Woudhuysen, 1989, p.235)

With these strictures in mind, Hawkins notes in the Preface to his adaptation of *Cymbeline* that the play is 'one of the most irregular productions of *Shakespeare*' (Vickers, 1976, p.374). As correctives, he changes the play, first, to celebrate what is 'truly *British* in the subject of it', and secondly, 'to new-construct this Tragedy almost upon the plan of *Aristotle* himself' (Vickers, 1976, p.374). Hawkins accordingly changes Shakespeare's version of the war between Britain and Rome: Hawkins's Cloten is a secret defector to the Romans; Giacomo (confusingly renamed Pisanio) is a Roman secret agent commissioned by Cloten to seduce Innogen; and the play ends not with Cymbeline obediently paying tribute to Augustus, but with complete victory for the Britons over Rome. The Epilogue offers a contemporary reference, and approves the marriage of Posthumus and Innogen:

> You can't for shame condemn old British wit,
> (I hope there are no Frenchmen in the pit)
> Or slight a timely tale, that well discovers,
> The bravest soldiers are the truest lovers.
>
> (Vickers, 1976, p.392)

David Garrick's popular production of *Cymbeline* two years later returned to Shakespeare's original text, but, crucially, suppressed Cymbeline's decision to pay tribute to the Romans. As Michael Dobson puts it, in their productions of *Cymbeline* Hawkins and Garrick are ratifying 'not the Pax Romana, but the Pax Britannica' (Dobson, 1992, p.207).

Whereas the weight of eighteenth-century critical opinion was against *Cymbeline*, the Romantics were rather more well disposed towards the play. Samuel Taylor Coleridge's little-known play *Zapolya*, for example, takes its temporal structure from *The Winter's Tale*, and its plot from *Cymbeline*, and there are clear echoes of particular well-known speeches from *Cymbeline* in the poetry of William Blake, John Keats and Lord Byron. The case for *Cymbeline*, however, is made most strongly by August Wilhelm Schlegel and William Hazlitt. For Schlegel, writing in 1811, *Cymbeline* is one of Shakespeare's 'most wonderful compositions' (Bate, 1992, p.297). Where the likes of Johnson and Lennox had seen anachronisms, incongruities and implausible storylines, Schlegel sees superb dramatic craftsmanship:

> He has here combined a novel of Boccaccio's with traditionary tales of the ancient Britons reaching back to the time of the first Roman Emperors, and he has contrived, by the most gentle transitions, to blend together into one harmonious whole the social manners of the newest times with olden heroic deeds, and even with appearances of the gods.

> (Bate, 1992, p.297)

Even the controversial final act, for Schegel, is unfairly criticized: 'all the numerous threads of the plot are united [so] that he might collect together into one focus the scattered impressions of the whole' (Bate, 1992, p.298). Hazlitt, in 1817, is also very complimentary about the play, commending its mood ('pathos ... of the most pleasing and amiable kind'); the characterization ('characters ... are represented with great truth and accuracy'); the skilful evocation of the countryside ('a fine relief to the artificial refinements of the court'); *and* the final act, which is 'crowded with decisive events brought about by natural and striking means' (Bate, 1992, pp.299, 300, 301, 299). Finally, Schlegel and Hazlitt inaugurate the ardent love affair of male critics with the character of Innogen. For Schlegel, in Innogen 'no one feature of female excellence is omitted', and for Hazlitt, the play's 'greatest charm is the character of Innogen' (Bate, 1992, pp.297, 300).[1]

The nineteenth century saw the infatuation with the character of Innogen continue (Figure 1). In the words of the critic Ann Thompson, the Victorians saw in Innogen 'the perfect *wife*, a model of domesticity, devotion, and self-sacrifice' (1991, p.211). The most acclaimed actress to play Innogen in Victorian England was Helen Faucit, who gave memorable performances of the role in 1843 and 1864. In her notes on the play, Faucit describes Innogen in glowing terms: 'her demeanour expresses, silently but eloquently, the purity and beauty of her soul' (Jackson, 1971, p.29). Indeed, Faucit's regard for Innogen was so deep that she suggested the play be renamed *Imogen, Princess of Britain.* Also of interest in Faucit's reflections on Innogen is her conviction that, in translating *Cymbeline* from the page to the stage, the actress playing Innogen carries as much creative responsibility as Shakespeare himself. The burden upon the actress is particularly heavy when her character is silent, as Faucit explains: 'It is [in the final act] that Shakespeare surpasses all dramatic writers. He has faith in his interpreters, and does not encumber them with words. None could express what was happening in Innogen's soul' (Jackson, 1971, p.32) (Figure 2). Uninhibited by false modesty, and unintimidated by the authority of the Bard, Faucit therefore claims equal credit for the successful dramatic realization of Innogen.

Innogen's romantic partner Posthumus, however, did not enjoy the same adulation, and he was often overshadowed in productions by the villain Giacomo. For example, in Garrick's 1761 version of play, which was performed 163 times before 1800, many of Posthumus's key scenes were cut, and Giacomo's humiliation and confession occupied the central place in the final act. Following Garrick's lead, major Shakespearean actor-managers of the Victorian stage like William Charles

---

[1] The 1986 Oxford edition of Shakespeare's collected works revealed that while the 1623 Folio edition of *Cymbeline* had settled on 'Imogen', the original productions of the play had used 'Innogen'. Post-1986 Shakespearean scholarship has as a result accepted 'Innogen', and rather than retaining 'Imogen', or even '[Imogen]', in my quotations of pre-1986 criticism, I have changed *all* references to 'Innogen'.

Figure 1 Innogen, *from Anna Jameson,* Characteristics of Women, Moral, Poetical and Historical, with Fifty Vignette Etchings, *Volume 2, Saunders & Otley, London, 1832, p.50. British Library 840.f.2. Reproduced by permission of the British Library, London.*

Macready and Henry Irving chose in their productions of *Cymbeline* to play Giacomo rather than Posthumus.

While the characters of Innogen and Giacomo might have been favourites of Victorian theatre audiences, *Cymbeline* reached a far wider audience with the introduction of Shakespeare into the education system in the middle of the nineteenth century. We can see this process particularly vividly in the educational policies and practices of the expanding British Empire. As a result of the unshakeable hold of Hinduism in early-nineteenth-century India, the teaching of English Literature was introduced in certain of the new university colleges as a substitute for Christian instruction. Colonial administrators like Charles Trevelyan were convinced that 'without ever looking into the Bible one of these Natives must come to a considerable knowledge of it from merely reading English Literature' (Viswanathan, 1989, p.94). Satisfied after a few years that the Indian experiment was

Figure 2 *Richard Westall,* Innogen, *1879, photograph, from* The Boydell Shakespeare Gallery, *W. Mansell, London, 1879, plate 44.*

a success, British educators from the 1850s onwards introduced English Literature in Britain, using it as a test for candidates seeking entry into the civil service and the professions. Seventeen such examinations in English Literature were in place by 1875, and they all demanded the memorizing of set literary texts, with Shakespeare most prominent. The Indian Civil Service examiner W.G. Dasent explained: 'If you give me a play of Shakespeare, I should take good care that I set my questions in such a way as to exhaust it. I can conceive nothing more trying than being really examined in a play of Shakespeare' (Johnson, 1996, p.59). At schools, too, the ability to memorize was everything, as Matthew Arnold summarized in 1880: 'English Literature, as it is too ambitiously called – in truth the learning by heart and reciting of a hundred lines or two of standard English poetry – continues to be by far the most popular' (Sutherland, 1973, p.59). Shakespeare and Milton dominated the selection of 'standard English poetry' set for schools, and of the Shakespeare passages set, soliloquies from *Hamlet*, *Macbeth*, *Julius Caesar* and *King Lear* were the most common. However, the sublime language of one particular passage from *Cymbeline* found favour with several examiners, namely Guiderius's and Arviragus's valediction for Innogen: 'Fear no more the heat o'th' sun, / Nor the furious winter's rages ...' (4. 2. 259–70). Ignorant of the plot and wider context of the play, Victorian school pupils dutifully memorized the passage in order continue their journey up the educational ladder. The valediction, under the title 'Fidele', was also anthologized in a hugely popular Victorian poetry volume, Francis Turner Palgrave's *The Golden Treasury of the Best Songs and Lyrical Poems in the English Language* (1861). In the Dedication, addressed to the Poet Laureate Alfred Lord Tennyson, Palgrave expresses the hope that the anthology will 'be found by many a lifelong fountain of innocent and exalted pleasure; a source of animation to friends when they meet [and] a storehouse of delight to Labour and Povety' (Palgrave, 1861, Dedication). In a short note on 'Fidele', he quotes Charles Lamb's praise: '''I never saw anything like this funeral dirge, except the ditty which reminds Ferdinand of his drowned father in *The Tempest*. As that is of the water, watery; so this is of the earth, earthy''' (Palgrave, 1861, pp.310–11).

For those Victorian school pupils who successfully memorized their 200 lines of Shakespeare, and continued their study of Shakespeare at university, a version of *Cymbeline* as expounded by Edward Dowden was their most likely reward. Dowden was the nineteenth century's most influential Shakespeare critic – at the time of his death 30 professors of English were ex-students of his – and he made a profound impact on how the late plays, and *Cymbeline* in particular, were interpreted. Dowden divided Shakespeare's plays into four periods: the first period he called 'In the Workshop'; the second 'In the World'; the third 'Out of the Depths'; and the fourth 'On the Heights'. *Cymbeline* is in the final period, and, writing in 1875, Dowden explained his designation 'On the Heights' as follows:

> [The name signifies] that in these exquisite plays Shakespeare had
> attained an altitude from which he saw human life in a clear and
> solemn vision, looking down through a pellucid atmosphere upon
> human joys and sorrows with a certain aloofness or disengagement, yet
> at the same time with a tender and pathetic interest.

> (Dowden, 1967 edn, p.2)

Not that the plays are without fault; at times Shakespeare's concentration flags, 'as if he were thinking of his own life, or the fields and streams of Stratford' (Dowden, 1967 edn, p.404). Such quibbles, however, are of minor import, as Dowden praises the language of certain passages in the play, the 'exquisite vivacity of feeling and fancy' (p.413) displayed by Innogen, and the moral force of the ending. For Dowden, the significance of the play's resolution 'is ethical and spiritual; it is a moral necessity' (p.407). Cymbeline, Posthumus and Giacomo have all learned valuable moral lessons, but whereas in a tragedy they would have been killed off to atone for their 'fatal flaws', in a romance like *Cymbeline* the plot gives them the opportunity to change.

While Dowden defended *Cymbeline* in reverential tones, his youthful contemporary George Bernard Shaw was iconoclastic. Shaw's views on the character of Innogen and on the final act are a bracing contrast to the orthodox Victorian views on the play. In a letter in 1896 to the actress Ellen Terry, who was preparing to play Innogen in Henry Irving's production of *Cymbeline*, he offers the following advice:

> All I can extract from the artificialities of the play is a double image [of Innogen] – a real woman *divined* by Shakspere [*sic*] without his knowing it clearly, a natural aristocrat, with a high temper and perfect courage, with two moods – childlike affection and wounded rage – ; and an idiotic paragon of virtue produced by Shakspere's [*sic*] *views* of what a woman ought to be, a person who sews, and cooks, and reads improving books until midnight, and 'always reserves her holy duty', and is anxious to assure people that they may trust her implicitly with their spoons & forks, and is in a chronic state of suspicion of improper behaviour on the part of other people, especially her husband, with abandoned females. If I were you I should cut the part so as to leave the paragon out and the woman in.

> (Laurence, 1965, pp.646–7)

Shaw's own views on feminine conduct come through strongly here, as he seeks to extract an exciting Victorian suffragette Innogen from the Elizabethan strait-jacket of feminine duty. Whether such a reading can be sustained is a question we return to later in the chapter. As regards the final act of *Cymbeline*, Shaw felt so strongly about its inadequacies that he rewrote it in 1936, and saw his version performed at the Embassy Theatre in London in 1937. In the Foreword to the play (reprinted in full as Text 5 in Appendix 1), he spells out his case against the final act in typically colourful terms:

> The more childish spectators may find some delight in the revelation that Polydore and Cadwal are Innogen's long lost brothers and Cymbeline's long lost sons; that Iachimo is now an occupant of the penitent form and very unlike his old self; and that Innogen is so dutiful that she accepts her husband's attempt to have her murdered with affectionate docility. I cannot share these infantile joys.

> (Laurence, 1974, pp.182–3)

What Shaw therefore does to the final act is to shorten it substantially, but whereas earlier adaptors like Hawkins had clear political motives for making changes, Shaw claims to be guided entirely by dramatic considerations. His complaint is not that *Cymbeline* fails to promote national unity in its final act; rather, its cardinal fault lies for him in the fact that it is *boring*.

With both the Shakespeare industry and the profession of literary criticism expanding rapidly in the twentieth century, critics in ever larger numbers have written about *Cymbeline*, and they have continued to disagree energetically about the merits of the play. Arguably the most influential critical interpretation of

Cymbeline in the first half of the century was the staunch defence of the play by G. Wilson Knight in *The Crown of Life*. Published in 1947, with the memory of World War II fresh, the book ignores Shaw's criticisms of *Cymbeline*, and focuses instead on themes of national interest. Conceding that the start of the play seems 'dull and ineffective, and the people uninteresting' (p.129), Wilson Knight insists that it ultimately produces a superb synthesis of personal transcendence and political reconciliation. Indeed, in *Cymbeline* Shakespeare integrates all of his significant concerns: the play blends the early comedy with his later tragedy; it 'is also concerned to blend Shakespeare's two primary historical interests, the Roman and the British'; personal, tragic interest is 'close-knotted' with feminine idealism; 'recent discoveries are incorporated into a national sentiment; and all is subdued within a melancholic harmony' (p.130). Wilson Knight concludes that *Cymbeline* should be cherished, as it represents the successful attempt of 'our supreme national poet ... to delve into the historic origins of the nation with a view to the interpretation of its destiny' (p.166).

Although there have been relatively few twentieth-century productions of *Cymbeline*, they too have fuelled debate about the play. As a result of the efforts of charismatic directors of the late Victorian and Edwardian period like William Poel, Harley Granville-Barker and Edwin Gordon Craig, Shakespeare productions eschewed cavalier adaptation, and increasingly sought to recreate authentic versions of the original Shakespeare, making the most of the few surviving records. Poel in particular insisted upon Jacobean costumes, bare stages and Renaissance music, so that for the first time since the Restoration Shakespeare was performed in theatrical conditions resembling the original. As if in reaction to this, in 1923 Barry Jackson's Birmingham Repertory Theatre produced a controversial *Cymbeline* in modern dress, setting a trend that was to continue into the 1930s. Subsequent directors of *Cymbeline* have opted for a variety of settings for the play: Ben Iden Payne in 1937 recreated a Jacobean setting, with a formal archway in the style of Inigo Jones framing the action; Michael Benthall in 1949 at Stratford set the play within the gloomy frame of massive Norman arches; in a second (and more acclaimed) production in 1956, Benthall dispensed with an elaborate set, and used no more than the lighting to define the bare stage; William Gaskill in 1962 at Stratford and Jean Gascon in 1970 at the Canadian Shakespeare Festival also successfully used bare stages and simple costumes; Robin Philips in 1986 in Ontario set the play in the 1940s in an attempt to highlight themes of European conflict; and Elijah Moshinsky in a 1986 BBC television production looked to the early-seventeenth-century paintings of Rembrandt and Vermeer in order to recreate the costumes and décor of Jacobean England. What these different settings provoke is a reassessment of Ben Jonson's famous tribute to Shakespeare: 'not of an age, but for all time' (see *The Norton Shakespeare*, p.3352). On the one hand, productions with contemporary allusions like those of Jackson or Philips confidently assume that Shakespeare, including *Cymbeline*, is indeed 'for all time', and choose modern settings accordingly. On the other hand, productions like those of Poel, Payne and Moshinsky implicitly suggest that Shakespeare is best understood as 'of his age', and although he might *also* be 'for all time', the differences between Jacobean and contemporary Britain are foregrounded. One aspect of twentieth-century productions of *Cymbeline* that displays a strong contemporary influence has been the playing of Innogen. Shaw's fears that she would remain trapped in the role of Victorian 'paragon' have proved unfounded, as a succession of actresses since Ellen Terry in 1896 have extracted every ounce of the 'real woman' from the part, from

Peggy Ashcroft in 1932 and 1957, to Vanessa Redgrave in 1962, Helen Mirren in 1986 and Geraldine James in 1988 (Figure 3).

The attempts in theatrical productions to rescue Innogen from female subordination have been matched in recent years by the work of feminist Shakespeare critics, who have been one of the major forces in redefining *Cymbeline* at the end of the millennium. In *The Woman's Part: Feminist Criticism of Shakespeare* (1980), Carolyn

Figure 3 *Geraldine James as Innogen with the body of Cloten in the National Theatre production of* Cymbeline *directed by Peter Hall, 1988. Photo: John Haynes.*

Lenz, Gayle Greene and Carol Thomas Neely draw the title of their pioneering collection from Posthumus's speech attacking Innogen's (perceived) infidelity. The editors juxtapose Posthumus's misogynistic tirade:

> Could I find out
> The woman's part in me – for there's no motion
> That tends to vice in man but I affirm
> It is the woman's part

(2. 5. 19–22)

with his contrite entreaty to Innogen in the final act – 'Hang there like fruit, my soul, / Till the tree die' (5. 6. 263–4) – and they argue that his expanded sense of 'the woman's part' provides a model for feminist criticism: 'Similarly, feminist critics of Shakespeare seek to recover a truer sense of women's parts and of men's. Enlarging our conception of relations between men and women in Shakespeare, we enlarge our conceptions of the plays, of ourselves, and of others' (Lenz *et al.*, 1980, p.14).

One of the many consequences of this fresh emphasis has been a revaluing of the late plays. However, whereas critics like Dowden and Wilson Knight liked *Cymbeline* because they saw it as resolving conflict and containing female aspirations within a traditional order, feminist critics have read the play as problematizing patriarchal authority by exposing its contradictions. In an influential essay (see Text 6), Janet Adelman reads Innogen's fate in the play as quite the opposite of female transcendence: 'Innogen begins the play as its primary defining figure, defining herself, her husband, and the dramatic focus of the audience; by the end, she has learnt her place' (1992, p.210). For Adelman, therefore, after a promising start, by Act 5 Innogen is subdued by the patriarchal authority structures.

A second and related concern central to Shakespeare critics of the last 20 years has been the desire both to historicize and to politicize explicitly the reading of Shakespeare. Critics have used a range of different strategies known as 'new historicism' in the United States of America and 'cultural materialism' in the United Kingdom in giving expression to these commitments. In the British context, perhaps the clearest statement of intent is the one provided by Jonathan Dollimore and Alan Sinfield, who declare that their

> belief is that a combination of historical context, theoretical method,
> political commitment and textual analysis offers the strongest challenge
> .... Historical context undermines the transcendent significance
> traditionally accorded to the literary text and allows us to recover its
> histories; theoretical method detaches the text from immanent criticism
> which seeks only to reproduce it in its own terms; socialist and feminist
> commitment confronts the conservative categories in which most
> criticism has hitherto been conducted; textual analysis locates the
> critique of traditional approaches where it cannot be ignored.

(1985, p.vii)

There are many examples in recent scholarship and criticism on the late plays that bear the mark of these concerns. Less obviously polemical than Dollimore and Sinfield's manifesto, Jonathan Goldberg's *James I and the Politics of Literature* (1983) provides an intricate sense of the relation between Jacobean theatre and its historical context, as well as careful deployment of French critical theory, and a close reading of the plays. Building on the work of Goldberg, Leah Marcus relates *Cymbeline* to its historical context in meticulous detail, noting that the play 'culminates in a vision of harmonious internationalism and accommodation that mirrors James's own policy' (1988, p.141). More recently, Jodi Mikalachki (see Text 7) has attempted to revise twentieth-century interpretations of *Cymbeline* as a nationalist drama by highlighting the contradictions and anxieties related to national identity in early modern England. In general, the presence of 'powerful and rebellious females in native historiography threatened the establishment of a stable, masculine identity for the early modern state' (1995, p.303), and in particular, the fervent nationalism of the Queen in *Cymbeline*, and her subsequent death, can be understood in this light.

Finally, recent criticism of *Cymbeline* has also been concerned to explore questions of sexuality, including homoeroticism, cross-dressing and transvestism. Between 1570 and the closing of the theatres in 1642, there were 81 plays by 40 dramatists in which women characters (played by boys) assumed male disguises (see Text 3 for a list of these plays) (Figure 4).

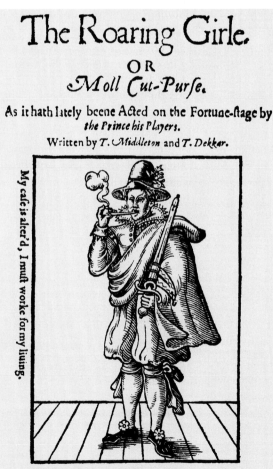

Title-page of the 1611 quarto

Figure 4 *Title page of Thomas Middleton and Thomas Dekker,* The Roaring Girle, *Thomas Archer, London, 1611. Corpus Christi College Library. Reproduced by permission of the President and Fellows of Corpus Christi College, Oxford.*

The implications of this widespread theatrical convention have been explored by a number of influential critics. Extending the argument in detail to particular plays, Michael Shapiro in *Gender in Play on the Shakespearean Stage* (1994) categorizes the different types of cross-dressing. *Cymbeline* fits into a category he defines as 'From Center to Periphery', and, much like Adelman, he believes that Innogen loses authority in the course of the play, *despite* the fact that she dresses as a page. He concludes that, unlike most comic heroines who don male attire, 'Innogen, an assertive woman who holds a central position in the opening scenes of the play, becomes one of many characters buffeted by providential events and dramaturgical ingenuity. Fidele, her male persona, is not a cheeky Lylian page but a frail waif' (Shapiro, 1994, p.173). Shapiro argues further that what excites the most anxiety for masculine authority in the play is *not* Innogen dressing as a man, but the thought of Innogen actively choosing to sleep with another man. What is most valued in *Cymbeline*, then, is that it dramatizes Jacobean male anxieties about infidelity and sexual identity, and although Innogen/Fidele is ultimately subdued by the heterosexist, patriarchal hierarchy, the play enables an interrogation of both mainstream and dissident sexual possibilities.

Having surveyed in some detail the reception history of *Cymbeline*, we are now able to draw together cases both for and against the play.

To start positively, which of *Cymbeline*'s qualities have won praise in the last 390 years?

1   The love story of Posthumus and Innogen is moving and powerful (Durfey in 1682).

2   The play celebrates the heroic origins of British nationalism (Hawkins in 1759; Wilson Knight in 1947). Alternatively, the play problematizes the complex representation of nationalism, internationalism and masculine authority in Jacobean England (Marcus in 1988; Mikalachki in 1995).

3   Although *Cymbeline* draws on diverse sources, and has a convoluted plot, Shakespeare integrates the many different elements of the play with great skill (Schlegel in 1811; Hazlitt in 1817; Dowden in 1875; Wilson Knight in 1947).

4   The character of Innogen is an appealing portrait of obedient femininity (Schelegel in 1811; Hazlitt in 1817; Dowden in 1875). Alternatively, the character of Innogen convincingly displays certain qualities of the resourceful independent woman (Shaw in 1896; twentieth-century actresses like Ashcroft, Redgrave, Mirren and James). A third alternative is that the fate of the character Innogen provides an instructive instance of how autonomous women characters in Jacobean drama, including even those who cross-dressed, were subdued by masculine authority (Adelman in 1992; Shapiro in 1994).

5   Certain passages in *Cymbeline* – notably the 'Fear no more the heat o'th' sun' speech – are amongst the greatest poetry penned by Shakespeare (Victorian English Literature examiners; Palgrave in 1861; Shaw in 1936).

6   *Cymbeline* offers salutary moral instruction to audiences, as its principal male characters – Cymbeline, Posthumus, Giacomo – suffer terribly for their 'near-fatal flaws', but are exemplary (and convincing) in their final commitment to change their ways (Dowden in 1875).

Against this substantial defence of *Cymbeline*, we need to ask: what criticisms – direct and implied – have been advanced against the play?

1   The play flouts the rules of classical aesthetics, and as a result has a flawed dramatic structure (Dryden in 1668; Rymer in 1693; Lennox in 1753; Samuel Johnson in 1765).

2   With its distracting political plot, the play provides insufficient sexual titillation (Durfey in 1682).

3   The play is unrealistic, combining a confusing mix of characters (Renaissance Italian Giacomo and Roman Lucius), and of sources (ancient British history, Roman history and Renaissance narrative) (Lennox in 1753; Johnson in 1765).

4   The political plot about the struggle between Britain and Rome is too contradictory, and can only be salvaged to celebrate British nationalism if subjected to severe editing (Hawkins in 1759; Garrick in 1761).

5   Innogen is only sporadically plausible as a character; for the most part, she is a tedious 'paragon' of feminine propriety (Shaw in 1896).

6   The final act of *Cymbeline* is long-winded, repetitious and boring (Shaw in 1936).

These disagreements about *Cymbeline* might be grouped under three more general headings. First, the fact that the play does not fit neatly into the existing categories or genres of drama has been seen alternately as a serious weakness (Johnson), or as an indication of Shakespeare's genius in developing new genres (Schlegel). Secondly, the representation of feminine and sexual identity in the case of Innogen/Fidele is seen either as exemplary (Hazlitt), or as insulting to independent women (Shaw), or as symptomatic of how Jacobean patriarchy controlled its unruly women (Adelman). Thirdly, the play's treatment of British nationalism is either embraced (Wilson Knight), seen as wanting in key respects (Hawkins), or praised for its complexity (Marcus). The balance of the chapter is structured in terms of the long-running arguments listed above, and we turn first to questions of genre raised by *Cymbeline*. With all the debates in mind, reread *Cymbeline* and then read two of the sources Shakespeare used in writing the play (see the extracts reprinted as Texts 1 and 2, from Raphael Holinshed, *The First Volume of Chronicles* (1587 edition), and Giovanni Boccaccio, *The Decameron* (1620 translation)).

The genre of Cymbeline

The first point to note is that there has long been disagreement amongst critics as to how *Cymbeline* should be classified. The Folio edition of Shakespeare's works of 1623 catalogued the plays under three headings – Comedies, Histories and Tragedies – with *Cymbeline*, despite its happy ending, being listed as Shakespeare's final tragedy. This division survived until 1725, when Alexander Pope rearranged the plays into four categories: Comedies; Tragedies; Histories; and Fables. *Cymbeline*, together with *Troilus and Cressida*, *Romeo and Juliet*, *Hamlet* and *Othello*, was reclassified as a Fable. Towards the end of the eighteenth century, influential editors like Edmond Malone went beyond the text of Shakespeare's plays and studied Shakespeare's predecessors and contemporaries, establishing a tradition of historical scholarship, which yielded new insights into the chronology and original genre-division of the plays. In 1832, the Reverend W.H. Black, for example, discovered evidence of performances of *Cymbeline* in 1611. With this gradual and piecemeal accumulation of new evidence throughout the nineteenth century, a new four-part chronological classification of the plays gradually gained acceptance: an early period dominated by the comedies; then the period of the histories; then the tragedies; and finally the 'late plays', including *Cymbeline*. Although Hazlitt in 1817 had described *Cymbeline* as 'a dramatic romance' (Bate, 1992, p.299), Dowden's designation in 1875 of *all* the late plays as 'romances' exerted a much stronger influence on how *Cymbeline* was to be classified. Finally, in the twentieth century, two further terms have been invented to try to account for the genre of *Cymbeline* and the late plays: 'retrospective' play and 'tragicomedy'. For critics like G.E. Bentley, Philip Edwards and Frank Kermode, the late plays were not so much a new development as a 'retrospective', a reworking of earlier material. *Cymbeline*, they argued, should be read principally as a revision of the earlier Jacobean play *King Lear*, although with a more cheerful ending to suit the mood of the court in 1609–10. More convincing has been the argument that *Cymbeline* should be placed within the emergent European genre of tragicomedy, a genre that gained even more popularity and authority in England in the work of Beaumont and Fletcher.

Before looking in detail at the more plausible generic classifications of *Cymbeline* – romance and tragicomedy – it is worth pausing to reflect on why other competing genres have on occasions claimed the play.

Cymbeline *as tragedy?*

In the Folio of 1623, *Cymbeline* was classified as a tragedy, and even allowing for the paucity of corpses in the final act, the reasons for such a classification are not too hard to find. Although the list of prerequisites for tragedy are disputed, it might be argued that *Cymbeline* satisfies at least the following ones: the play is about kings and princes; its protatgonist (Cymbeline, Posthumus or even Cloten) suffers a 'fatal flaw'; the spectacle of his suffering excites pity and fear in the audience; order is restored during a cathartic conclusion in which anti-social elements are purged from the body politic (not only the Queen and Cloten, but also Cymbeline's false pride, Posthumus's misogyny and Giacomo's sexual deviousness). Further, on a number of previous occasions, Shakespeare had transformed fragments of Holinshed's *Chronicles* from historical accounts into tragedies, and the story of Cymbeline (Cunobellus in Holinshed) and his reign offered ample scope for such a reworking. According to Holinshed, Cymbeline enjoyed a close relationship with Rome, but as a result of a refusal to pay the tribute, Cymbeline's son Guiderius was killed in battle. However, the principal reason finally for excluding *Cymbeline* from the canon of Shakespearean tragedies is the simple fact that Cymbeline and Posthumus survive the final act in good health, and although Cloten dies, his character is weighed down by too many fatal flaws. Indeed, as a secondary reason, it has often been argued that Cymbeline, Posthumus and Cloten as characters are all two-dimensional, and lack the necessary tragic gravitas.

Cymbeline *as history?*

In deriving his characters and part of the plot for *Cymbeline* from Holinshed's *Chronicles*, Shakespeare returned to the principal source for his history plays of the 1590s. The names of most of the characters, as well as one of the main storylines –

Britain's conflict with Rome – are drawn directly from Holinshed's *Chronicles* (see Text 1). Furthermore, like the history plays, *Cymbeline* evokes a sense of national pride in offering a positive vision of Ancient Britain. What complicates any attempt to read the play purely as a history, however, is the central presence in the play of storylines drawn from fictional sources. Editors of *Cymbeline* are now in broad agreement that for the wager story Shakespeare borrowed from the ninth novel of the second day in Boccaccio's *Decameron* (see Text 2) and the anonymous prose tale *Frederyke of Jennen* (1560). For the tale of Belarius and the abducted princes, he was indebted to the Elizabethan play *The Rare Triumphs of Love and Fortune* (performed 1582, printed 1589). A second factor that distinguishes *Cymbeline* from the earlier history plays is that it presents a rather more complicated attitude towards British nationalism. Far from uncritically endorsing pride in Britain, Shakespeare has the two most unpleasant characters in *Cymbeline* – the Queen and Cloten – as the most fervent nationalists, and in the final act Cymbeline agrees to subordinate Britain to Rome by continuing to pay the tribute to Rome.

Cymbeline as comedy?

The reuniting of Posthumus and Innogen in the happy ending of *Cymbeline* is the main reason we might group it with the earlier Shakespearean comedies, but there are also other compelling reasons for treating the play as a comedy. Sticking once again to relatively uncontroversial generic markers, we note that *Cymbeline* qualifies as a comedy insofar as it takes as its material the conflict between generations (Innogen versus Cymbeline); its thematic centre is the renewal and regeneration of the social order (the marriage of Posthumus and Innogen); its festive conclusion is achieved by the youthful characters transcending a rigid or unreasonable law (defeat for Cymbeline's opposition to Posthumus and Innogen's union); and finally, for the audience, emotions of relief and pleasure supersede those of pity and terror. The main objection to classifying *Cymbeline* as a comedy is that one of the main characters (Cloten) is killed, and that with the exception of a couple of short scenes the mood of the first four acts is profoundly tragic. Compared to the young lovers in Shakespeare's early comedies like *A Midsummer Night's Dream* and *Twelfth Night*, the suffering protagonists in *Cymbeline* endure far more prolonged and harrowing ordeals. They are up against more than the single figure of authority found in those plays (Egeus, Malvolio); they confront what Howard Felperin describes as 'a universal law of frustration' (1972, p.61), and fashioning a happy ending therefore requires the intervention of the gods. Posthumus's change of heart at the end of *Cymbeline* constitutes a more profound personal transformation than any experienced by the protagonists of the early comedies. Recent productions have overwhelmingly opted for the tragic mode, although David Frost's 1970 amateur production in Cambridge in the style of – as he describes it – 'high camp' (1986, p.37) did its best to exploit the play's comedic potential.

Cymbeline as Roman play?

Shakespeare's fascination with Ancient Rome is reflected in his choice of Roman settings and characters in one of his narrative poems, *The Rape of Lucrece* (1593–4), and in five of his plays: *Titus Andronicus* (1593–4), *Julius Caesar* (1599), *Antony and Cleopatra* (1606–7), *Coriolanus* (1607–8) and *Cymbeline* (1609–10). As it is set in Britain, with the exception of one short scene in Rome (3. 7), *Cymbeline* has not always been grouped with the Roman plays. In recent years, however, a number of critics have argued persuasively that it shares many of the generic markers of Shakespeare's unambiguously 'Roman plays'. David M. Bergeron, for example, has pointed out how closely the characters in *Cymbeline* parallel figures from Roman history well known to Shakespeare: both Cymbeline and the emperor Augustus lack male heirs and are angry with their female heirs; the Queen in her scheming ambition resembles Augustus's wife Livia; like the military commander Agrippa, Posthumus is banished and ultimately reconciled with the king; and Cloten has much in common with the cruel and lustful emperor Tiberius (see Bergeron, 1980, pp.36–41). More substantially, Robert S. Miola suggests that the moral code in *Cymbeline* echoes the Roman emphasis on constancy, honour and individual accountability, with Posthumus's fate in particular framed by the dictates of the Roman gods (see Miola, 1984, p.51): Jupiter, the principal Roman god, descends in the masque sequence in the final act to re-establish order. Most recently, Coppélia Kahn has pointed to the normative function within the play of Roman definitions of masculinity, although she insists that they are also complemented by British ideals of male courage. She notes that in defeating the Romans in the narrow lane, Posthumus, Belarius, Arviragus and Guiderius achieve 'a British independence and authentic manly virtue [that] is indebted to native and Roman models of valor' (1997, p.164). Kahn's acknowledgement here (conceded by the other critics too) of the central place of Britain both as imaginative resource and as aspiration in *Cymbeline* sets a clear limit on the extent to which the play might be defined as 'Roman'. Furthermore, whereas in the earlier Roman plays Shakespeare endorsed the Roman code of honour, in *Cymbeline* that code is shown to be wanting, with British mercy prevailing over Roman stoicism in the final act.

Cymbeline as romance?

The contributions of Dowden and Hazlitt in labelling *Cymbeline* as a romance have been noted, and it is a classification that has been repeated and refined many times since. For example, the editor of the second Arden edition of *Cymbeline*, J.M. Nosworthy, defines the play as an 'experimental romance' (1955, p.xlviii), and more recently, Judiana Lawrence has seen it as an 'ethical romance' (1994, p.447). Even more influential, perhaps, has been Northrop Frye's insistence upon the centrality of romance not only in Shakespeare's late plays, but in *all* forms of story-telling. For Frye, romance is the ultimate source and paradigm of all narrative, and other genres are fragments or sub-genres of romance (1976, pp.28–31). He defines romance as a quest for fulfilment that will transcend present realities, and he provides the following frame:

> The hero of romance is analogous to the mythical Messiah or deliverer who comes from an upper world, and his enemy is analogous to the demonic powers of a lower world. The conflict however takes place in, or at any rate concerns, *our* world, which is in the middle, and which is characterised by the cyclical movements of nature. Hence the opposite poles of the cycles of nature are assimilated to the opposition of the hero and his enemy. The enemy is associated with winter, darkness, confusion, sterility, moribund life, and old age, and the hero with spring, dawn, order, fertility, vigor, and youth.

(pp.187–8)

With such a wide definition, not only the late plays, but even Shakespeare's tragedies and comedies might be shoehorned into the genre of romance. In the case of *Hamlet*, Hamlet the elevated intellectual hero engages with his demonic enemy Claudius in Denmark ('the middle'), and the action is structured by the quest for the truth about the death of Hamlet's father. In the case of *Twelfth Night*, Viola is the questing hero-figure who has to overcome her adversary Malvolio to achieve personal fulfilment. A narrower definition of romance is provided by Felperin, who specifies the following requirements: 'romance is a success story in which difficulties of any number of kinds are overcome, and a tall story in which they are overcome against impossible odds or by miraculous means' (1972, p.10). Moving on to locate his definition more precisely in the context of Shakespearean romances, Felperin identifies three earlier romance genres, which he argues converge in Shakespearean romance: the third-century classical prose romances like Longus's *Daphnis and Chloë* and Heliodorus's *Aethiopica*; the chivalric romances of the Middle Ages like Chrétien de Troyes's *Lancelot* (c.1172) and Thomas Malory's *Morte d'Arthur* (c.1469–70); and the miracle and morality plays like *The Castle of Perseverance* (c.1405–25).

While quite clearly *Cymbeline* would fit Frye's wide definition of romance, the play also satisfies Felperin's more precise definition. Either Posthumus or Innogen qualify as the hero-figure on a quest; the Queen is the opposing axis of evil; the obstacles to the hero-figure's success are numerous (Giacomo's attempted seduction of Innogen, the Roman invaders, and Cloten's designs on the throne and Innogen); and in overcoming these impossible odds, the miraculous intervention of Jupiter ensures success. Are there any substantial objections, then, to settling on the genre of *Cymbeline* as romance? On Frye's definition there could be no objections, but on Felperin's narrower definition the play might not be assimilated to the category of 'romance' quite so effortlessly. In particular, the ambivalences and contradictions in the play resist the archetypes and moral absolutes of 'good' and 'evil' central to romance. For example, the complexity of characterization in the case of Posthumus makes him at many points an uncomfortable candidate for hero status (recall his 'woman's part' speech), and Innogen's passivity as a character also ill-qualifies her for successful 'questing'. Secondly, if the political narrative is to be taken seriously, it fails to deliver the kind of binary opposition favoured in romances. Rather than a 'Good Britain' counterpoised against an 'Evil Rome', *Cymbeline* discloses a contradictory political universe where uneasy compromise rather than the triumph of good over evil is the prevailing trope.

Cymbeline *as tragicomedy?*

The final genre to have been associated with *Cymbeline* is tragicomedy. The most famous definition of tragicomedy from the period itself is the one provided by John Fletcher in his Preface 'To the Reader' for his unsuccessful play *The Faithful Shepherdess* (c.1610). He claims that tragicomedy 'wants deaths, which is inough to make it no tragedie, yet brings some neere it, which is inough to make it no comedie' (Bowers, 1976, p.497). To refine Fletcher's rather wide definition, the term 'tragicomedy' in the Jacobean period referred to plays derived from Greek romances or Italian pastorals, performed before the court and at the Blackfriars playhouse. Such plays might more accurately be distinguished as 'pastoral tragicomedies', a sub-genre of tragicomedy which gained great currency after 1610. Proponents of pastoral tragicomedy saw it as a substantial advance on tragedy, as Giambattista Guarini's rhetorical question in *The Compendium of Tragicomic Poetry* (1601) makes clear:

> ... what need have we today to purge terror and pity with tragic sights, since we have the precepts of our most holy religion .... Hence these horrible and savage spectacles are superfluous, nor does it seem to me that today we should introduce tragic action for any other reason than to get delight from it.

> (Simonds, 1992, p.31)

During the seventeenth century, the category 'tragicomedy' gradually expanded into Fletcher's definition, to include plays not performed exclusively at court, which combined elements of tragedy and comedy. The prestige of tragicomedy is most accurately captured in William Hole's emblematic engraving on the title page of *The Workes of Beniamin Jonson*, which depicts the five muses of English drama – tragicomedy, satire, pastoral, tragedy and comedy (Figure 5).

Note the dominant positioning of the figure representing TRAGI COMOEDIA, wearing a crown and sceptre, and presiding like a superior deity over the other four genres. Note too how in terms of dress the figure of TRAGI COMOEDIA combines

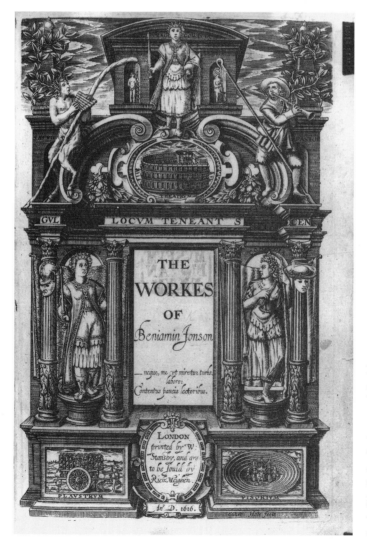

Figure 5 *Title page of* The Workes of Beniamin Jonson, *William Stansby, London, 1616, engraved by William Hole. British Library c.39.k.9. Reproduced by permission of the British Library, London.*

elements both of the figure of TRAGOEDIA (bottom left) in the expensively embroidered cloak and of COMOEDIA (bottom right) in the modest tunic.

In the most detailed study of *Cymbeline* in relation to tragicomedy in recent years, Peggy Munoz Simonds defines Renaissance tragicomedy as 'a courtly, a philosophical, and a highly ritualistic form of theater requiring considerable sophistication from its audience' (1992, p.32). She then goes on to list the following nine characteristics of Renaissance tragicomedy:

(1) a strong emphasis on either pastoralism or primitivism;
(2) the use of satyrs or Wild Men as the primary instruments of satire;
(3) allusions to well-known literary sources and especially to previous tragicomedies, which remind the audience of the artificialities of the genre;
(4) heroic self sacrifice;
(5) formal commentaries on the nature and power of love and on the fortunate workings of providence;
(6) provocative social equalizing achieved through love;
(7) the setting of a wilderness cave as the place of psychic transformation and as a symbol of both womb and tomb;
(8) the celebration of one or more blood rituals reflecting the Platonic theology in order to make possible the required happy finale through a change in human perspective; and
(9) an interest in the Orphic art of poetry itself and the problem of transforming sense into intelligence or images into Platonic Ideas.

(p.36)

Most of these nine characteristics can be identified in *Cymbeline*, but rather than run through and relate all nine of them to the play, we might simply note a couple of its 'tragicomic' qualities. For one, the tragicomic interest in pastoralism is strongly present in the tale of Belarius and the two princes, with a clear opposition set up in the play between the corrupt court and the vital innocence of the country. Further, Belarius's wilderness cave functions in *Cymbeline* as a 'womb' for Arviragus and Guiderius, and also for Innogen, but as a 'tomb' for the slain Cloten. Posthumus fights against the Romans in a spirit of 'heroic self sacrifice', and the final happy union of Posthumus and Innogen celebrates both the 'power of love' and 'the fortunate workings of providence'.

If we cast our minds back for a moment to the quest motif of romance, and apply it to our current search for the genre of *Cymbeline*, we might at this stage be tempted to feel that with tragicomedy our search was over. As a genre located in the Jacobean context of the play, tragicomedy would appear to account for the many peculiarities of *Cymbeline*. However, as with all the other genres we have tried to relate to *Cymbeline*, the genre of tragicomedy also fails to contain all the aspects of the play. In particular, the historical and political complexities of *Cymbeline* – especially the ambivalent attitudes to British nationalism contested in the play – exceed Simonds's definition of tragicomedy.

Why have we failed to identify *Cymbeline* conclusively with a particular genre?

At one level, the answer is easy: *Cymbeline* combines a number of genres, and therefore does not fit neatly into any one. Indeed, the genres it does fit most closely – romance and tragicomedy – are themselves less prescriptive, and include refugees from the more long-established genres.

However, there are more complex reasons for our failure to settle on the genre of *Cymbeline*, and they relate to the nature of genre criticism itself. Three major objections have been raised to the activity of genre criticism, one theoretical, the second historical, and the third political. We need to consider all three of these objections, and to think about how they might relate to our attempts to classify *Cymbeline* in terms of genre. Further, we need to consider how such classification might have affected *Cymbeline*'s marginal position within the Shakespeare canon.

Theoretical objections

The theoretical objection to genre criticism is that it prescribes laws that impose punitive limitations upon the variety of literary productions. The French critic–philosopher Jacques Derrida observes that 'As soon as the word "genre" is sounded, as soon as it is heard, as soon as one attempts to conceive it, a limit is drawn. And when a limit is established, laws and interdictions are not far behind' (1980, p.203). To continue Derrida's legal metaphor, once laws of genre have been established, they become institutionalized over time, and new cases are brought before the court of genre to be judged by their norms or criteria. Problems arise when the laws no longer meet the specifics of the new cases. Shifting metaphors, Derrida quotes Gerard Genette's arresting formulation of the problem: 'The history of genre-theory is strewn with these fascinating outlines that inform and deform reality, a reality often heterogeneous to the literary field, and that claim to discover a "natural" system wherein they construct a factitious symmetry heavily reinforced by fake windows' (Derrida, 1980, p.207). For Derrida and Genette, then, genre theory creates theoretical models that both 'inform and deform' reality; these models of genre claim to disclose a natural symmetrical system of order within the literary field, but they can only sustain themselves by constructing empty categories. These ideas become clearer when we relate them to an example we know well, namely the case of *Cymbeline*. When the word 'genre' is invoked, laws defining and distinguishing tragedy, comedy, history, Roman play, romance and tragicomedy are laid down. These laws of genre assume a natural, eternal appearance, and literary works are brought before the court of genre to be classified and judged. As new instances like *Cymbeline* emerge, however, the law of genre founders because the play simply does not fit the existing genres. Genre theory deforms reality and constructs neat though bogus aesthetic models, and will always fail to account for a complex reality that includes texts like *Cymbeline*. To offer a second example, we might compare the generic instability of *Cymbeline* to that of a modern film like *Pulp Fiction*. The film industry lays down laws which insist that all films fit into to a limited range of genres (comedy, horror, romance, science fiction, art house and so on). A film like *Pulp Fiction* combines a number of genres, and therefore defies the 'factitious symmetry' of the existing genre divisions with its innovative film version of 'heterogeneous reality'.

Historical objections

The second objection to genre theory has been voiced by Marxist critics like Fredric Jameson, who have sought to locate the rise and decline of genres in relation to their historical contexts. The idea that genres transcend time and space – Frye's claims for romance are an obvious example – is rejected in favour of a historically and socially inflected discussion of genre. Jameson defines genres as 'essentially literary *institutions*, or social contracts between a writer and a specific public, whose function is to specify the proper use of a particular cultural artifact' (1981, p.106). When he turns his attention to the genre of romance, Jameson is therefore interested less in providing a universal definition of romance than in tracing how romances have circulated in different contexts. Jameson describes romance as 'the imaginary resolution of the objective conditions', and as 'an imaginary "solution" to [the] real contradiction' (p.118), by which he means the contradiction between, on the one hand, older notions of good and evil and, on the other, emergent class affiliations. He then goes on to identify different 'objective conditions' that have produced romances, from the Middle Ages and the Renaissance in Europe, and post-World War II in the United States of America. Again the argument becomes clearer if applied to a specific instance like *Cymbeline*. On Jameson's approach, our question 'what is the genre of *Cymbeline*?' is misconceived. What we should be asking instead are two questions. First, 'how do the dominant dramatic genres in London in 1609 imaginatively resolve the contradictions of that society?' The critic Glynne Wickham's reflections on Shakespeare's shift from tragedy to tragicomedy might provide a useful starting-point. According to Wickham, the shift

> has its origins in the political consciousness of the British people saved from foreign invasion and civil war by the peaceful accession of James I in 1603, by the timely discovery of the Gunpowder Plot in 1605, and the final ratification of the Union of the two Crowns by Act of Parliament in 1608.

> (1973, p.36)

As the 'political consciousness' changes, so a new genre emerges which imaginatively resolves the new set of contradictions in that society. The second question for Jameson would then be: 'how does *Cymbeline* combine/reproduce/ modify the dominant dramatic genres of its time?' In the same spirit, our approach to *Pulp Fiction* would be directed to its relation to the contradictions in American society in the 1990s as well as to its formal generic mix.

Political objections

Attention to the history of how genres mutate alerts us to the third objection to genre theory, namely the fact that in the process of classifying genres, certain genres have been routinely privileged at the expense of others. In the context of Shakespeare studies, for example, the tendency for centuries has been for the tragedies to be elevated above the comedies. Feminist critics have argued convincingly that accepting such a hierarchy entails a political choice, and they note how generations of Shakespearean critics have embraced masculine concerns in the tragedies – war, heroism, state politics, sword-fighting – while at the same time dismissing or patronizing the greater feminine presence in the comedies. Such hierarchies are rejected by Linda Bamber, for example, who argues in *Comic Women, Tragic Men: A Study of Gender and Genre in Shakespeare* (1982) that Shakespeare 'must be a hero for feminists ... because in every genre except history he associates the feminine with whatever it is outside himself he takes most seriously. Whatever most seriously challenges the masculine self – whatever matters in tragedy, comedy, and romance – Shakespeare associates with the feminine' (1982, p.6). On account of its substantial traces of the tragic, *Cymbeline* has not been dismissed from the core canon of Great Shakespeare Plays quite as peremptorily as the early comedies. At the same time, however, its lack of a dominant tragic hero in the mould of Macbeth, Lear or Hamlet has ensured that it has never been included either.

In addition to highlighting the gender biases implicit in discussions of *Cymbeline*'s genre, recent feminist criticism of the play has also focused in detail on the characters of Innogen and the Queen. We need now to turn our full attention to the second four-century long debate about *Cymbeline*, namely how are feminine and sexual identities represented in the play? Is Innogen/Fidele to be seen as an exemplar (Hazlitt), as insulting to independent women (Shaw), or as symptomatic of how Jacobean patriarchy controlled its unruly women (Adelman)?

Feminine and sexual identities in Cymbeline

A necessary preliminary is to establish how Innogen is described by the other characters in the play. **Note down briefly how each of the other main characters perceives Innogen, both initially and as the play progresses.**

The essentials of the cast and plot are introduced by the two Gentlemen in the opening scene, who direct audience sympathies firmly in favour of Posthumus and Innogen, and against the Queen and Cloten. When Posthumus and Innogen then enter to say their farewells, Posthumus dwells on Innogen's qualities of beauty and constancy. For her father Cymbeline, however, her indifference to his authority outweighs her virtues:

> O disloyal thing,
> That shouldst repair my youth, thou heap'st
> A years's age on me.

> (1. 1. 132–4)

In his anger, he goes on to describe her as 'mad' (148) and 'foolish' (151). His harsh judgement of Innogen is reinforced in the next scene, where Cloten's dismay at being spurned in favour of Posthumus is indulged by the sycophantic First Lord, who says of Innogen 'her beauty and her brain go not together' (1. 2. 25–6).

The scene after next (1. 4) is crucial in confirming the criteria for judging Innogen. Posthumus arrives in Rome as the guest of Philario, and in recalling a disagreement involving Posthumus in France some years before, the Frenchman present at the banquet sums up the feminine qualities most valued. According to the Frenchman, Posthumus argued 'upon warrant of bloody affirmation' (1. 4. 50) that English women are 'more fair, virtuous, wise, chaste, constant, qualified, and less attemptable than any the rarest of our ladies in France' (51–2). The repetition of adjectives related to sexual fidelity – 'virtuous', 'chaste', 'constant', 'less attemptable' – hints at Posthumus's fear of being cuckolded, and also establishes the terms of his wager with Giacomo. First Giacomo and then Posthumus describe Innogen in terms that reduce her to the status of sexual trophy. Giacomo compares her to a pond hosting many different birds ('strange fowl light upon neighbouring ponds' (78)); a trinket that might be stolen ('A cunning thief or a that-way accomplished courtier would hazard the winning both of first and last' (80–2)); and a fencing opponent who might be defeated ('I should get ground of your fair mistress, make her go back even to the yielding' (90–2)). In defending Innogen's honour, Posthumus likens Giacomo to an explorer facing a challenging journey – 'if you make your voyage upon her' (138–9) – with Innogen by implication little more than a blank space testing masculine endeavour.

Giacomo's image of Innogen is elaborated in three succeeding scenes: the attempted-seduction scene (1. 6); the trunk-in-bedroom scene (2. 2); and the scene in which he returns to Posthumus to claim victory in the wager (2. 4). The qualities he attributes to Innogen, however, remain very much within the terms set out by the Frenchman. That Innogen is 'fair' Giacomo confirms with interest, describing her in terms that recall the inflated conventions of the courtly love tradition. When he first meets Innogen, Giacomo in an aside exclaims at her beauty:

> All of her that is out of door most rich!
> If she be furnished with a mind so rare
> She is alone, th'Arabian bird
>
> (1. 6. 15–17)

and then continues to pay her lavish compliments, comparing her to 'the radiant sun' (1. 6. 87), and a 'Fresh lily, / And whiter than the sheets!' (2. 2. 15–16). Even more important to him than her beauty, however, is the question of whether she will sleep with him. Innogen, of course, rejects Giacomo's offer to 'dedicate myself to your sweet pleasure' (1. 6. 137), but defeat does not diminish his obsession with her. He continues to describe her in sexual terms, both in conversation with Innogen herself:

> The love I bear him
> Made me to fan you thus, but the gods made you,
> Unlike all others, chaffless
>
> (1. 6. 177–9)

and subsequently when he returns to Posthumus (a 'night of such sweet shortness which / Was mine in Britain' (2. 4. 44–5), and 'her bedchamber – / Where I confess I slept not' (66–7) (Figure 6).

The most brutal descriptions of Innogen, however, are not those of Giacomo, but those of Posthumus and Cloten. When confronted with Giacomo's evidence of Innogen's 'infidelity', Posthumus explodes with a barrage of crude insults – 'She hath bought the name of whore thus dearly' (2. 4. 128); 'She hath been colted by him' (133) – which culminate in his famous 'woman's part' speech (2. 4. 152–87). In this frightening speech, his unjust anger with Innogen is extended to *all* women, as he projects his own inadequacies onto 'The woman's part in me' (2. 4. 172). In his subsequent letter instructing Pisanio to kill Innogen, Posthumus continues to describe her as 'the strumpet in my bed' (3. 4. 21–2), and complains of 'her dishonour' (29). When he finally realizes he has wronged Innogen, Posthumus reverts to a version of the 'madonna–whore' binary, and his descriptions of her switch from images of illicit physical desire to ones of spiritual virtue. He describes Pisanio as a 'sacrilegious thief' (5. 6. 220) he had commissioned to kill Innogen, and he likens her to a 'temple / Of virtue' (220–1).

Figure 6 *LeWan Alexander as Giacomo and Monica Bell as Innogen in the Utah Shakespearean Festival production of* Cymbeline *directed by Kent Thompson, 1988. Reproduced by permission of the Utah Shakespearean Festival.*

By comparison, Cloten's descriptions of Innogen eschew any spiritual pretensions, as he consistently and flagrantly focuses on her as a sexual object. Attempting to woo Innogen with music, Cloten's sexual innuendoes are anything but subtle:

> I am advised to give her music o' mornings; they say it will penetrate.
> Come on, tune. If you can penetrate her with your fingering, so; we'll
> try with tongue too.

(2. 3. 10–13)

Later on, when plotting Posthumus's demise, he anticipates raping Innogen before taking her back to the court as his wife: 'when my lust hath dined ... to the court I'll knock her back, foot her home again' (3. 5. 138–40). Finally, most commentators draw a firm distinction between the worthy Posthumus and the repulsive Cloten, but if we compare Posthumus's 'woman's part' speech (2. 4. 152–87) and Cloten's explanation of his love for Innogen (3. 5. 70–9), an uncomfortable symmetry between the two of them is apparent. In both speeches, the idea that an individual's identity is assembled from 'parts' is central: Posthumus associates the '[part] that tends to vice in man' (2. 5. 21) with women, and Cloten sees Innogen as made up of 'courtly parts more exquisite' (3. 5. 71). Indeed, exclusively on the basis of these two speeches, Cloten's image of Innogen and of women in general is less insulting than that of Posthumus.

Of the remaining characters, we can sum up their descriptions of Innogen-as-Innogen (as opposed to Innogen-as-Fidele) more briefly. The Queen emphasizes Innogen's disobedience to her father, and also her feminine frailty in a male-dominated world. She asks Pisanio:

> Weeps she still, sayst thou? Dost thou think in time
> She will not quench, and let instructions enter
> Where folly now possesses?

> (1. 5. 46–8)

Much later she explains Innogen's weakness to Cymbeline as follows:

> She's a lady
> So tender of rebukes that words are strokes,
> And strokes death to her.

> (3. 5. 39–41)

The Second Lord, by contrast, sympathizes with Innogen's suffering, and like Posthumus, compares her to a temple threatened with violation:

> ... poor princess,
> Thou divine Innogen, what thou endur'st
> ... The heavens hold firm
> The walls of thy dear honour, keep unshaked
> That temple, thy fair mind.

> (2. 1. 53–4, 59–61)

In the same vein, Pisanio refuses to believe Posthumus's accusing letter, and defends Innogen's honour vigorously (Figure 7):

> She's punished for her truth, and undergoes,
> More goddess-like than wife-like, such assaults
> As would take in some virtue.

> (3. 2. 7–9)

Before considering in detail Innogen's response to these events and pressures, we need to try and derive from the accumulated remarks of all these different characters the body of rules that dictates her actions. **In other words, what rules or social imperatives – backed by considerable sanctions – are informally laid down for Innogen in *Cymbeline*?**

1   Obey your father (Cymbeline, the Queen, Cloten).

2   Obey your heart (Posthumus, Pisanio, Giacomo).

3   Obey your husband. Crucially, never have sex – or even be *suspected* of having sex – with *anyone* except your husband (Posthumus).

4   Although not quite qualifying as a fourth rule, being 'fair' is presented as a distinct advantage (Posthumus, Giacomo, Guiderius, Lucius).

Figure 7 *John Hopper,* Innogen and Pisanio, *1879, photograph, from* The Boydell Shakespeare Gallery, *W. Mansell, London, 1879, plate 43.*

This set of injunctions controlling Innogen's conduct is not unique to *Cymbeline*. Beaumont's and Fletcher's contemporaneous play, *Philaster, or Love Lies a-Bleeding* (first performed *c*.1609; first printed 1620) discloses the same preoccupation with feminine sexuality, and replicates many of *Cymbeline*'s features. Most notably, Act 2, Scene 2 of *Philaster* (see Text 4) is a variation on Giacomo's attempted seduction of Innogen. In *Philaster*, the Giacomo-figure is the Spanish prince Pharamond, who first tries unsuccessfully to seduce Galatea, 'a wise modest lady attending the princess', and then enjoys swift success with Megra, 'a lascivious lady' (Beaumont and Fletcher, 1975 edn, p.3). At the close of a typically convoluted Jacobean plot, Galatea is rewarded for her virtue, and Megra expelled from the court. Linda Woodbridge explains these constraints on women characters like Innogen, Galatea and Megra by reference to the wider changes attending James I's accession to the English throne in 1603. In particular, James's pursuit of peace with Spain saw a change in the culture, from one privileging '"masculine" military values to peacetime values traditionally female', and Shakespeare's Jacobean plays 'reflect the unease attending this action [and] are full of aborted battles and confused sex roles' (Woodbridge, 1984, p.161). The transition from war to peace was accompanied by improved economic mobility for women in London, but the results of these social changes were contradictory. Woodbridge concludes that 'Economic changes were producing new lifestyles for city women, which brought down on them the antifeminist wrath of those whose conservatism could not accommodate such changes' (p.176). Is Shakespeare's *Cymbeline* an expression of 'antifeminist wrath'? The punishing and policing of the two women characters in the play might encourage such a conclusion, although the sympathetic presentation of Innogen's defiance in the opening acts complicates such a judgement.

The impact of the formidable array of social pressures upon Innogen can be measured to some extent by attending to how she describes her own sense of self as the play unfolds. **Summarize briefly how Innogen describes herself in each of the five acts.**

In the opening act, Innogen refers to herself in the third person actively rejecting both Giacomo and Cloten. She says to Giacomo that she is 'a lady that disdains / Thee and the devil alike' (1. 6. 148–9); and to Cloten she apologizes half-heartedly for 'forget[ting] a lady's manners / By being so verbal' (2. 3. 100–1). After reading Posthumus's letter charging Pisanio to kill her for being unfaithful, however, this initial exuberance disappears, and she sees herself first as 'stale, a garment out of fashion' (3. 4. 50), and then as an object of sacrifice. Asking Pisanio to kill her, she says, 'Prithee, dispatch. / The lamb entreats the butcher' (94–5), and soon after describes herself as 'Th'elected deer before thee' (108). She sounds the same note when discovered by Belarius and the two princes, describing herself as an unsuccessful and self-destructive thief: 'I'll rob none but myself; and let me die, / Stealing so poorly' (4. 2. 15–16). The most powerful image of her sense of annihilation, however, occurs when she awakens next to Cloten's decapitated body, and explains herself to Lucius: 'I am nothing; or if not, / Nothing to be were better' (4. 2. 369–70). What makes this judgement resonate with particular poignancy is the fact that at an earlier stage Innogen had described the hated Cloten as 'that harsh, churlish, noble, simple nothing' (3. 4. 132). In describing *herself* as 'nothing', she occupies the same debased level as Cloten. In the final scene, Innogen ascends from 'nothing', but rather than reverting to her original spirited self, she meekly accepts her position subordinate to father, husband, brothers, and even to Belarius and Lucius. Her last words in the play are directed to Lucius, and encapsulate her reformed obedient self: 'My good master, / I will yet do you service' (5. 6. 404–5).

What is the function of Innogen's cross-dressing?

Innogen's one response to her predicament is to disguise herself as a boy. Pisanio's speech explaining the advantages of cross-dressing is instructive:

> You must forget to be a woman; change
> Command into obedience, fear and niceness –
> The handmaids of all women, or more truly
> Woman it pretty self – into a waggish courage,
> Ready in gibes, quick-answered, saucy and
> As quarrelous as the weasel.

> (3. 4. 154–9)

Pisanio's faith in the advantages for Innogen of dressing as a boy continues a substantial tradition of successful cross-dressing in Elizabethan and Jacobean theatre, a tradition to which Shakespeare himself contributed richly (Viola in *Twelfth Night*, Portia in *The Merchant of Venice*, to name but two examples). According to Michael Shapiro, despite the fact that it was punished by imprisonment in Jacobean

London, female cross-dressing on stage nonetheless 'encouraged some women to use male clothing symbolically, to challenge sartorial markers of gender boundaries in order to challenge moral and spiritual inequalities, as well as secure greater social liberties' (1994, p.23). In Innogen's case, however, it is difficult to detect any advantage gained by donning male attire. No displays of 'waggish courage' are forthcoming. Continuing to be buffeted by external forces, all she achieves – and this hardly demands any agency on her part – is to have Guiderius, Arviragus and Lucius love her for her beauty and tender ways. In a remark that triggers anxieties for the audience of homoerotic love *and* incest, Guiderius says 'Were you a woman, youth, / I should woo hard' (3. 6. 66–7). Later, he commends Innogen/Fidele's 'neat cookery' (4. 2. 50), and when Arviragus enters with the unconscious body of Innogen/Fidele announcing that 'The bird is dead' (4. 2. 198), he repeats Giacomo's metaphor of the lily, although with a tragic inflection:

> O sweetest, fairest lily!
> My brother wears thee not one half so well
> As when thou grew'st thyself.

> (4. 2. 202–4)

While Guiderius and Arviragus ultimately settle on loving Innogen/Fidele 'as my brother' (3. 6. 69), for Lucius the Roman consul she becomes both a surrogate son – he claims he would 'rather father thee than master thee' (4. 2. 397) – and the best of servants ('Never master had / A page so kind, so duteous, diligent' (5. 6. 85–6)). Even disguised as a boy, Innogen therefore continues to be defined by her beauty and sense of duty. Shakespeare also explores the ambiguity of gender identity and the appeal of homoerotic love – suggested here in Innogen's cross-dressing scenes – in the different genre of the sonnet, a concern Richard Danson Brown looks at in Chapter 2.

How is the feminine identity of the Queen dramatized?

The route chosen by Innogen is, of course, not the only one available for the women characters in *Cymbeline*, although the more defiant alternative taken by the Queen does end in a horrible death off-stage. The Queen's first words reveal an acute self-knowledge, when she says to Innogen:

> ... be assured you shall not find me, daughter,
> After the slander of most stepmothers,
> Evil-eyed unto you.

> (1. 1. 71–3)

Roger Warren, editor of the 1998 Oxford World's Classics edition of *Cymbeline*, sensibly suggests that although no written versions of *Snow White* before 1609 have been discovered, it is very likely that the versions of the tale circulated in oral form. The character of the Queen resembles the Wicked Stepmother in *Snow White*, and Innogen's flight from her, sanctuary in the country, 'death' and miraculous revival, and the final death of the Queen, confirm the parallel. Despite her initial appeal for understanding, the Queen never again tries to defend her self-interested actions, and all the other characters consistently describe her in very negative terms. Innogen refers to her as 'this tyrant / [who] Can tickle where she wounds!' (1. 1. 85–6); Cornelius declares in an aside 'I do not like her ... I do know her spirit, / And will not trust one of her malice' (1. 5. 33–5); the Second Lord calls her 'a crafty devil'

(2. 1. 49); and on hearing of her treachery from Cornelius after her death, Cymbeline himself first describes her as a 'most delicate fiend' (5. 6. 47), and then in keeping with his misogyny asks 'Who is't can read a woman?' (48).

There is one crucial aspect of the presentation of the Queen, however, which does not entirely coincide with her Wicked Stepmother image, and that is her stout defence of Britain and unremitting hostility to Rome. In order to look at this apparent anomaly in more detail, we need to move on to the third and final debate about *Cymbeline* identified above, the play's presentation of nationalism.

Nationalism in Cymbeline

How is 'Britain' imagined in *Cymbeline*? There are at least two aspects of British national identity to consider in *Cymbeline*, one that deals with Britain's relationship with Rome, and a second that deals with Britain's relationship with Wales.

Britain and Rome

The Queen's defiant speech to the Roman consul Lucius is a useful starting-point for our discussion of Britain's relation with Rome. Explaining why Britain's tribute to Rome remains unpaid, the Queen declares:

> That opportunity
> Which then they had to take from 's, to resume
> We have again. Remember, sir, my liege,
> The kings your ancestors, together with
> The natural bravery of your isle, which stands
> As Neptune's park, ribbed and paled in
> With banks unscalable and roaring waters,
> With sands that will not bear your enemies' boats,
> But suck them up to th' topmast. A kind of conquest
> Caesar made here, but made not here his brag
> Of 'came and saw and overcame'. With shame –
> The first that ever touched him – he was carried
> From off our coast, twice beaten; and his shipping,
> Poor ignorant baubles, on our terrible seas
> Like eggshells moved upon their surges, cracked
> As easily 'gainst our rocks; for joy whereof
> The famed Cassibelan, who was once at point –
> O giglot fortune! – to master Caesar's sword,
> Made Lud's town with rejoicing fires bright,
> And Britons strut with courage.

> (3. 1. 14–33)

As a patriotic call-to-arms, the Queen's speech compares favourably to the more famous of such speeches in Shakespeare, like that of John of Gaunt in *Richard II* (2. 1. 31–68), and that of King Harry before Agincourt in *Henry V* (4. 3. 20–67). The Queen appeals to the memory of brave British heroes (Cassibelan), sneers at the bravado of old adversaries (Julius Caesar), and evokes powerful images of a Britain defended by Nature ('banks unscalable', 'roaring waters', and wild seas that dash enemy ships against the rocks). There are, however, three important differences between the Queen's speech here, and those of John and Harry. In the first instance, *Richard II* and *Henry V* belonged to a relatively recent past and remained part of popular consciousness, whereas *Cymbeline* was drawn from a distant past in which the boundaries between myth and history had become blurred. In the second instance, *Cymbeline* was performed in 1609–10, when James I's diplomatic efforts were directed to securing treaties with European powers, whereas both *Richard II* (1595) and *Henry V* (1598–9) were performed a decade earlier, when Elizabeth I and Britain's international relations were dominated by war and the threat of war. Nationalist sentiment in the earlier plays would be indulged, and indeed encouraged, whereas by 1610 in extreme forms it might be viewed as an obstacle to international peace. The third difference between the Queen's speech and those of John and Harry is the fact that it is spoken by a *woman*. Mikalachki has noted that there are a number of Jacobean dramas like *Cymbeline* set in Roman Britain, which end with a masculine embrace uniting Rome and Britain, and the death of a female character who had advocated British resistance to Rome. Mikalachki explains this pattern as an attempt to exorcize or at least contain the histories of powerful female leaders in pre-Roman Britain, as any approval for such founding figures would threaten 'the establishment of a stable, masculine identity for the early modern nation' (1995, p.303). In other words, the same masculine order in *Cymbeline* that taught Innogen her place, expels the war-like Queen, who threatens to reincarnate the likes of Boadicea, or even the female figure of Britannia herself. Of interest in this regard is the cover of John Speed's book of maps of Britain, *The Theatre of the Empire of Great Britaine* (Figure 8), which was published in 1611, soon after *Cymbeline*'s first performance. The central figure of 'A Britaine' is male, and the prominent depiction of past invaders – Romans, Danes, Saxons and Normans – represents in visual terms the integration of old foes into an expanded British national identity.

How are sentiments of patriotism or national pride presented in the play?

The Queen, of course, is not alone in voicing patriotic feelings. Cloten and Pisanio also pledge their commitment to Britain, with Cloten especially vehement. In concert with the Queen's speech, Cloten tells Lucius that:

> Britain's a world
> By itself, and we will nothing pay
> For wearing our own noses

(3. 1. 12–14)

and that

> If Caesar can hide the sun from us with a blanket, or put the moon in his pocket, we will pay him tribute for light; else, sir, no more tribute

(3. 1. 41–3)

and he warns that, if Rome attacks Britain,

> you shall find us in our salt-water girdle. If you beat us out of it, it is yours; if you fall in the adventure, our crows shall fare the better for you; and there's an end.

(3. 1. 77–9)

Figure 8 *Title page of John Speed,* The Theatre of the Empire of Great Britaine, *John Sudby and George Humble, London, 1611. British Library G.7884. Reproduced by permission of the British Library, London.*

Less bellicose than Cloten, Pisanio, too, clings to the call of the nation when all else is confused:

> These present wars shall find I love my country
> Even to the note o'th' King, or I'll fall in them.
> All other doubts, by time let them be cleared:
> Fortune brings in some boats that are not steered.

> (4. 3. 43–6)

Posthumus's nationalism follows a more complex path. The wager with Giacomo, as well as the much earlier dispute recalled by the Frenchman, are both prompted by Posthumus's defence of the honour of British women. While in Rome, he dismisses Philario's optimistic prediction that Britain will pay the tribute, arguing on the contrary that 'this will prove a war' because 'our not-fearing Britain' (2. 4. 17, 19) has become a more formidable military force than when Julius Caesar subdued them. His heroic deeds in the final battle against the might of Rome, however, are undercut by his over-riding desire to redeem himself in the memory of Innogen. It is also his obsessive guilt in relation to Innogen that prompts him to allow himself to be taken as a Roman prisoner by the victorious Britons. The ease with which Posthumus switches national allegiance by changing clothes from 'Italian weeds' to those of 'a Briton peasant' (5. 1. 23–4), and then back again, throws into doubt the essentialist definitions of nationality favoured by the Queen and Cloten.

Like Posthumus, Innogen is ambiguously associated with British national identity. On the one hand, as a sexual trophy she is strongly connected to Britain. Unsettled by Giacomo's lies about Posthumus's philandering, she explicitly links her fate with that of Britain when she sighs, 'My lord, I fear, / Has forgot Britain' (1. 6. 113–14), and in exposing Giacomo she likens his sordid plot to 'a Romish stew' (153). Posthumus reinforces the association of Innogen's honour and Britain's sovereignty when before the battle he pledges

> 'Tis enough
> That, Britain, I have killed thy mistress-peace;
> I'll give no wound to thee.

> (5. 1. 19–21)

For Kahn, the 'narrow lane' defended by Belarius, Guiderius, Arviragus and Posthumus can be read as sexual terrain 'for the plot of Britain's relations with Rome is at every point in close alignment with the love story of Posthumus and Innogen' (1997, p.164). Innogen's ejection of Giacomo parallels the brave four's defeat of the Roman invaders. On the other hand, Innogen herself strikes a very different note when Pisanio advises her to leave Britain to save her life:

> Hath Britain all the sun that shines? Day, night,
> Are they not but in Britain? I'th' world's volume
> Our Britain seems as of it but not in't,
> In a great pool a swan's nest. Prithee, think
> There's livers out of Britain.

> (3. 4. 136–40)

Innogen's distressed state of mind might be put forward as a possible explanation for this unexpected refusal of British patriotism, but seen in the wider context of the evil Queen's narrow nationalism and the concluding rapprochement with Rome, her sentiments cohere with the 'internationalist' moral structure of the play.

Why does Cymbeline pay the tribute to Rome in the final scene?

In the first instance, it is important to register that Cymbeline shares the Queen's defiant patriotism that triggers the war with Rome. He says to Lucius:

> You must know,
> Till the injurious Romans did extort
> This tribute from us we were free. Caesar's ambition,
> Which swelled so much that it did almost stretch
> The sides o'th' world, against all colour here
> Did put the yoke upon 's, which to shake off
> Becomes a warlike people, whom we reckon
> Ourselves to be.
>
> (3. 1. 44–51)

After such brave words, how are we to explain his capitulation in the final scene? It is here that he recants:

> Although the victor, we submit to Caesar
> And to the Roman empire, promising
> To pay our wonted tribute, from the which
> We were dissuaded by our wicked queen.
>
> (5. 6. 460–3)

As many critics have observed, the answer lies in the identification of Cymbeline with James I. Augustus was the Roman emperor most admired in Jacobean England, with James explicitly identifying himself with Augustus, and seeking to achieve a Pax Britannia comparable to Augustus's Pax Romana. In submitting to Rome, Cymbeline is submitting to the authority of Augustus, an act of deference congruent with the dominant ideology of the time. In the play, what gives the settlement with Rome particular authority is the intervention of Jupiter, and the predictions of the Soothsayer. Again, this form of intervention satisfied Jacobean notions of wise royal governance. As Marcus points out, 'James I more than once descended upon Parliament like Jove with his "thunderbolts" to chide its members for their sluggishness with a pet project of his, the creation of Great Britain through the union of England and Scotland' (1988, p.134). The parallels with Jupiter's descent in the final act of *Cymbeline* are obvious.

Britain and Wales

How are we to explain the substantial Welsh section of the plot in *Cymbeline*? At a superficial level, the answer lies in the fact that James I had Welsh ancestors: he was a direct descendant of Henry VII, who was a Welshman. The most obvious allusions in *Cymbeline* to James's Welsh origins are the repeated references to Milford Haven. Henry VII had landed at Milford Haven in 1485 on returning from exile in Brittany, and on his way to defeating Richard III, thus establishing the Tudor dynasty. As Henry consolidated power during his reign, Welsh-speakers moved to London in significant numbers. Beyond the personal histories of the monarchs, there were also religious ties between Wales and the English throne. Donna B. Hamilton, who argues that the key to understanding *Cymbeline* lies principally in the religious conflicts between Protestant and Catholic, notes that the primitive British church was strongly associated with Wales. Further, James I enjoyed much support in Wales, which was 'the well-known power base for some of the great protestant gentry' (1992, p.153). For Terence Hawkes, however, Shakespeare's Welsh characters are to be explained in political – and particularly nationalist – terms, as their presence is due finally to the gradual incorporation of Wales into England, culminating in the sixteenth century. As Hawkes explains, 'when it came to the construction of a new entity called "Britain", that massive ideological project which obsessed both the Tudors and Stuarts and on which the history plays focus with consuming intensity, Wales's fate would ultimately prove to be more a matter of incorporation than confederacy' (1998, p.125). What gave the incorporation of the Welsh characters into a greater Britain in *Cymbeline* an added resonance in 1609 was the fact that James I was in the process of overseeing a second such act of union, namely the incorporation of Scotland into an expanding Britain.

Whereas characters like Posthumus and Innogen appear to move from an exclusively 'British' consciousness to a more international one, the Welsh characters of Belarius, Guiderius and Arviragus move from pastoral isolation to embrace Britain. After killing Cloten, Guiderius stoutly rejects Belarius's despairing 'We are all undone' (4. 2. 124), and declares:

> Why, worthy father, what have we to lose
> But that he swore to take, our lives? The law
> Protects not us: then why should we be tender
> To let an arrogant piece of flesh threat us,
> Play judge and executioner all himself,
> For we do fear the law?

(4. 2. 125–30)

With the prospect of Roman invasion, however, they soon change their tune. Guiderius concludes that the Romans will 'for Britains slay us' (4. 4. 5), and with very little encouragement, Arviragus and Belarius also commit themselves to fight in defence of Britain. Even if Belarius concludes with somewhat less enthusiasm – 'If in your country wars you chance to die, / That is my bed, too, lads, and there I'll lie' (4. 4. 51–2) – the three of them, together with Posthumus of course, go on to save Britain. In defeating Rome, the glory accrues not to the soldiers of Wales, but to· Cymbeline's Britain, which in turn defers to Roman authority.

Conclusion

Why, finally, has *Cymbeline* been neglected? The reception history illustrates how arguably more than any other Shakespeare play its reputation has shifted as critical fashions have changed. For reasons attributed both to its uncertain genre and to its awkward content, its fortunes have fluctuated wildly. This is a pattern that continues to the present, for at least part of the reason for its return in this volume lies in its status as a fascinating seventeenth-century treatment of what are much-debated contemporary obsessions: gender politics, sexual identity and nationalism.

The clearest indication of how our reading of *Cymbeline* here has been influenced by current concerns lies in the focus on nationalism. British political life in the last few decades has been dominated by arguments about nationalism, focusing both on Britain's troubled relationship with an expanding Europe, and on the separatist aspirations of Wales, Scotland and Ireland. *Cymbeline* is an early modern text that dramatizes in complex fashion similar contradictions and tensions. A glib version of the argument might suggest:

Rome in 1609 = Brussels in 2000;
Milford Haven in 1609 = the Welsh Assembly in 2000.

Such neat analogies might serve as a provocation, but underlying them deeper and ongoing questions about British nationalism persist, and *Cymbeline* provides a sophisticated version of how they were expressed at a key historical moment. The same might certainly be said of how *Cymbeline* represents for its own age anxieties about gender politics and sexual identities that continue unresolved in mutated forms in contemporary society. In Chapter 2 on *Shakespeare's Sonnets*, Richard Danson Brown takes these questions further, and focuses in particular on how the sonnets articulate Shakespeare's preoccupations of 1609 in poetic form.

References

Adelman, J. (1992) *Suffocating Mothers: Fantasies of Maternal Origin in Shakespeare's Plays, 'Hamlet' to 'The Tempest'*, London and New York: Routledge.

Bamber, L. (1982) *Comic Women, Tragic Men: A Study of Gender and Genre in Shakespeare*, Stanford: Stanford University Press.

Bate, J. (ed.) (1992) *The Romantics on Shakespeare*, Harmondsworth: Penguin.

Beaumont, F. and Fletcher, J. (1975 edn) *Philaster, or Love Lies a-Bleeding*, ed. D.J. Ashe, London: Edward Arnold (first published 1610).

Bergeron, D.M. (1980) '*Cymbeline*: Shakespeare's last Roman play', *Shakespeare Quarterly*, vol.31, pp.31–41.

Bowers, F. (ed.) (1976) *The Dramatic Works in the Beaumont and Fletcher Canon*, Volume 3, Cambridge: Cambridge University Press.

Derrida, J. (1980) 'La loire du genre/The Law of Genre', *Glyph Textual Studies*, vol.7, pp.176–232.

Dobson, M. (1992) *The Making of the National Poet: Shakespeare, Adaptation and Authorship, 1660–1769*, Oxford: Clarendon Press.

Dollimore, J. and Sinfield, A. (eds) (1985) *Political Shakespeare: New Essays in Cultural Materialism*, Manchester: Manchester University Press.

Dowden, E. (1967 edn) *Shakespeare: A Critical Study of His Mind and Art*, London: Routledge & Kegan Paul (first published 1875).

Felperin, H. (1972) *Shakespearean Romance*, Princeton: Princeton University Press.

Frost, D. (1986) '"Mouldy tales": the context of Shakespeare's *Cymbeline*', *Essays and Studies*, pp.19–38.

Frye, N. (1957) *The Anatomy of Criticism*, Princeton: Princeton University Press.

Frye, N. (1976) *The Secular Scripture*, Cambridge: Harvard University Press.

Goldberg, J. (1983) *James I and the Politics of Literature*, Baltimore: Johns Hopkins University Press.

Greenblatt, S., Cohen, W., Howard, J.E. and Maus, K.E. (eds) (1997) *The Norton Shakespeare*, New York: W.W. Norton.

Hamilton, D.B. (1992) *Shakespeare and the Politics of Protestant England*, Kentucky: University of Kentucky Press.

Hawkes, T. (1998) 'Bryn Glas', in *Post-colonial Shakespeares*, ed. A. Loomba and M. Orkin, London and New York: Routledge, pp.117–40.

Jackson, R. (1971) '*Cymbeline* in the Nineteenth Century', M.A. dissertation, University of Birmingham.

Jacobi, D. (1998) *Classic FM Favourite Shakespeare*, intro. J. Brunning, London: Hodder & Stoughton.

Jameson, F. (1981) *The Political Unconscious: Narrative as a Socially Symbolic Act*, London: Methuen.

Johnson, D. (1996) *Shakespeare and South Africa*, Oxford: Clarendon Press.

Kahn, C. (1997) *Roman Shakespeare: Warriors, Wounds, and Women*, London and New York: Routledge.

Kirsch, A.C. (ed.) (1966) *Literary Criticism of John Dryden*, Lincoln: University of Nebraska Press.

Knight, G.W. (1947) *The Crown of Life*, Oxford: Oxford University Press.

Laurence, D.H. (ed.) (1965) *Bernard Shaw: Collected Letters, 1874–1897*, London: Max Reinhardt.

Laurence, D.H. (ed.) (1974) *The Bodley Head Bernard Shaw: Collected Plays with their Prefaces*, Volume VII, London: The Bodley Head.

Lawrence, J. (1994) 'Natural bonds and artistic coherence in the ending of *Cymbeline*', *Shakespeare Quarterly*, vol.35, no.4, pp.440–60.

Lenz, C.R.S., Greene, G. and Neely, C.T. (eds) (1980) *The Woman's Part: Feminist Criticism of Shakespeare*, Chicago: University of Illinois Press.

Marcus, L. (1988) '*Cymbeline* and the unease of topicality', in *The Historical Renaissance: New Essays on Tudor and Stuart Literature and Culture*, ed. H. Dubrow and R. Strier, Chicago: University of Chicago Press, pp.134–68.

Mikalachki, J. (1995) 'The masculine romance of Roman Britain: *Cymbeline* and early modern English nationalism', *Shakespeare Quarterly*, vol.46, no.3, pp.301–22.

Miola, R.S. (1984) '*Cymbeline*: Shakespeare's valediction to Rome', in *Roman Images: Selected Papers from the English Institute, 1982*, New Series No. 8, ed. A. Patterson, Baltimore: Johns Hopkins University Press, pp.51–62.

Nosworthy, J.M. (ed.) (1955) *Cymbeline*, The Arden Shakespeare, London: Methuen.

Palgrave, F.T. (1861) *The Golden Treasury of the Best Songs and Lyrical Poems in the English Language*, Cambridge and London: Macmillan.

Shapiro, M. (1994) *Gender in Play on the Shakespearean Stage: Boy Heroines and Female Pages*, Ann Arbor: University of Michigan Press.

Simonds, P.M. (1992) *Myth, Emblem, and Music in Shakespeare's 'Cymbeline'*, Newark: University of Delaware Press.

Sutherland, G. (ed.) (1973) *Matthew Arnold on Education*, Harmondsworth: Penguin.

Taylor, G. (1989) *Reinventing Shakespeare: A Cultural History for the Restoration to the Present*, London: The Hogarth Press.

Thompson, A. (1991) '*Cymbeline*'s other endings', in *The Appropriation of Shakespeare: Post-Renaissance Reconstructions of the Works and the Myth*, ed. J.I. Marsden, New York: St Martin's Press, pp.203–20.

Vickers, B. (ed.) (1976) *Shakespeare: The Critical Heritage, Volume 4, 1753–1765*, London: Routledge & Kegan Paul.

Viswanathan, G. (1989) *Masks of Conquest: Literary Study and British Rule in India*, London: Faber & Faber.

Warren, R. (ed.) (1998) *Cymbeline*, Oxford: Oxford University Press.

Wickham, G. (1973) 'From tragedy to tragi-comedy: *King Lear* as Prologue', *Shakespeare Survey*, vol.26, pp.33–48.

Woodbridge, L. (1984) *Women and the English Renaissance: Literature and the Nature of Womankind, 1540–1620*, Brighton: The Harvester Press.

Woudhuysen, H.R. (ed.) (1989) *Samuel Johnson on Shakespeare*, Harmondsworth: Penguin

SHAKESPEARE'S SONNETS

Chapter 2

Richard Danson Brown

Aims

The central purpose of this chapter is to enable you to meet the challenges of Shakespeare's non-dramatic poetry through an examination of *Shakespeare's Sonnets*.[1] We shall investigate the sonnet form as it came down to Shakespeare and how he modifies that form. Then we shall explore how the sonnets have been interpreted since their first publication and consider how these poems have influenced perceptions of Shakespeare. Finally, we shall attempt to read the sonnets as complex representations of conflicting experiences of love. Throughout the chapter, close attention is paid to the literary language used in these poems, and this should facilitate your understanding of Shakespeare's poetry and drama.

Introduction

This chapter has a different focus from David Johnson's chapter on *Cymbeline* and from this book's companion volume, *Shakespeare: Texts and Contexts*, in examining poetic rather than dramatic texts. We are taking this approach because Shakespeare's poetic *oeuvre* is often overlooked by students and scholars, and paying close attention to the poetry can refocus how we read the plays, as well as extending our sense of the breadth of Shakespeare's writing. It will become clear that there are important connections between the plays and the sonnets as literary representations of love and sexuality. Yet because the sonnets were not produced in cultural isolation when they were first published in 1609 by Thomas Thorpe, we also need to read sonnets by other writers who had an influence on Shakespeare. As we shall see, *Shakespeare's Sonnets* can be viewed both as a late response to the Elizabethan vogue for sonnet sequences, and as a response to the literary and cultural conditions of the Jacobean period in which the volume was published. So in this chapter you will find detailed readings of the sonnets alongside parallels drawn both from Shakespeare's plays and from the poetry of earlier writers and contemporaries that influenced him.

Reading a sonnet sequence is not like reading a play or a novel. If you try to read each sonnet consecutively, you will soon become exhausted and dispirited. Every

---

[1] *Shakespeares Sonnets* is the full title of the first publication of the sonnets in 1609. In this chapter we use a modernized version of this title to indicate the published collection of 154 sonnets. In referring generally to the poems in the volume we use the form: the sonnets.

sonnet is a complex and independent poetic unit within a larger whole and the 'story' of a sonnet sequence is rarely as developmental as the plot of a play. Ideally, you should become familiar both with specific sonnets and with the broader sequence, but at this stage **read the poems that will be discussed in this chapter: Sonnets 18, 65, 138, 1, 118, 20, 35, 126, 129 and 146. It would help you to develop a sense of *Shakespeare's Sonnets* as a sequence to read the poems in their numerical order as well as in the order of their discussion in the chapter.**

From Cymbeline *to Sonnet 18*

Where *Cymbeline* is a relatively unfamiliar part of the Shakespearean canon, *Shakespeare's Sonnets* includes some of the most famous short poems to have been written in any language. What are the critical implications of moving from an obscure play to a collection of sometimes notorious poems? Let's consider Sonnet 18 as a test case – a poem that almost single-handedly seems to embody Shakespeare as a love poet. In Evelyn Waugh's satirical novel *The Loved One* (1948), a dilettante English poet living in Hollywood attempts to seduce an American mortician by passing off famous English poems as his own work inspired by her:

> At first he had tried writing poems for her himself but she showed a preference for the earlier masters. Moreover, the Muse nagged him. He had abandoned the poem he was writing ... Sooner or later the Muse would have to be placated. She came first. Meanwhile Aimée must draw from the bran-tub of the anthologies. Once he came near to exposure when she remarked that *Shall I compare thee to a summer's day* reminded her of something she had learned at school.

> (Waugh, 1951 edn, p.84)

Waugh's joke is that 'Shall I compare thee to a summer's day?' (Sonnet 18) is one of the most celebrated love poems written in any language. It is as famous a piece of Shakespeare as Hamlet's 'To be or not to be' soliloquy. A more recent example of its fame would be its use in John Madden's film *Shakespeare in Love* (1999), in which the love-struck Will Shakespeare takes time out from struggling over *Romeo and Juliet* to write the sonnet for the glamorous heiress-cum-actor Viola De Lesseps. In watching Shakespeare write the sonnet for Viola, the audience experiences a satisfying illusion of biographical explanation: 'so *that's* why he wrote it'. In Waugh's novel, the fact that his protagonist, Dennis Barlow, is able to get away with this level of literary imposture aptly demonstrates the cultural naïvety of his heroine, Aimée Thanatagenos (her name means roughly 'the beloved dead thing', punning on her job as a beautifier of corpses). Yet even Aimée half recognizes this poem. Although *The Loved One* is animated by Waugh's disdain for twentieth-century America, he has to concede that Shakespeare's most famous sonnet has reached California. Indeed, Dennis's American rival – the ludicrously named Mr Joyboy – later exposes his plagiarism.

The Loved One's story of literary theft raises the question of how far the sonnets have become a part of the cultural mainstream. By contrast with *Cymbeline*, whose checkered performance and reception histories fully justify us seeing it as a neglected play, the sonnets seem to be a more stable part of the Shakespearean canon. Waugh's text implies one answer to this question. Dennis takes his poems not from a volume of Shakespeare's collected works or an edition of *Shakespeare's Sonnets*, but from the *Oxford Book of English Verse*; as Waugh snidely puts it, 'Aimée must draw from the bran-tub of the anthologies'. In other words, Aimée's familiarity with Sonnet 18 does not tell us that all of the sonnets are equally well known. Rather, it points to the fact that some poems have achieved a wider dissemination than others because they have been reprinted in influential anthologies. *Shakespeare in Love* plays a similar game: other more complicated sonnets would not have been either as familiar to the cinema audience or as applicable to Will's heterosexual passion for Viola. 'Shall I compare thee to a summer's day?' is both extremely popular even among non-poetry readers and sufficiently general to be appropriated to any kind of love affair. As the example of Sonnet 18 shows, certain poems have come to embody a very general idea of the emotions of being in love.

It would also be unwise to claim that the sequence as a whole has not enjoyed extensive attention during the twentieth century. As long ago as 1964, W.H. Auden observed: 'Probably, more nonsense has been talked and written, more intellectual and emotional energy expended in vain, on the sonnets of Shakespeare than on any other literary work in the world' (1973, p.88). But, as Auden goes on to clarify, much of this 'intellectual and emotional energy' has been 'expended' on attempts to unravel the biographical mystery – whether or not the poems are disclosures of Shakespeare's own love life – that surrounds the volume. Writing in 1987, Heather Dubrow makes a similar point: although there are many studies of the sonnets, most 'still focus on biographical questions at the expense of ... rhetorical issues' (p.29). Formal consideration of the sonnets as poetry has been overshadowed by the investigation of them as a *roman-à-clef*, which, if ever satisfactorily unlocked, would disclose the secrets of Shakespeare's love life.

One of the central aims of this chapter is to enable you to appreciate the complex poetic qualities of the sonnets. Yet we should recognize that the formalist ambition to read the sonnets solely as poetry is in itself as illusory as the desire to unlock the poems' biographical meaning. Poetry is a very specialized use of language with its own rules and forms, but it is not insulated from outside pressures and influences. Indeed, if it were simply a self-sustaining 'art' language, it would have few claims on our interest. Although I would suggest that it is unwise to read *Shakespeare's Sonnets* in the hope of discovering the amatory proclivities of the 'real' William Shakespeare, the 1609 volume includes prominent autobiographical pointers which seem to invite the reader to speculate about the relationship between the activities described in the poems and the life of their writer (see Walter Cohen's similar observation in *The Norton Shakespeare* (Greenblatt *et al.*, 1997), pp.1920–1). Shakespeare may not have anticipated the speculative industry that has tried to identify the young man and the 'woman coloured ill' (144.4)[2] who generate the poems, yet he does aggressively draw the reader's attention to his first name in some of the sequence's most erotically charged poems: 'Will will fulfill the treasure of thy love' (136.5).

We will need, then, to adopt a range of approaches to the sonnets, balancing attention to the forms that organize the poems with a sense of the traditions, interests and irrecoverable events that stimulated their writing. The study of poetry requires different skills from the study of drama, but applying these skills will also

---

[2] The convention adopted throughout this chapter when referring to quotations from sonnets is to cite sonnet number followed by line number(s) after a full point.

enrich our understanding of Shakespeare's plays. Discussion of the sonnets is typically isolated from discussion of the plays beyond the observation of verbal reminiscences (as we shall see, the fourth line of Sonnet 1 recalls a phrase from *Cymbeline*). But the sonnets are connected to *Cymbeline* not just because they were first published in the same year that the play was first performed, but also because of the selective ways in which they – like *Cymbeline* – have been interpreted by later readers. This means, I suggest, that despite the fame of some sonnets, we may read these poems as another less familiar area of the Shakespearean landscape.

Bearing this information in mind, let's now examine Sonnet 18 (Figure 9) in detail.[3]

Read Sonnet 18 through carefully. It is a good practice to read any new poem at least twice, and, if possible, to read it out loud to get a more intimate sense of the sounds and patterns within the verse. Now look at the poem's structure: how do you think the content is organized in this sonnet? Try to isolate the moment where the focus of the poem shifts from the beloved to poetry itself.

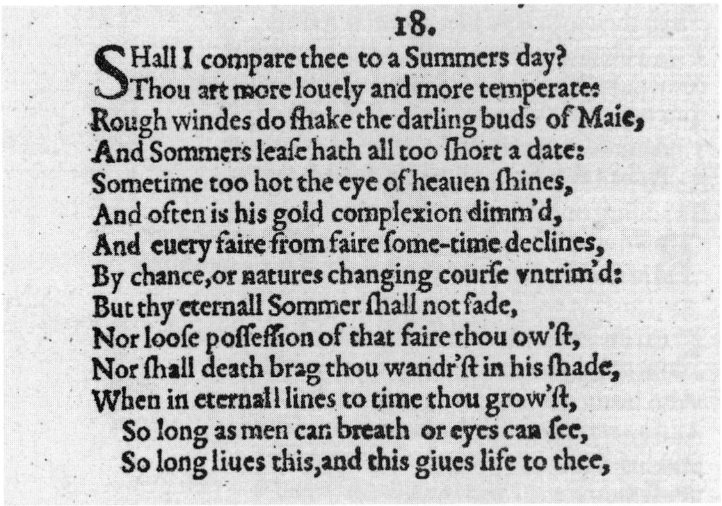

18.

SHall I compare thee to a Summers day?
 Thou art more louely and more temperate:
Rough windes do ſhake the darling buds of Maie,
And Sommers leaſe hath all too ſhort a date:
Sometime too hot the eye of heauen ſhines,
And often is his gold complexion dimm'd,
And euery faire from faire ſome-time declines,
By chance,or natures changing courſe vntrim'd:
But thy eternall Sommer ſhall not fade,
Nor looſe poſſeſſion of that faire thou ow'ſt,
Nor ſhall death brag thou wandr'ſt in his ſhade,
When in eternall lines to time thou grow'ſt,
 So long as men can breath or eyes can ſee,
 So long liues this,and this giues life to thee,

Figure 9 *Sonnet 18 in* Shake-Speares Sonnets ... , *G. Eld for T.T., London, 1609, reproduced from* Shakespeare's Sonnets; ... facsimile ... from the unrivalled original in the library of Bridgewater House ..., *Lovell Reeve, London, 1862.*

The vast majority of the sonnets follow the same basic design as Sonnet 18.[4] They are composed of three quatrains (four-line stanzas with alternate rhymes) followed by a closing rhymed couplet. In the quotation of Sonnet 18 that follows, I embolden the rhyme words or sounds and indicate by means of a letter which other line they rhyme with. I also separate the quatrains and couplet from one another to give you a clearer picture of the design Shakespeare employs.

[3] We have reprinted texts from the first edition of *Shakespeare's Sonnets* so that you can compare them with the versions in *The Norton Shakespeare.*

[4] The poems that do not conform to this scheme are Sonnet 99 (which has an extra opening line introducing the poem) and Sonnet 126 (a 12-line poem composed of rhyming couplets). Sonnet 145 is exceptional because its lines are shorter than those of every other sonnet: instead of the five stress lines of the majority of sonnets (usually known as iambic pentameter), this has four stress lines (iambic tetrameter). Compare the first line of Sonnet 144 ('Two **loves** I **have**, of **comfort and despair**') with the first line of Sonnet 145 ('Those **lips** that **love's** own **hand** did **make**').

Shall I compare thee to a summer's **day**?	(A)
Thou art more lovely and more tempe**rate**.	(B)
Rough winds do shake the darling buds of **May**,	(A)
And summer's lease hath all too short a **date**.	(B)
Sometime too hot the eye of heaven **shines**,	(C)
And often is his gold complexion **dimmed**,	(D)
And every fair from fair sometime de**clines**,	(C)
By chance or nature's changing course un**trimmed**;	(D)
But thy eternal summer shall not **fade**	(E)
Nor lose possession of that fair thou **ow'st**,	(F)
Nor shall death brag thou wander'st in his **shade**	(E)
When in eternal lines to time thou **grow'st**.	(F)
So long as men can breathe or eyes can **see**,	(G)
So long lives this, and this gives life to **thee**.	(G)

We could say that a Shakespeare sonnet is a poem of 14 lines with seven rhymes, organized as above. This form is often known as the Shakespearean or English sonnet in contrast to the Petrarchan sonnet, which has a major break in sense between the first eight lines (the octave, usually rhyming ABBA ABBA) and the final six lines (the sestet, typically rhyming CDE CDE).[5]

But the question I asked was more specific: how is the content organized in this sonnet? It is important to remember that poetic lines and sentence structure do not invariably coincide. Although in this text each line can be read as a self-contained unit of meaning ('Sometime too hot the eye of heaven shines' and 'And often is his gold complexion dimmed' are simultaneously independent statements and parts of the same sentence), this is not always the case. In Sonnet 65, for example, sentence structure and line length are disrupted and distorted as the thought becomes more troubled: 'O fearful meditation! Where, alack, / Shall time's best jewel from time's chest lie hid' (65.9–10). Line 10 here only makes sense as a part of a longer sentence. You can see similar effects in Shakespeare's dramatic verse: earlier plays like *A Midsummer Night's Dream* have a greater preponderance of self-contained and rhyming lines, whereas later plays like *Cymbeline* have more lines in which the sense seems to overflow the five-beat line. Compare Helena's

> Happy is Hermia, wheresoe'er she lies;
> For she hath blessèd and attractive eyes

> (*A Midsummer Night's Dream* 2. 2. 96–7)

with Innogen's

> I would have broke mine eye-strings, cracked them, but
> To look upon him till the diminution
> Of space had pointed him sharp as my needle.

> (*Cymbeline* 1. 3. 17–19)

---

[5] For an example of this kind of poem, see the sonnets by Sir Philip Sidney quoted below.

The layout of Sonnet 18 above shows its poetic design and suggests that the poem is made up of four separate but interconnected units. Yet is this really our experience of reading it? Sonnet 18 begins with a question, which the next seven lines debate. Let's try to paraphrase this part of the poem, remembering that, as John Barrell observes, such an exercise 'can do little more ... than point one way through a poem, privileging those meanings which the paraphraser thinks it most important to draw attention to' (1988, p.32); the paraphrase is not, in other words, an exhaustive or objective guide to the meaning of Sonnet 18:

> Shall I compare you to a summer's day? Well, it sounds flattering, but you are actually more lovely and moderate ('temperate'); furthermore, summer's days are often scorchingly hot, while such beautiful things of their very nature disappear all too quickly; through all of these examples, I am not sure how like a summer's day you really are.

It seems that lines 1–8 constitute a connected thought about the beloved object. (It is worth noting at this point that the first 126 sonnets are clearly addressed to a young man; we will discuss the full implications of this later in the chapter.) I would suggest that the major change in this poem comes with the 'But' that begins line 9. It is here that we switch from exploring the comparison to a more assertive mode. The young man's 'eternal summer shall not fade' because it will be preserved in the 'eternal lines' of the poem we are reading. Unlike a summer's day, the young man will not 'lose possession of that fair thou ow'st' because of the endless succession of later readers this poem imagines for itself; as the couplet puts it, 'So long as men can breathe or eyes can see, / So long lives this, and this gives life to thee'.

Sonnet 18, then, turns from the beloved to poetry in line 9. This effectively means that it follows the structure of a Petrarchan sonnet in having a significant break or change in meaning between the first eight and final six lines, even though it follows a simpler rhyme scheme.

From this exercise you should be able to see that the sonnet form Shakespeare deploys is a design that is capable of a range of different permutations. If Sonnet 18 looks Petrarchan, Sonnet 66, for example, piles up a series of complaints in its first 12 lines before shifting semantic and poetic gears in the couplet. Equally, there are poems like Sonnet 73, which fit more easily into the design of having four separate movements that coincide with the quatrains and the couplet. Each sonnet is in some ways a new attempt on Shakespeare's part to negotiate the challenges of the sonnet form; each reading that you make, therefore, needs to be alert to the poetic strategies he employs. You may have wondered why Shakespeare or Thomas Thorpe did not simplify the reader's job by printing the sonnets as separate quatrains and couplets. The simplest answer to this question (beyond the practical necessity of saving space in the book) is that to print the poems in this way would suggest that they all follow that particular semantic permutation. Printing each of them as a continuous paragraph with an indented couplet suggests both that these texts share the same overall format, and that each separate poem constructs its own rules for itself.

Before leaving Sonnet 18, I would like to return to the issue of the immortality that this poem promises its subject. On the face of it, Sonnet 18 makes a startling claim. Although summer's days and other beautiful things are mortal and transient, the young man will cheat death through the fame of the poem. It almost sounds as though Shakespeare had in fact anticipated the enormous posthumous success of this poem. Yet, in making this promise, Sonnet 18 is participating in a very ancient literary strategy, which is also used in many of the other sonnets. As E.R. Curtius puts it, 'Poetry perpetuates' (1990 edn, p.476): poets from the ancient Greek Homer (8 BCE) onwards have drawn attention to the power of their art to preserve both its subjects and its practitioners. At the end of the *Metamorphoses* (CE 8), the Roman poet Ovid asserted 'all the world shall never / Be able for to quench my name' (Martin, 1998, p.75; see Text 1 in Appendix 2). This emphasis on the fame provided by poetry became a stock part of the persuasive rhetoric of Renaissance sonneteers. Across national and linguistic boundaries, poet after poet produces his – and sonneteers were usually, although not exclusively, men – own version of a kind of poetic bribery.[6] 'If you will love me,' the poet says to his putative girl, 'I will immortalize you': as Edmund Spenser puts it 'my verse your vertues rare shall eternize [immortalize], / and in the hevens wryte your glorious name' (Evans, 1977, p.146). In reading Sonnet 18, we are immediately engaging with Shakespeare's treatment of what was by 1609 a well-worn literary cliché. Does this suggest that the sonnets are simply reduplications of ideas that may have been better expressed elsewhere?

I would now like you to read Sonnet 65, and compare it first with Sonnet 18 and then with Spenser's 'One day I wrote her name upon the strand' (Text 2), Sonnet 75 from his *Amoretti and Epithalamion* (1595). What are the major differences you notice between the way these texts treat the idea of literary immortality?

In Sonnet 18, poetry's ability to preserve the young man is asserted with a swagger. Death will not 'brag thou wander'st in his shade' because Shakespeare's poem will last 'So long as men can breathe or eyes can see', thus giving a metaphoric 'life' to the poem's subject. By contrast, the bulk of Sonnet 65 (Figure 10) states that the 'power' of 'sad mortality' is so great that nothing can resist the process of decay. The notion that poetry could exempt the speaker's love from time's onslaught then appears as a 'miracle'. Shakespeare opposes the physically insignificant 'black ink' of his text against the enormous destructive power of time. The point is that, whereas in Sonnet 18 poetry is itself a powerful agent, in Sonnet 65 its powers are more tenuous. The survival of his love through poetry is a miraculous postulate the speaker desperately wants to believe in, even though he is conscious that 'summer's honey breath' cannot 'hold out / Against the wrackful siege of battering days'. Sonnet 65 trades the confident assertions of the earlier poem for a more troubled faith in poetic miracles.

There are two differences between Sonnet 65 and 'One day I wrote her name upon the strand' that I would particularly emphasize. First, Spenser asserts poetry's power to 'eternize' without any of the uncertainties that are so manifest in Shakespeare's text; Spenser's poem is closer to Sonnet 18 than Sonnet 65. When the woman in *Amoretti* 75 reminds the poet–speaker of her mortality, he blithely assures her not only that she will 'live by [poetic] fame', but also that the couple's love will 'later life renew' after their own deaths. In this hyperbolic assertion, poetry has acquired an unspecific capacity to regenerate the dead. Secondly, Spenser's poem is a kind of miniature drama, an anecdote with dialogue. Sonnet 65, by contrast, is a 'fearful meditation', in which the speaker broods intensely over a series of questions

---

[6] With the growth of gender studies in the late twentieth century, there has been an increasing realization that early modern women did write poetry, including love sonnets. Their work, however, has been doubly marginalized – first, by the patriarchal societies of which they were a part and which construed poetry as a predominantly male activity, and, secondly, by the formation of the literary canon by later critics, who were often ignorant of or insensitive to the writings of women. Impressive love sonnets were written by women like Lady Mary Wroth, whose *Pamphilia to Amphilanthus* (1621) are poems written by a female speaker to a male subject, and the sixteenth-century French writer Louise Labé.

> 65
>
> ꟊInce braffe, nor ſtone, nor earth, nor boundleſſe ſea,
> But ſad mortallity ore-ſwaies their power,
> How with this rage ſhall beautie hold a plea,
> Whoſe action is no ſtronger then a flower?
> O how ſhall ſummers hunny breath hold out,
> Againſt the wrackfull ſiedge of battring dayes,
> When rocks impregnable are not ſo ſtoute,
> Nor gates of ſteele ſo ſtrong but time decayes?
> O fearefull meditation, where alack,
> Shall times beſt Iewell from times cheſt lie hid?
> Or what ſtrong hand can hold his ſwift foote back,
> Or who his ſpoile or beautie can forbid?
> O none, vnleſſe this miracle haue might,
> That in black inck my loue may ſtill ſhine bright.

Figure 10 *Sonnet 65 in* Shake-Speares Sonnets ... , *G. Eld for T.T., London, 1609, reproduced from* Shakespeare's Sonnets; ... facsimile ... from the unrivalled original in the library of Bridgewater House ..., *Lovell Reeve, London, 1862.*

relating to 'sad mortality'. Where Spenser's poem presents a specific occasion as a witty interaction between the poet and the woman, Shakespeare's renders an anguished process of thinking in which the potential immortality of poetry is the last hope against the realization of the transience of all things. Although both texts participate in the same tradition, their treatment of that tradition is radically dissimilar.

So I would argue that, reading the sonnets alongside the work of Shakespeare's contemporaries, it becomes clear both that his poems were shaped by the patterns of earlier writers, and that he treats this inheritance idiosyncratically. As Jonathan Bate points out, Renaissance literary culture did not insist that new texts should have the kind of unprecedented originality that post-Romantic and nineteenth-century writers aimed for. Shakespeare's treatment of Ovid, for example, demonstrates his awareness of 'a cardinal principle of Renaissance poetics' that 'good imitation involves difference as well as similarity' (Bate, 1993, p.87). In other words, Shakespeare can model his poems on a pre-existing text or tradition yet assimilate its influences into his own poetic vocabulary.

In general, the sonnets do not try to embody particularly abstruse ideas. The thinking in Sonnet 65's 'meditation' is familiar and readily apprehensible: human life and beauty are transient. Indeed, as we have seen, Sonnet 65 is in many ways a more introspective reworking of the same ideas explored in Sonnet 18: life passes, poetry perpetuates. Yet Shakespeare's expression of these ideas is characteristically rich. Consider the dense metaphors and conflicting sounds packed into 'Against the wrackful siege of battering days': time is an ultimately ruinous ('wrackful') 'siege' in which the passage of 'days' is likened to the 'battering' of a ram against the gates of a besieged city. The metaphor then spreads outwards into the following lines' images of 'rocks impregnable' and 'gates of steel', which are all subject to the depredations of time. Almost all of the poems in *Shakespeare's Sonnets* simultaneously enact and demand this kind of intense concentration. There is nothing particularly new about sonnets that utilize the idea that poetry provides a metaphoric form of memorialization. In the sixteenth century, such poems were commonplace. But Shakespeare's poems – which directly engage the reader in unpacking the speaker's interiorized meditations – have actually made good their often tentative claims to immortality.

'Antique song': the history of the sonnet

This reading of Sonnets 18 and 65 is a useful way into the study of the sequence as a whole, because it illustrates that, to make sense of these poems, we need to be aware of the complex literary traditions of which Shakespeare was both a product and a part. You will not fully understand the sonnets unless you are prepared to read them alongside the work of other writers who were Shakespeare's influences and contemporaries. So this section explores the history of the sonnet form in early modern Europe to give a more detailed sense of the literary mode of *Shakespeare's Sonnets*.

Petrarch and his imitators

Where, then, does the sonnet come from? The form of the 14-line love poem was a creation of thirteenth-century Italian poets; the Tuscan Dante Alighieri (1265–1321) is the most celebrated of these early sonneteers. His collection *La vita nuova* (*The New Life*, *c*.1292), which recounts the story of his idealized love for Beatrice, includes several sonnets. But the European vogue for long sequences of sonnets was prompted by the later Tuscan poet Franceso Petrarch (1304–74). He wrote over 300 sonnets between the 1330s and the 1360s, recording his hopeless love for the vague figure of Laura, which were collected as the *Rime sparse* (*Scattered Rhymes*). Although Petrarch's collection includes other kinds of lyric, his sequence differs crucially from Dante's in lacking any external explication of the poems. *La vita nuova* contains a prose commentary, which contextualizes each poem within the overall narrative of Dante's love for Beatrice and his development as a poet. By contrast, the *Rime sparse* simply progress from one poem to another. The reader must infer the changes and developments in the speaker's feelings for Laura through the poems themselves. Moreover, the only action that takes place in Petrarch's long sequence is that Laura dies; conventionally, the sequence is divided between poems written while Laura was alive and those written after her death (see Durling, 1976, p.8).

Stories told through sequences of lyric poems are usually precisely that – lyrical. Petrarch's sonnets, like those of his many imitators, anatomize the complex and fluctuating emotions of the poet–speaker; unlike a play, they do not circumstantially relate a concrete narrative. As an example of this, you might compare Sonnet 18 with the sonnet Romeo and Juliet speak to one another at the Capulet ball (*Romeo and Juliet* 1. 5. 90–103). Although the words the lovers speak take the form of a sonnet, their passionate exchange is dramatically framed by Tybalt's argument with Capulet about Romeo's presence at the ball. The sonnet is a small component of a larger dramatic action, whereas Sonnet 18 is a self-contained unit within a text made up of such units.

Petrarch made the lyric expression of anguished interiority an attractive and readily imitable poetic mode. The poet loves a woman he cannot have; this situation enables him to generate texts reiterating and exploring that dilemma. Between the fourteenth and sixteenth centuries, sonnet writing became a fashionable activity in a wide range of European languages. In this sense, the diffusion of the sonnet form indicates the wider diffusion of the Renaissance – the so-called 'rebirth' of an interest in classical culture – throughout early modern Europe. The sonnet was not a classical form, but its association with Petrarch, who was also an influential exponent of the classics, gave it a neo-classical lustre. When later poets wrote love sonnets they were participating in a complex literary and cultural game for which Petrarch had written the rules.

Let's try to get a more specific sense of what the rules of the sonnet game were. Read Robert Durling's modern prose translation of Petrarch's 'Pace non trovo' as well as the translation of this same poem by Sir Thomas Wyatt (*c.*1503–42) (Texts 3 and 4). How would you characterize the speaker's state of mind?

My answer would be that the speaker in both versions is conflicted. This sense of conflict is progressively elaborated in each new line as Petrarch piles up an accumulating body of antitheses and paradoxes: although he burns he is made of ice; although he grasps nothing he embraces all the world; and, crucially, he loves another and hates himself. Love forces the speaker into a paradoxical mode of being and expression. The Petrarchan speaker is typically extreme, veering between contrary emotional states as love disrupts his sense of self.

This emotional turmoil leads to a poetic language that is similarly exaggerated yet tightly controlled. Wyatt's translation catches this well: 'That looseth nor locketh, holdeth me in prison / And holdeth me not, yet can I scape no wise'. A modern English paraphrase of these lines could be: 'I am imprisoned yet I am not held; I am free and yet I cannot escape'. Even in this version, you should see that this is not a conversational idiom. Rather, it is a rhetorical register that draws attention to its artfulness through its balanced self-contradictions. As Wyatt's translation demonstrates, such conflicts became the raw materials of later poets. Petrarch's sonnets gave a series of templates that could be modified according to the demands of new situations. What Sir Philip Sidney ironically calls '*Petrarch*'s long deceased woes' (Evans, 1997, p.8) in a love sonnet of his own were recycled by different poets addressing their poems to ladies as unyielding as Laura.

It is also worth noting that this hyperbolical style was not restricted to poetry. It became a ready resource for dramatists who were representing lovers. The self-deluding quality of the antithetical style, which is implicit in the Petrarch sonnet, is made explicit in Shakespeare's early comedy *The Two Gentlemen of Verona* (*c.*1591–2). Proteus, an archetypal Elizabethan himbo whose name advertises his fickleness, persuades himself that he is justified in leaving Julia for his best friend Valentine's beloved, Silvia, through antithetical reasoning:

> I cannot leave to love, and yet I do.
> But there I leave to love where I should love.
> Julia I lose, and Valentine I lose.
> If I keep them I needs must lose myself.
> If I lose them, thus find I by their loss
> For Valentine, myself, for Julia, Silvia.

> (2. 6. 17–22)

Petrarchan extremity provides the basis for Proteus's tenuous self-extenuation. Like Petrarch, he adopts the position of a helpless victim of all-powerful love, although in this case his identity is at the mercy of each new attachment. Proteus is the Protean lover who 'cannot … prove constant to [him]self' or anyone else (2. 6. 31).

The sonnet in England

Wyatt and his fellow courtier Henry Howard, Earl of Surrey (*c*.1517–47) were among the first English sonneteers. Yet their sonnets were not part of larger sequences and seem to have been written as occasional pieces in the context of their careers as courtiers. Stephen Greenblatt goes as far as to claim that Wyatt's love poetry is best understood as an expression of his shaping as a man and a writer by the forces of 'secular power' in the Henrican court (1980, p.154). The connections between what is ostensibly amatory poetry and political discourse have become an increasing preoccupation of readers of English Renaissance sonnets. Barrell, for example, argues that Sonnet 29 does not exhibit the timelessness of love as a human value, but rather betrays the fact that 'love' in this poem is implicated in the early modern discourse of patronage (see Text 9).

Sonnet sequences of the scope and ambition of Petrarch's first appear in English during the 1580s and 1590s. It became one of the supremely fashionable literary modes of the period: between 1591 and 1595, first editions of Sir Philip Sidney's *Astrophel and Stella*, Samuel Daniel's *Delia*, Michael Drayton's *Idea* and Spenser's *Amoretti* were published. In addition to these works by canonical figures, sequences appeared by lesser-known writers such as Henry Constable, Barnabe Barnes, Richard Barnfield, Giles Fletcher the Elder, Thomas Lodge, and even more obscure figures like B. Griffin, or the anonymous writer of *Zepheria* (1594).[7] If you were an ambitious, well-educated Englishman in the 1590s, writing a sequence of sonnets to a Stella, Delia or even Fidessa may have seemed a plausible way of exhibiting your rhetorical talents. Shakespeare satirizes many such young men in his comedies of the 1590s, for example Orlando in *As You Like It* or, more spectacularly, the King and his three lords in *Love's Labour's Lost*. The writing of love sonnets almost seems to have been an aristocratic disease. Indeed, Arthur Marotti has explained the Elizabethan vogue for sonnets in terms of bids for patronage: 'courtly authors ... used love poetry as a way of metaphorizing their rivalry with social, economic, and political competitors' (1980, p.398). According to Marotti, love sonnets to unattainable women were especially apposite to the Elizabethan court culture of the 1580s and 1590s, which operated through the coded flirtation between rival courtiers and Queen Elizabeth. But in the Jacobean court of the 1600s, this code lost its relevance. As we shall see, however, sonnet sequences did not disappear as abruptly as Marotti suggests.

How, then, do Shakespeare's poems connect with the Elizabethan sonnet vogue? There are many different and contradictory answers to this question. The first thing to note is that most explanations depend on the fraught issue of dating the sonnets. Are these poems deposits of Shakespeare's earlier poetic work, or do they represent material he had been working on in the period in and around 1609? The Quarto volume, *Shake-speares Sonnets: Neuer before Imprinted* (Figure 11) was first published in 1609 by Thomas Thorpe, yet whether or not Shakespeare authorized this edition is a matter of academic dispute (see Cohen's Textual Note in *The Norton Shakespeare*, pp.1921–2). Scholars who date the poems early emphasize their connections with sequences like Sidney's *Astrophel and Stella*; those who date them nearer to 1609 try to explain them in terms of Jacobean rather than Elizabethan literary culture. There

[7] These sequences were: Constable's *Diana* (1592); Barnes's *Parthenophil to Parthenophe* (1593); Barnfield's *Cynthia* (1595); Fletcher's *Licia* (1593); Lodge's *Phillis* (1593) and Griffin's *Fidessa* (1596). See Evans, 1977, pp.185–226, for full details.

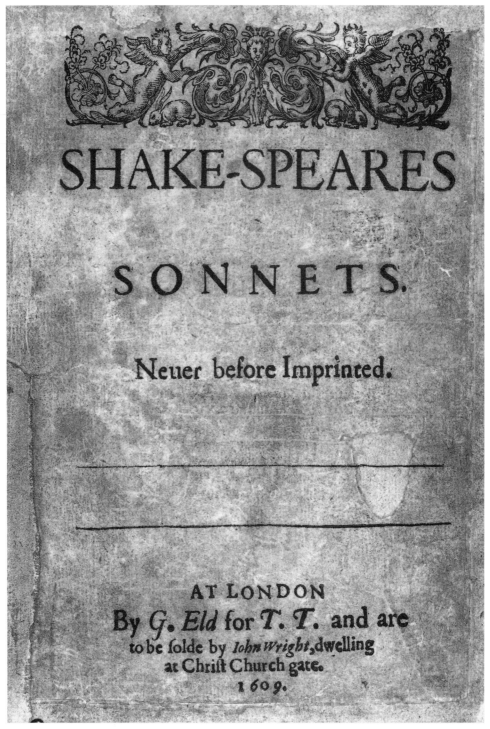

Figure 11 *Title page of* Shake-Speares Sonnets: Neuer before Imprinted, *G. Eld for T.T., London, 1609. British Library c.21.c.44. Reproduced by permission of the British Library, London.*

is a small amount of primary evidence about when the poems were written. In 1598, Francis Meres asserted that 'the sweete wittie soule of Ovid lives in melliflous & honytongued *Shakespeare*, witnes ... his sugred Sonnets' (*The Norton Shakespeare*, p.3324). This remark has been taken to indicate that some or all of the sonnets were circulating in manuscript in the late 1590s. Further support for this hypothesis is the publication in 1599 of a collection of poems entitled *The Passionate Pilgrim* by William Jaggard. This miscellaneous volume, which attempted to cash in on Shakespeare's growing celebrity by attributing all its contents to him, includes versions of Sonnets 138 and 144 (see *The Norton Shakespeare*, pp.1986–7). On the basis of this evidence, earlier commentators tended to see *Shakespeare's Sonnets* as another unofficial publication, recycling poems Shakespeare had written many years earlier during the height of the Elizabethan sonnet craze, anywhere between the mid-1580s and the mid-1590s. Yet all *The Passionate Pilgrim* unequivocally tells us is that Shakespeare had written versions of two of the sonnets by 1599.

Furthermore, the example of Petrarch shows that sonnet sequences could easily be – and were often – composed over a long period of time. The work of Drayton gives a contemporaneous example of this process. In 1594, he published a sequence of 51 sonnets, *Ideas Mirrour*, but this text underwent a series of radical revisions in later editions. As Maurice Evans summarizes: 'The subsequent editions in 1599, 1600, 1602, 1605 and 1619 embody a process of revision in which thirty-two of the more conceited or plaintive sonnets of the original were omitted, and forty-four new sonnets were added' (1977, p.202). In other words, the sequence called *Idea* we read as part of Drayton's *Poems* of 1619 was a substantively different document from the *Ideas Mirrour* of 1594. Drayton's 25-year reworking of the sequence also charts his desire to remodel it to reflect changing poetic fashions. We can further illustrate the tendency for sonnet sequences to be revised over time by considering the twentieth-century American poet Robert Lowell. His sonnet sequence *Notebook 1967–68* was first published in 1969, then revised as just *Notebook* in 1970, before being completely overhauled and relaunched as two separate volumes, *History* and *For Lizzie and Harriet*, in 1973. As Lowell apologetically noted half-way through this process, while also explaining that *Notebook* contained at least 90 new poems, 'I am sorry to ask anyone to buy this poem twice. I couldn't stop writing, and have handled my published book as if it were a manuscript' (1970, p.264). The same could be said for Drayton and Daniel. Although Lowell immersed himself in the writing of sonnets from the late 1960s through to the early 1970s (Hamilton, 1982, pp.392–3), it should be clear that the writing of a sonnet sequence is typically a slow and accretive process, with the poet adding to, subtracting from, and reshaping the emerging sequence over a longer period of time.

To illustrate this process, compare the *Passionate Pilgrim* (1599) text of Sonnet 138 with the 1609 text of the sonnet, both on page 1986 of *The Norton Shakespeare* (top: 1609 text; below: *Passionate Pilgrim* text). What would you say are the major differences between the two versions?

At a first glance, you might think that the two texts are virtually interchangeable. The first three lines are identical, and the rhyme sounds remain the same in each version. But looking more closely you should be able to see that almost every change in the 1609 version (Figure 12) is an improvement, enriching the verbal texture of the sonnet. Take two examples: first, in the 1599 text, line 4 begins 'Unskilful', which is changed by 1609 to 'Unlearnèd'. This may look like a trivial detail, but in context 'Unlearnèd' more vitally picks up the image of the speaker's

138

> W Hen my loue sweares that she is made of truth,
>   I do beleeue her though I know she lyes,
> That she might thinke me some vntuterd youth,
> Vnlearned in the worlds false subtilties.
> Thus vainely thinking that she thinkes me young,
> Although she knowes my dayes are past the best,
> Simply I credit her false speaking tongue,
> On both sides thus is simple truth supprest :
> But wherefore sayes she not she is vniust ?
> And wherefore say not I that I am old ?
> O loues best habit is in seeming trust,
> And age in loue, loues not t'haue yeares told.
>   Therefore I lye with her, and she with me,
>   And in our faults by lyes we flattered be.

Figure 12 *Sonnet 138 in* Shake-Speares Sonnets ... , *G. Eld for T.T., London, 1609, reproduced from* Shakespeare's Sonnets; ... facsimile ... from the unrivalled original in the library of Bridgewater House ..., *Lovell Reeve, London, 1862.*

pretence in line 3 that he is 'some untutored youth'. Although 'Unskilful' conveys the idea of the speaker's invented naïvety, 'Unlearnèd' cunningly emphasizes that it is specifically an educational innocence the speaker is pretending to have. A similar dynamic underlies the change at the end of line 4 from 'forgeries' to 'subtleties'. This is the subtle poetry of a subtle speaker, who is – as the poem amply demonstrates – well versed 'in the world's false subtleties'. A more radical reshaping takes place in lines 7–8, where 'I, **smi**ling, **cre**dit **her** false-**spea**king **tongue**, / Outfacing faults in love with love's ill rest' becomes '**Sim**ply I **cre**dit **her** false-**spea**king **tongue**; / On both sides thus is simple truth suppressed' (I have emphasized the stressed syllables). Again, Shakespeare's second thoughts improve the poem: he loosens the rhythm of the beginning of line 7 to give it a more conversational feel, while line 8, by repeating 'simple' from the previous line, again draws the reader's attention to the poem's central concern with false simplicity. By contrast, the earlier version of the line is more melodramatic ('love's ill rest') and less pertinent to the poem's overall agenda: that the speaker and his mistress are colluding in the fiction that he is not as old as in fact he is. We have no means of knowing when Shakespeare made these changes, but from this evidence it seems clear that he continued to work on individual sonnets after first writing or circulating them among his friends. Moreover, unlike many later poets, in Shakespeare's case it is clear that such revision did lead to artistic improvements.

The extent to which the poems in *Shakespeare's Sonnets* are a sequence like *Idea* or *Astrophel and Stella* has also been questioned. Writing in 1934, L.C. Knights insisted that '"Shakespeare's Sonnets" is a miscellaneous collection of poems, written at different times, for different purposes, and with very different degrees of poetic intensity' (Jones, 1977, p.75). Readers of the sonnets should therefore 'assess each poem independently, on its merits as poetry' (Jones, 1977, p.75). Knights represents an influential strand in sonnets criticism, partly taken up in recent years by Helen Vendler (1997). A summary of this formalist position would be: 'The sonnets are primarily poetry. Let's try to forget this aura of mystery which surrounds their initial publication and who they may or may not have been written for and concentrate on interpreting them as verbal contraptions.' Although this is often a helpful way of approaching individual sonnets, it depends, as the work of John Kerrigan (1986) and Katharine Duncan-Jones (1997) has shown, on the assumption that *Shakespeare's Sonnets* is an unauthorized miscellany. There are other, more plausible, ways of reading the 1609 Quarto, which connect it more firmly to the sonnet sequences written by Shakespeare's contemporaries.

In their editions of the sonnets, Kerrigan and Duncan-Jones reconsider the form of the Elizabethan sonnet sequence, and from this the question of whether the 1609 volume had Shakespeare's approval. Their central claim is that Shakespeare's sequence follows the two- or three-part form of earlier English sequences, and, in particular, of Daniel's *Delia*. The 1592 edition of *Delia* has three interconnected components: 55 love sonnets, a short ode in a stylized meter known as anacreontics,[8] and *The Complaint of Rosamund*, Daniel's retelling of the tragic story of Henry II's mistress Rosamund Clifford. According to Kerrigan, sequences in the 'Delian tradition' (1986, p.14), like Lodge's *Phillis* and even Spenser's *Amoretti*, carefully incorporate parallels between their different components. In *Amoretti*, while the courtship between the speaker and his mistress appears to break down inconclusively in the final sonnets (numbers 86–89), the third part of the sequence, the marriage hymn *Epithalamion*, gives the volume an unexpected point of closure through the celebration of the lovers' wedding. Shakespeare's volume appears to fit this tripartite design. As Kerrigan summarizes:

> When those first Jacobean readers opened Shakespeare's volume in 1609, they found something perfectly familiar. Here was a sequence of a hundred and fifty-two sonnets in two groups, followed by two sonnets of anacreontic matter [Sonnets 153 and 154] ... the whole being brought to a conventional close in *A Lover's Complaint*. Modern critics may be baffled by the heterogeneity of Shakespeare's volume; Shakespeare's audience had a framework for reading it ... They would have read the volume *as* a volume, and their sense of the parts would have been modified by the whole.
>
> (1986, p.14)

This innovative emphasis on the form of 1590s sonnet sequences has led to the first careful consideration of *A Lover's Complaint* in nearly 400 years. Earlier critics like Knights assumed that this poem was, like the weaker sonnets in the sequence, probably not by Shakespeare (Jones, 1977, p.76). But if the whole 1609 publication knowingly recalls a traditional Elizabethan form of sequence plus anacreontics plus complaint, it then follows that *A Lover's Complaint* is an authentic part of Shakespeare's design. Kerrigan has gone so far as to edit a critical anthology of contemporaneous 'Female Complaints' to provide a more systematic contextualization of this poem than has so far been available. For our purposes, the importance of the work of Kerrigan and Duncan-Jones is twofold. First, it suggests that the Quarto of 1609 was working in a recognized poetic tradition dating from the 1590s. Second, it implies that the Quarto was a carefully designed publication. At this point it would be helpful to read Cohen's Textual Note on the

[8] Anacreontics were poems written in the meter or style of the Greek poet Anacreon. His love poems typically focus on the kind of mythological double entendre Shakespeare experiments with in Sonnets 153 and 154; see Kerrigan, 1986, pp.387–8.

sonnets and *A Lover's Complaint* in *The Norton Shakespeare* (pp.1921–2), which articulates the growing sense that 'it is very likely that Shakespeare arranged and authorized the publication of the volume'.

These conclusions have important implications for how we read *Shakespeare's Sonnets*. If it is not 'a miscellaneous collection', then we should try to understand it as a sequence. Equally, if the design of the 1609 volume reflects Shakespeare's reading of the work of his contemporaries, then we need to explore those influences. Before turning to the question of how we should read the sonnets as a sequence, I would like to pursue the question of how we should contextualize Shakespeare's poems, by reading selected sonnets alongside the work of two of his Elizabethan and Jacobean contemporaries.

Compare the first sonnet of Sidney's *Astrophel and Stella* (first published 1591) (Text 5) with Shakespeare's first sonnet. What do you think is the main difference between the speakers of these poems? What different expectations do you think the poems set up about their respective sequences?

Sidney's poem explores the preoccupation of its speaker, Astrophel, with Stella, the 'deare she' of this sonnet. As such, it is an introductory poem for the whole sequence. Astrophel loves the unattainable Stella and wants to use his poetry to persuade her to take pity on him. By contrast, Shakespeare's first sonnet (Figure 13) is addressed to another person, the 'thou' of line 5. Instead of introducing another variant on the Petrarchan story, this poem attempts to persuade the 'thou' to a specific course of action. The speaker urges his addressee away from the selfishness of not procreating – as the couplet puts it, 'Pity the world, or else this glutton be: / To eat the world's due, by the grave and thee'. By not breeding, the addressee is a 'glutton' in that he is 'eat[ing] the world's due' himself. Instead of giving the world children, he (we will soon find out that the addressee is male) reserves this 'due' to himself. In contrast to *Astrophel and Stella*'s poetic speaker and obdurate lady, this poem is an arresting piece of advice: have sex, procreate, preserve your beauty for posterity through having children. Equally striking is the fact that the speaker is not inviting the addressee to his own bed for this purpose. What is at issue in this poem is not so much the speaker's love or desire, but the preservation of 'beauty's rose'. Indeed, as becomes clear by Sonnet 3, these poems are addressed to a young man, whom the speaker is trying to persuade to sleep with a young woman: 'where is she so fair whose uneared womb / Disdains the tillage of thy husbandry?' (3.5–6)

From *Astrophel and Stella* 1, you could reasonably conclude that Astrophel is a typically Petrarchan speaker, hopelessly in love with an unattainable woman, and that the sequence as a whole will amplify this situation. In fact, Sidney's sequence is a highly self-conscious exercise in Petrarchan writing, which interlinks the frustration of Astrophel–Sidney's political and amatory desires. In stark contrast, Shakespeare's first sonnet is much less of an introductory poem. Instead of sketching a fictional background, it begins a persuasive strategy that the next 16 sonnets develop. We should also notice that, in comparison with Sidney's poem, Shakespeare's is much denser and more metaphorical – he forces the reader to work to unpack his metaphors. For example, 'thou ... Feed'st thy light's flame with self-substantial fuel' suggests that the young man is a candle who is consuming himself – that is, the 'fuel' of his own 'substance' – by not breeding; like a candle, he will leave no trace of himself after his 'flame' is extinguished.

Yet these poems are not wholly dissimilar. They are both elaborate exhibitions of their writers' command of rhetorical language. Sidney employs a rhetorical figure in

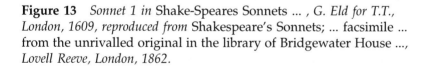

Figure 13 *Sonnet 1 in* Shake-Speares Sonnets ... , *G. Eld for T.T., London, 1609, reproduced from* Shakespeare's Sonnets; ... facsimile ... from the unrivalled original in the library of Bridgewater House ..., *Lovell Reeve, London, 1862.*

which succeeding phrases build on a repeated word: note how 'pleasure' produces 'reading' which in turn produces 'knowledge' and 'pitie'. Although the sonnet culminates with the apparently anti-rhetorical advice that Astrophel should 'looke in [his] heart and write', at every line Sidney cannily displays his awareness that it is rhetorical language that organizes the poem. Similarly, Shakespeare's poem is structured both as a detailed argument and through paradoxes like 'tender churl'. This formulation encapsulates what the speaker thinks is wrong with the young man: he is caught between his beautiful youth (his tenderness) and his miserly, or selfish, behaviour in not breeding. For Shakespeare, as for Sidney before him, there is no tension between rhetorical and poetic language: poetry is in fact an elaborate medium which is constructed through such formal devices. We may find the climactic building of phrases in Sidney's sonnet stilted and unnatural, but his contemporary, Abraham Fraunce, praised the poem precisely because of its exhibition of a rhetorical trope (Ringler, 1962, p.459).

This exercise should show you that while Shakespeare's poems are close to the practice of Elizabethan sonneteers like Sidney, there are crucial differences between them. As we have seen, Shakespeare's poem is metaphorically denser than Sidney's;

equally, Shakespeare here moves away from the Petrarchan situation of frustrated heterosexual desire to a less familiar register in which a male speaker addresses another man. We could also note, along with Kerrigan (1986, p.170), that the phrase 'tender heir' is rephrased at the end of *Cymbeline*, when the Soothsayer refers to Innogen as 'The piece of tender air thy virtuous daughter' (5. 6. 446). In each text, Shakespeare uses the same pun: Innogen is the young ('tender') heir ('air') of Cymbeline; Sonnet 1 similarly imagines the young man's child as his own 'tender heir'. Although this detail does not prove that the sonnets were written like *Cymbeline* in about 1607–9, it does suggest both that we should explore connections between these poems and Shakespeare's plays, and that we should read the poems in the broader context of Jacobean as well as Elizabethan literature.

Duncan-Jones has recently made such comparisons. She argues that the vogue for the sonnet sequence was not an exclusively Elizabethan phenomenon: there was a 'second wave' (1997, p.29) of sonnets after the accession of James I in 1603, which were harder and more epigrammatic than the Petrarchan register of the Elizabethan sonnet. Duncan-Jones suggests that the acerbic sonnets of poets like Alexander Craig, John Davies of Hereford and, indeed, Drayton provide more pertinent analogies to Shakespeare's poems than the sequences of Sidney and Spenser. So, do Drayton's Jacobean sonnets bear a stronger resemblance to Shakespeare's work than, say, Spenser's Elizabethan sonnets? Let's have a look at one of the poems Drayton added to his sequence in 1605.

Read Drayton's 'As in some Countries, farre remote from hence' (*Idea* 50, 1605 edition) (Text 6). How does this poem convey its attitude towards its subject? Then read Shakespeare's Sonnet 118. What connections do you see between the two poems?

Drayton's sonnet compares the practice of foreign countries in which 'Surgeons' use condemned men as subjects for vivisection with the treatment the speaker receives from his mistress. Like most English writers of the period, Drayton exports ideas of savage behaviour 'farre ... from hence': you may see parallels with the foreign settings of plays like *Hamlet* and *The Tempest*. Drayton provides a graphic and horrifying image that fuses amatory experience with torture: 'Ev'n so my Mistres workes upon my Ill, / By curing me and killing me each How'r'.

Given that traitors in early modern England were executed by the agonizingly attenuated process of hanging, drawing and quartering, you may find Drayton's assertion that such practices only take place 'in ... Countries, farre remote from hence' frankly implausible. As an example of English punitive practices, consider Figure 14, which shows the punishment known as 'pressing to death', in which the victim was literally pressed to death by having stones laid on his or her body; this extraordinary form of execution was used against felons who refused to plead.

Sonnet 118 works through a different sort of comparison. Shakespeare compares the medicinal practice of purging, or taking laxatives – that is, making yourself sick to avoid the risk of greater sickness – with his practice in love. The poem seems to be saying: 'In order to avoid getting sick of you, I purged myself by indulging in "bitter sauces"'. Vendler sees this as a 'specious ... apology for infidelity' (1997, p.449). The speaker offers the purging analogy as a self-consciously inadequate way of explaining his own inexcusable behaviour. As lines 9–10 put it, this strategy, by anticipating 'ills that were not, grew to faults assured'. Yet as Kerrigan notes, the couplet adds a further innuendo: 'The black joke seems to be not just that the poet *fell sick* of being *healthful* and took *Drugs* to make himself *ill* ... but that the poet has

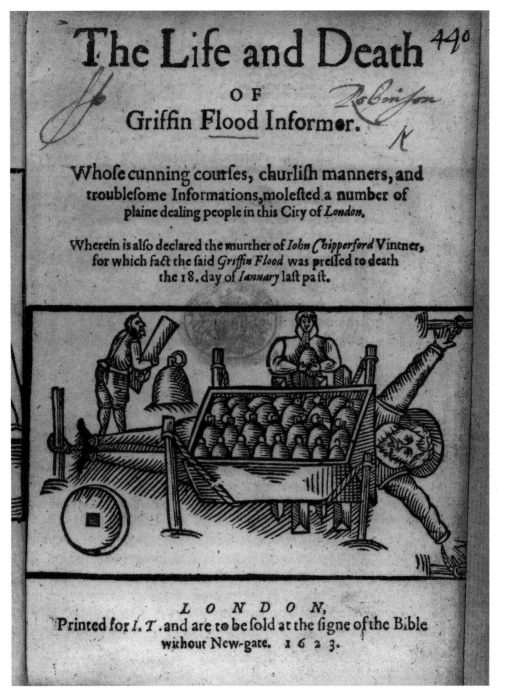

Figure 14 *Title page of* The Life and Death of Griffin Flood Informer, *I.T., London, 1623. British Library 11320.a.45. Reproduced by permission of the British Library.*

proven by his experience that being in love with the young man is an incurable though benign disease' (1986, p.337).

What connects these sonnets is the use of violent and disturbing analogies for the experience of being in love. It is either like the excruciating pain of vivisection, or it is a kind of self-imposed sickness – a drug habit that there is apparently no means of kicking. In each case, the violence of the comparison seems to embody a change in how love is being treated poetically: instead of the 'sweet' Petrarchan lyricism of Sidney or Spenser, these poems leave us with a bitter after-taste.

Yet as Stephen Booth notes in his commentary on Sonnet 118: 'The unflattering harshness of the suggestion that the speaker no longer finds the beloved appealing is somewhat softened by its kinship with the traditional ... courtly-love conceits by which love or the beloved is likened to a disease ... e.g. Spenser's *Amoretti* 50' (1977, p.398). Similarly, Drayton's image of his mistress as a surgeon-cum-torturer is related to the Petrarchan image of the beloved as a 'cruel fair' – a woman who is as cruel as she is beautiful. As we have already seen, such extreme imagery is in itself part of the traditional armoury of the sonneteer. Is there, then, anything that distinguishes these sonnets published in the 1600s from the sonnets of the 1590s? Put another way, is Duncan-Jones correct that the 'second wave' of English sonnets is different from the first?

Reread Drayton's 'As in some Countries, farre remote from hence' and Sonnet 118 alongside *Amoretti* 50, 'Long languishing in double malady' (1595) (Text 7). Now consider Booth's point that Sonnet 118's 'kinship' with the tradition softens the harshness of its depiction of the relationship between the speaker and the young man. Do you think that this is a convincing reading, or is there a real difference between Shakespeare's use of this tradition and Spenser's?

Spenser's poem is the same kind of miniature drama as his 'One day I wrote her name upon the strand'. The speaker is sick of a 'double malady' afflicting his heart and his body. Predictably enough, he identifies his mistress as his 'lyfe's Leach' who has the unique ability to heal 'with one salve both hart and body'. Spenser uses medical analogies similar to Sonnet 118; broadly, Booth is correct that these poems are part of the same tradition. In each case, the metaphor of disease opens up the speaker's interior world – what Spenser calls 'the inward languuour' – to the reader. Yet Shakespeare's poem is harder and harsher than Spenser's. For Spenser, the idea of love as a disease re-emphasizes the speaker's dependence on the good will of his mistress: the disease he experiences is being unrequitedly in love with her. But for Shakespeare, disease is a condition he has brought on himself through purging and through his involvement with the young man; as Bruce Smith states, what distinguishes Shakespeare's poems from the sonnets of the 1590s is 'they are focused on what love is like after sexual consummation' (1994, p.229). Although Shakespeare draws on the same tradition as Spenser, he transforms the metaphor of disease into a more inclusive statement of the speaker's predicament. He is sick through the 'bitter sauces' he has ingested and of the young man's 'ne'er cloying sweetness'.

The added emotional complexity of Shakespeare's interpretation of this tradition is neatly shown by the Quarto's spelling of this last phrase: 'nere cloying sweetnesse' (Figure 15). As Booth observes: 'Both *ne'er-cloying* (i.e. "never-cloying") and "near cloying" make sense here, and their paradoxical amalgamation in a single self-negating expression constitutes an emblem of the whole poem' (1977, p.395). Indeed, if the young man's sweetness is *'near* cloying', it is in itself becoming a fundamental part of the speaker's ailment. Put another way, he is both 'sick' of his beloved in the sense that he is tired of him, and ill through his association with him. Whereas Spenser's poem points towards healing – by becoming the speaker's lover, the mistress will cure him – Shakespeare's remains mired in physical addictions that the speaker cannot kick.

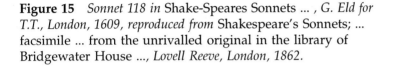

Figure 15 *Sonnet 118 in* Shake-Speares Sonnets ... , *G. Eld for T.T., London, 1609, reproduced from* Shakespeare's Sonnets; ... facsimile ... from the unrivalled original in the library of Bridgewater House ..., *Lovell Reeve, London, 1862.*

My own answer, then, would be that while it is helpful to connect Sonnet 118 with texts like *Amoretti* 50, direct comparison actually stresses how different Shakespeare's poem is from earlier work. So although we cannot be sure when the sonnets were written, there is indeed a Jacobean quality to them. They are not all universally applicable anthology pieces like Sonnet 18. Rather, as the comparison with Drayton's later sonnets suggests, the sonnets include more disturbing material than is often recognized. This emphasis on the darker sides of sexuality is very much in keeping with Shakespeare's Jacobean drama: the insecure heterosexual passion of Sonnets 127–152 is highly congruent with the psychosexual anxieties of *Cymbeline*'s Posthumus Leonatus. Consider, too, Claudio's addictive account of his sexual relations with Juliet in *Measure for Measure* (c.1603):

> Our natures do pursue,
> Like rats that raven down their proper bane,
> A thirsty evil; and when we drink, we die.

(1. 2. 108–10)

Like Sonnet 118, these lines equate sexuality with poison: human beings in search of sex are, apparently, like rats gobbling poison. As we shall see below, it is precisely the disturbing quality of *Shakespeare's Sonnets*, and the transgressive sexualities that are so ingrained in the sequence, that has led to its often bizarre reception by later readers. Yet such concerns are equally prominent in the drama Shakespeare was writing in the first decade of the seventeenth century. As a further example of this, you might look back at David Johnson's discussion of the representations of sexual identities in *Cymbeline*, to see how far you think these poems are congruent with the attitudes exhibited in the play.

Unlocking Shakespeare's heart? The sonnets and their readers

In the last section, we looked at the history of the sonnet sequence and how Shakespeare's poems relate to the work of his immediate contemporaries. In the course of this survey, I suggested that *Shakespeare's Sonnets* are best understood as a coherent collection rather than as a miscellany, and that the collection was probably assembled and reworked in about 1609. Now we need to think about the poems' after life. Instead of charting precisely how the sonnets were read from 1609 to the late twentieth century, I am going to look at the most prominent and influential ways in which they have been interpreted. This should help you to see the extraordinary impact the sexual dimension of the sequence has had on its reception.

Moral outrage

In contrast with their popularity in the twentieth century, the sonnets were not a spectacular success in the seventeenth century. Unlike Drayton's *Idea*, for example, the poems were not reprinted during their author's lifetime. Given that by 1609 Shakespeare was a celebrated playwright and poet, we might have expected his 'Neuer before Imprinted' sonnets (Figure 11) to have sold well. What little evidence survives of Jacobean readings suggests that the poems' sexual content may have been a literary turn-off. One early reader of the 1609 volume wrote after Sonnet 154: 'What a heap of wretched Infidel stuff'; another scored out the whole text of Sonnet 129, which graphically anatomizes phallocentric desire (Duncan-Jones, 1997, pp.69–70). Similarly, the publisher of the second edition of the sonnets in 1640, John Benson, changed some of the pronouns within the poems so that the young man conveniently became a young woman (see Cohen's Textual Note in *The Norton Shakespeare*, p.1921). These elliptical reactions anticipate the bewilderment and often outright hostility the sonnets have generated in later readers. The eighteenth-century editor George Steevens asserted that 'the strongest act of Parliament that could be framed, would fail to compel readers into [the sonnets'] service'; even William Wordsworth, who as a poet was fascinated by the sonnet form, wrote in 1803: 'They are abominably harsh, obscure, and worthless' (Jones, 1977, pp.37, 41; see Text 10).

What was it about the sonnets that prompted this kind of response? The moral outrage that runs through these reactions seems to be a product both of the explicit heterosexual content of Sonnets 127–152 and of the implied homoeroticism of Sonnets 1–126. Again, Steevens is instructive. Commenting on Sonnet 20 – as we shall see, a crucial document for assessing the sequence's homoeroticism – he wrote in 1780: 'It is impossible to read this fulsome panegyrick [poem of praise], addressed to a male object, without an equal mixture of disgust and indignation' (Smith, 1994, p.230). What disgusted Steevens was clearly the unsettling feeling that Shakespeare may have been sexually aroused by the 'master–mistress' Sonnet 20 celebrates.

To get around this 'disgust and indignation', many critics have imitated the ingenious manoeuvrings of Samuel Taylor Coleridge. In the same copy of Shakespeare's works in which Wordsworth had recorded his disappointment in the sonnets, Coleridge wrote a note to his son Hartley in 1803, which attempts to exculpate Shakespeare from the imputation of homosexuality: 'O my son! I pray fervently that thou may'st know inwardly how impossible it was for a Shakespeare not to have been in his heart's heart chaste' (Jones, 1977, p.42; see Text 10). In this reading, Shakespeare's love for the young man was a 'pure' non-sexual passion. Although sexual attitudes and mores have liberalized substantially since the late eighteenth century, the question of the sonnets' homoeroticism is still contentious. As an example of this, consider again the work of Auden. Auden himself was openly homosexual, yet his preface to William Barto's 1964 edition of the sonnets essentially follows Coleridge in claiming that these are poems of idealized, non-sexual love. But in the same year this edition was published, Auden apparently admitted at a party that 'it won't do just yet to admit that the top Bard was in the homintern' (Smith, 1994, p.231). ('Homintern' – a play on 'Comintern' – is a coinage used by Auden in deriding the attempt by homosexual readers to appropriate Shakespeare as their 'patron saint'; see Auden, 1973, p.99.) Even in the more liberal climate of the late twentieth century, the sonnets have the power to arouse strong emotions, since they open troubling prospects to readers who retain a conventional veneration for 'the top Bard': a homoerotic Shakespeare, an unchaste Shakespeare – perhaps, indeed, a Shakespeare susceptible like the majority of his readers to various sexual desires, rather than a lofty and idealized cultural idol. Again, although the film *Shakespeare in Love* humanizes Shakespeare as a struggling playwright with a haphazard emotional life, it is interesting that the film-makers chose not to present him as a homosexual.

Biographical keys

The main section title above rephrases a poem by Wordsworth published in 1827, which defends the literary dignity of the sonnet. Shakespeare is one of Wordsworth's chief witnesses for this defence: 'with this Key / Shakespeare unlocked his heart' (Gill, 1984, pp.356–7). As we have just seen, discussion of the morality of the sonnets quickly shades into discussion of the characters in the poems. Wordsworth assumes the speaker is literally Shakespeare. As he put it in prose in 1815, in the sonnets 'Shakespeare expresses his own feelings in his own person' (Jones, 1977, p.42). Indeed, given the insistent punning on the speaker's first name – 'Will' – in Sonnets 135 and 136, such an approach is logical. The volume seems to invite us to read it as erotic autobiography. This was the practice of Oscar Wilde in his 1889 short story, 'The Portrait of Mr. W. H.', which playfully explores the thesis that the young man was a boy actor called Willie Hughes. For Wilde, biographical reading enables the coded exploration of 'the love which dare not speak its name': 'the sonnets are addressed to an individual, – to a particular young man whose personality for some reason seems to have filled the soul of Shakespeare with terrible joy and no less terrible despair' (Murray, 1979, p.146).

But this is a view of the sonnets (and literature) that can be contested. Although the volume gestures towards the life of a poet called William, it never states 'these poems are about the love life of the dramatist William Shakespeare'. As a point of contrast, consider the late Ted Hughes's *Birthday Letters* (1998), where the dust-jacket of the first edition states that the poems 'are addressed ... to Sylvia Plath, the American poet to whom he was married'. Shakespeare's volume gives no such unequivocal statement. In this context, the nineteenth-century poet Robert Browning famously replied to Wordsworth '"*With this same key / Shakespeare unlocked his heart*, once more!" / Did Shakespeare? If so, the less Shakespeare he!' (Jones, 1977, p.10).

In essence, biographical readers see the volume as a novel written in code. Their task is to crack that code. By trying to identify, first, the young man of Sonnets 1–126 and relate him to the 'Mr W. H.' of the publisher Thomas Thorpe's dedication (Figure 16), and, second, the mistress of Sonnets 127–152, such readers hope to pick the lock that apparently conceals Shakespeare's private life within the poems.

Bate usefully makes the point that biographical criticism is of relatively recent origin:

> It certainly did not occur to [eighteenth-century Shakespeareans] to seek in the plays for hidden clues to Shakespeare's amorous inclinations. They did not regard literature as encoded autobiography. This was an idea which only emerged towards the end of the [eighteenth] century and which was at the centre of the great cultural shift we call the Romantic movement.

(1997, p.36)

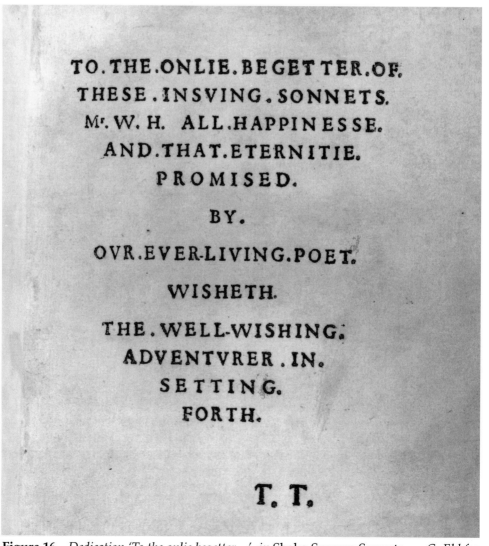

Figure 16 *Dedication 'To the onlie begetter ...', in* Shake-Speares Sonnets ... , *G. Eld for T.T., London, 1609. British Library c.21.c.4. Reproduced by permission of the British Library, London.*

Yet primary evidence about the sonnets is minimal. Biographical readers are therefore forced either to make that evidence work extremely hard to fit their theories – poor 'Mr W. H.' has been manipulated to fit a wide range of possible identities even though as Bate notes he could be a creation of a misprint (see Bate, 1997, pp.63–4) – or to suggest unprovable hypotheses that *might be* true. Bate ironically performs the latter manoeuvre in his whimsical attempt to link the sonnets with one of the longest-lasting 'Mr. W. H.' suspects, Henry Wriothesley, Earl of Southampton (Figure 17): 'I would like to propose that our understanding of the sonnets will be assisted if we *suppose* – not if we confidently assert – that they are tied to some rather sordid intrigue in the Southampton household around 1593–4' (1997, p.54).

This is an important point: although there is no new evidence about who the poems may or may not be about, there has been no real decline in the desire of even respected critics like Bate and Duncan-Jones (who plumps for the main rival 'Mr. W.H.', William Herbert, Earl of Pembroke (Figure 18)) to provide biographical 'keys' to the sonnets.

But, as Bate's sentence indicates, this is a criticism of supposition not proof. Especially in the twentieth century, this post-Romantic approach has generated strenuous objections from readers less inclined to see literary texts as coded autobiography.

The sonnets as poetic form

The objections to biographical criticism can be easily summarized. Although 'it seems reasonable to infer a troubled author behind the poetic "I" of the sonnets, biographical reading ... has so little purchase on these poems that criticism directed along such lines soon finds itself spinning off the text into vacuous literary chit-chat' (Kerrigan, 1986, p.11).

Kerrigan's metaphor is revealing: in seeking to decode the sonnets, biographical criticism slides away from the poems Shakespeare wrote. During the twentieth century, this perception produced a formalist reaction, a determination to return to the task of reading Shakespeare's poems in detail. Vendler's recent work distills the practice of such formalism:

> The true 'actors' in lyric are words, not 'dramatic persons'; and the drama of any lyric is constituted by the successive entrances of new sets of words, or new stylistic arrangements (grammatic, syntactic, phonetic) which are visibly in conflict with previous arrangements used with reference to the 'same' situation.
>
> (1997, p.3)

As I pointed out earlier, Vendler's methodology can be traced back to the work of 1930s critics like Knights and, more importantly, William Empson, whose ground-breaking *Seven Types of Ambiguity* (1930) used selected sonnets as brilliant illustrations of the ambiguities he sought to identify in poetic language.

Figure 17 *John de Critz the Elder*, Henry Wriothesley, Third Earl of Southampton, *1603, oil on canvas, 105.41 x 87 cm, Boughton House. Reproduced by kind permission of His Grace the Duke of Buccleuch, K.T. from his collection at Boughton House, Northamptonshire, England.*

Figure 18 *Isaac Oliver,* William Herbert, Third Earl of Pembroke, *1611, watercolour with body colour on vellum, oval, 5.3 x 4.3 cm, The Folger Shakespeare Library, Washington, D.C.*

The task of the critic is, as Vendler sees it, to pay scrupulous attention to the 'true "actors"' of lyric poetry, the words that constitute poetic texts. Formalist approaches to the sonnets concentrate on the close reading of individual poems in often laborious detail. Vendler's book of nearly 700 pages provides consecutive readings of each sonnet; similarly, Booth's 'analytic' edition is 'Elaborately annotated, on the ultra-Empsonian principle that any extractable meaning is significant' (Kerrigan, 1986, p.65).

But such approaches are themselves vulnerable to criticism. Although the professed aim of Booth's edition is to 'resurrect ... a Renaissance reader's experience of the 1609 Quarto' (1977, p.ix), formalists have, in general, suffered mixed fortunes in their attempts to contextualize their readings. Since formalism tries to display the workings of poems as what Auden called 'verbal contraptions' (Vendler, 1997, pp.10–11), the major drawback of this approach is the opposite of the problem Kerrigan identifies in biographical criticism: that of becoming so immured in the text that broader contexts are either ignored or misused. As an example of the misuse of context, consider Booth's gloss of Sonnet 35, line 5, 'All men make faults, and even I in this':

> *make faults*. Shakespeare's contemporaries may have heard a pun here on 'make farts' (a pun that would give cogency to a complementary pun on *in sense* in line 9) ... a similar but farfetched play may have been audible in 148.14 ['Lest eyes, well seeing, thy foul faults should find!'].

> (1977, p.190)

Although Booth tries to dress this astonishingly unhelpful gloss as something 'Shakespeare's contemporaries *may* have heard' (my emphasis), the admission that the pun could be 'farfetched' in Sonnet 148 gives the game away. Booth's suggestion that a lavatorially minded Jacobean would have heard 'All men make farts' in this line fails to distinguish between a meaning that is pertinent to the understanding of the poem, and one that is distracting. Do farts illuminate Sonnet 35? Are they necessary to make sense of it? Or do they instead distract attention from the doubts the poem articulates about the young man and the narrator's collusion in his faults? The suggestion that such a double meaning is present in Sonnet 148 is equally distracting: how does Booth imagine that the 'eyes' of this line could 'find' the 'foul farts' he wants us to imagine? Exhaustive commentary can paradoxically lead to nonsensical readings. Barrell (see Text 9) makes the related criticism that the modernized spelling of Booth's edition actually 'edits out' the historically specific discourse of patronage within Sonnet 29.

The sonnets as dramatic form

The reaction against the biographical tradition of sonnet criticism has not been confined to critics like Booth, who focus exhaustively on the sonnets' poetic form. There was also a substantial reaction from a second group of formalist critics, who argued that the key to understanding the sonnets lay in reading them as essentially dramatic texts. As we have seen, modern scholarship tends to regard the 1609 volume as an authorized publication, or at least as a sequence whose order embodies Shakespeare's design. At first sight, the volume can look more like Knights's 'miscellaneous collections of poems' (Jones, 1977, p.75) than a unified sequence. Unlike *Astrophel and Stella*, *Shakespeare's Sonnets* is not a chronological account of a relationship. Instead, the sonnets can be grouped in clusters, like Sonnets 1–17 (which persuade the young man to procreate), or Sonnets 78–86 (in which a rival poet vies with the narrator for the young man's affections), or, indeed, Sonnets 127–152 (which focus on a sexually incontinent woman). For readers like Knights, the discontinuities between different poems and parts of the sequence undermine claims made for its coherence. I suspect that this response rests on the idea that sonnet sequences provide – or should provide – narratives of the same type as plays or novels. But this is a highly debatable position.

It is in this context that there has been a critical debate about the sonnets' dramatic qualities (see Vendler's remark quoted above). On the one hand, there is the widespread view that Shakespeare's work as a playwright necessarily informs his non-dramatic poetry. As G.K. Hunter wrote in 1953:

> ... the approach to the Sonnets as lyric, narrative, or metaphysical exercises ... is misdirected ... when Shakespeare writes [the sonnets] ... he is not misdirecting his talent, not being a quaint and elaborate lyrist, a failed and soured Petrarchan ... or a passionate autobiographical poet whose confessions are cut short by his conceits, so much as – what one would expect – a *dramatist*.
>
> (Jones, 1977, pp.120–1; see Text 11)

In his influential essay, Hunter juxtaposes the sonnets with poems by writers like Sidney and Drayton to suggest that Shakespeare's poems are 'more affecting', in that he uses conventional poetic imagery to articulate and dramatize 'felt human situation[s]' (Jones, 1977, p.125). Hunter's point is not that the sonnets are the speeches of characters like the characters from Shakespeare plays (as T. Walter Herbert (1980) later claimed), but that Shakespeare's poems enable the reader to participate in the emotional dilemmas that individual poems voice:

> Shakespeare's 'plots' differ from those of contemporary sonneteers in that we are seldom given visual descriptions of the persons involved. This difference does not involve him in a modern 'psychological' presentation: when the lover appears before the reader there is no self-dramatization in the sense that he is presented as a significant and interesting individual. When we hear of him
>
> > Beated and chopped with tanned antiquity   [62.10]
> >
> > Desiring this man's art and that man's scope   [29.7]
> >
> > As an unperfect actor on the stage   [23.1]
>
> we are no nearer any conception of his personality. The dramatic power of conveying personal tensions is achieved by patterning the persons, not by analysing them.
>
> (Jones, 1977, p.123)

So the sonnets do not present psychological analyses of rounded characters like Hamlet; rather, the poems 'convey ... personal tensions' by giving a dramatic pattern, or outline, of the poet–speaker (whom Hunter calls 'the lover') and his dilemmas. At first sight, this may seem a convincing approach. As we have seen, there are shared concerns between the sonnets and the plays; it would seem almost self-evident that Shakespeare's dramatic work would inform his poetry. Yet this conception of the sonnets as 'dramatic' has been challenged in recent years by Dubrow. Using the same tools as Hunter (comparing Shakespeare's poems with those of his contemporaries), Dubrow questions the basis of Hunter's thinking: 'in literary criticism, as in so many other human activities, we are prone to see what we expect to see, and nothing else' (Dubrow, 1987, p.172; see Text 12). Because Shakespeare was a dramatist, we expect his sonnets to be dramatic. Dubrow argues the reverse: in comparison with the sonnets of his contemporaries, Shakespeare's poems are strikingly undramatic. They do not stage miniature dramas, narrate specific incidents or even quote the narrator's lovers directly, as is the common practice of sonneteers like Drayton or Spenser (look again at Text 2 and Sonnet 65). According to Dubrow, the organizing principle of Shakespeare's sequence is not narration or dramatic speech but the exploration and reiteration of the speaker's emotional dilemmas. Her analysis concentrates on the sonnets as miniature pieces of rhetoric, re-elaborating the speaker's emotional dilemmas:

> Most of Shakespeare's sonnets are not narrative ... in the sense that the speaker is not recounting a story to the reader or to any other implied audience. And they are not dramatic in the sense that we are not witnessing a confrontation that occurs at a specific place and time between a speaker and a particular listener or even between two clearly distinguished personages within the speaker. Instead, the lyric mode predominates ... The speaker in Shakespeare's sonnets often seems to be thinking aloud, to be at once speaking audibly and meditating. But ... in one crucial way the sonnets differ from the soliloquies that are so frequently embedded in their author's plays: the soliloquy normally takes place at a unique moment and is often provoked by a clearly defined event that has preceded it, whereas most of the sonnets are signally lacking in those types of particularization.

(pp.181–2)

From this refutation of Hunter's approach, Dubrow claims that 'The nondramatic mode of the sonnets ... functions dramatically in that it directs our attention to the speaker's temperament' (p.190). In other words, the unifying thread of the sequence is the voice that speaks each poem. Even though these poems are the work of Shakespeare, they are not scripts for dramatic performance. Instead of giving parts to a broad range of characters, they concentrate relentlessly on the fluctuating moods of one speaker alone.

Again, the critical issue we should consider is not just whether Hunter or Dubrow is right; in many ways, their methods of reading overlap and their conclusions are not as diametrically opposed as Dubrow initially suggests. Both critics agree that the speaker or the lover is at the centre of Shakespeare's sequence and that this figure – and this speaking voice – unites the disparate poems within the collection. We should be cautious, however, about making this speaker a sort of anonymous substitute for Shakespeare. When I discuss the 'speaker' or 'narrator', I am trying to convey the sense that there does seem to be a recognizable voice that speaks throughout the sequence, while being aware of the caveat that these lyrics do not construct what Barrell calls 'a transcendent, autonomous identity' (1988, p.42), however much they may seem to point in that direction.

The sonnets in historical context

One way of getting out of the problems encountered by formalist critics concerned with the literary qualities – both poetic and dramatic – of the sonnets is to historicize the sonnets more systematically by reading them alongside the work of Shakespeare's contemporaries, while remaining alert to the ambiguities of tone and context. The section above on the history of the sonnet form approached Shakespeare's poems in these terms. This is in itself a venerable critical strategy. In his 1916 *Life of William Shakespeare*, Sir Sidney Lee goes to great lengths to read the sonnets not as 'personal confessions' (Jones, 1977, p.55), but as exercises in the continental tradition of sonneteering. In Lee's case, the undeclared object of this project is once again to cleanse the Bard from the taint of (perceived) sexual perversion (see Bate, 1997, pp.42–3). Nonetheless, his work anticipates the comparatives studies of later writers like J.B. Leishman (1963) and Anne Ferry (1983), which explore the literary contexts of the sonnets with increasing complexity.

In common with other canonical works, Shakespeare's sonnets have been subjected to a series of major reinterpretations in recent years. A major shift in the interpretation of the sonnets – as of the whole of Renaissance literature – since the 1980s has come from new historicist and cultural materialist perspectives. As David Johnson has already indicated, such approaches have exhibited 'the desire both to historicize and to politicize explicitly the reading of Shakespeare'. What, then, is the difference between the historicism of a writer like Lee, and of, say, Smith? As Peter Jones summarizes, the historical importance of Lee's work was that it was the first major attempt to read the sonnets 'as poetry, to get beyond the fruitless debates about "characters"' (1977, p.19). Lee writes as a late Victorian 'man of letters', intent on revealing to a sceptical readership the poetic value of the sonnets by explaining their literary contexts in depth, and, incidentally, to persuade readers that Shakespeare was not a homosexual. If the poems are in fact imitations of Ovid, Sidney, Daniel and others, then 'the autobiographic element ... shrink[s] to slender proportions' (Jones, 1977, p.55). Lee's politics and prejudices are implicit rather than directly articulated. In contrast, Smith writes with an avowed political aim. He describes his book, *Homosexual Desire in Shakespeare's England* (1944), as 'an attempt to consolidate gay identity in the last decade of the twentieth century to help men whose sexual desire is turned toward other men realize that they have not only a present community but a past history' (p.27). But, as you can see from the extract from Smith's book reprinted as Text 13, he reads the sonnets in ways that are not altogether dissimilar from the practice of Lee: Shakespeare's texts are juxtaposed against the work of other writers who have influenced him. What chiefly demarcates Smith from Lee is that Smith's historicism is informed by his absorption of recent theoretical models, and by his insistence that the questions he asks of early modern texts have a bearing on late-twentieth-century ideas of gender and sexuality. Smith's work brings us to the wider range of theoretical reinterpretations in literary studies since the 1980s. The writers of book-length studies of the sonnets, Joseph Pequigney (1985) and Joel Fineman (1986), used psychoanalytic theories to read the poems – in Pequigney's case to claim them as homosexual texts, and in Fineman's to argue that through these texts (especially Sonnets 127–152) Shakespeare 'invents a genuinely new poetic subjectivity' (1986, p.1).

It should be clear that the interpretation of the sonnets has come a long way since that anonymous seventeenth-century reader described them as 'a heap of wretched Infidel stuff'. We can now see them as moving verbal artefacts, and as products of complex literary traditions and social practices. Nonetheless, these theoretical approaches are by no means the final word on the subject and have themselves generated further debate. Vendler provides a trenchant critique of the work of new historicist and 'psychoanalytically minded' critics (1987, p.3). She argues that both approaches are actively insensitive to the genre of the sonnets as lyric poems:

> Contemporary emphasis on the participation of literature in a social matrix balks at acknowledging how lyric, though it may *refer* to the social, remains the genre that directs its *mimesis* [representational strategy] toward the performance of the mind in *solitary* speech ... [the sonnets] do not fully reward psychological criticisms (or gender criticism, motivated by many of the same characterological aims) any more than they do political criticism. Too much of their activity escapes the large sieves of both psychology and politics, disciplines not much concerned to examine the basis of lyric: subgenre, structure and linguistic play.

(pp.1–3)

In other words, the sonnets are primarily lyric poems, whose 'activity' is 'linguistic play': they are not representations of social or psychological conflict. Vendler suggests that critics excited by these issues want to turn lyric poems into novels or plays. More importantly, such criticism has a tendency to ignore or minimize the sonnets' unique aesthetic value. What Vendler is really saying is that 'social' and 'psychoanalytic' critics are tone deaf to the beauties of Shakespeare's poetry.

Yet, as you can see from Barrell's essay (Text 9), this attack on recent theoretical perspectives provokes as many questions as it answers. For example, are 'social' critics really as actively insensitive to the complexities of Shakespeare's literary language as Vendler suggests? As we have seen, Barrell's argument emerges from a critique of Booth's 1964 edition of the sonnets. Barrell offers a reading of Sonnet 29 that draws attention to the presence in this text of the discourse of patronage – the idea that the poem's speaker is short of influential 'friends' who will promote and reward him – in order to query the assumption of critics like Booth (and Vendler) that such poems are timeless embodiments of a transcendent conception of love. In this sense, Barrell's reading is profoundly political, yet it also exhibits a scrupulous attention to the text alongside an interest in what makes Sonnet 29 a compelling poem. According to Barrell, it is precisely the poem's historical specificity that makes it effective:

> I find it moving by virtue of its *attempt* ... to assert an ideal of transcendent love, and of a transcendent, autonomous identity, and to grasp at these as the means and the result of an escape from the oppression of the system of patronage and the constraints it imposes on the freedom of the narrator.

(1988, p.42)

We could argue that a reading that minimizes 'the participation of literature in a social matrix' risks draining poems of precisely the energies and concerns that caused them to be written.

This section has surveyed some of the major ways in which the sonnets have been interpreted. Some are more important as records of how Shakespeare has been read than as guides to how we should approach the poems now. Biographical criticism, for all the clues the 1609 volume seems to provide, is dependent on facts and identities that are probably now irrecoverable; similarly, the subjective 'moral' response of writers like Steevens or Coleridge is now extremely dated. What approach, then, should we adopt?

To help you evaluate competing critical strategies, I would like you now to read Sonnet 20 alongside the extracts from Smith and Vendler (Texts 13 and 14). What are the major differences you see in the two approaches to this poem?

The first thing to notice is that Sonnet 20 (Figure 19) is an extremely slippery text: as both critics agree, it is larded with puns and sexual innuendo. Spotting the poem's 'linguistic play', however, is easier than working out its full implications. But innuendo – what the poem nudges us into thinking – is crucial here precisely because Sonnet 20 addresses the question of the narrator's erotic feelings towards the young man. A paraphrase of the last six lines could be: 'since *nature* gave you a *prick* so you can sleep with *women*, I cannot have sex with you'. Read like this, the poem fits with Vendler's idealizing reading: 'Once one has separated love from the act of sex, love can ... stand alone ... inhabiting the realm of [Platonic] ... Forms' (1997, p.129). Yet, as even she recognizes, the poem remains problematic, both because of its aggression (note its dismissive presentation of women) and what a reader like Steevens might have called its indelicacies of expression. How can we read those final six lines at face value? As well as the pun on 'pricked', there is an equally strong play on 'nothing'. Duncan-Jones explains: 'The primary suggestion is that the added feature is of no value to the loving poet. But since *nothing* also referred to female genitalia ... the line could yield a paradox that supports a homoerotic reading: "the one thing that nature added is, for my purposes, equivalent to a woman's sexual parts"' (1997, p.151). The extract from Smith constitutes an approach to the homoeroticism of Sonnets 1–126 rather than just Sonnet 20, but his emphasis is clear enough: '*What* Shakespeare's speaker says is

> **20**
> A Womans face with natures owne hand painted,
> Haste thou the Master Mistris of my passion,
> A womans gentle hart but not acquainted
> With shifting change as is false womens fashion,
> An eye more bright then theirs, lesse false in rowling:
> Gilding the obiect where-vpon it gazeth,
> A man in hew all *Hews* in his controuling,
> Which steales mens eyes and womens soules amaseth,
> And for a woman wert thou first created,
> Till nature as she wrought thee fell a dotinge,
> And by addition me of thee defeated,
> By adding one thing to my purpose nothing.
> But since she prickt thee out for womens pleasure,
> Mine be thy loue and thy loues vse their treasure.

Figure 19 *Sonnet 20 in* Shake-Speares Sonnets ... , *G. Eld for T.T., London, 1609, reproduced from* Shakespeare's Sonnets; ... facsimile ... from the unrivalled original in the library of Bridgewater House ..., *Lovell Reeve, London, 1862.*

above reproach; *how* he says it has left many readers since George Steevens uneasy' (1994, p.250). You have, then, a choice between a reading of the poem as a 'little myth of origin', which takes its assertions of sexual disinterestedness at face value (Vendler), and a reading that invites you to question the tone and purpose of the speaker's statement (Smith).

The object of this exercise is not to say that one critic is right while the other is wrong. For the record, I would say that both Smith and Vendler can be faulted: Vendler's reading takes the poem too much at face value, while conversely Smith depends too strongly on the often dubious double entendres Booth discerns throughout the sonnets. The fact that Sonnet 20 counts on us hearing double meanings in words like 'pricked' and 'nothing' does not mean that these words are *always* used sexually in the rest of the sequence. As the discussion above indicates, although Smith and Vendler have different critical priorities in reading Sonnet 20, they are in agreement about its use of puns, and, implicitly, about its aesthetic value.

Rather, this exercise has two related purposes: first, to illustrate that the erotic element of the sonnets remains contentious and depends on how you read individual poems and phrases; second, to suggest through the comparison of formalist and historicist readings that these approaches are not mutually exclusive. Despite Vendler's attack on 'social' critics, the best historicist commentators retain an awareness of the sonnets' poetic value, as the work of Smith and Barrell ably demonstrates.

So, what approach should we adopt to these poems? My own view is that we need to engage in readings that are sensitive to the literary and social contexts in which the poems were produced, as well as to their linguistic inventiveness as literary texts.

Reading the sonnets

The popular image of the sonnets as universal love poems, mocked in *The Loved One* and recycled by *Shakespeare in Love*, should now seem a long way off. This chapter has investigated the literary contexts underlying the poems and their often erratic reception by later readers. Already we have looked at the addictive emotional dynamics of Sonnet 118 and the implied homoeroticism of Sonnet 20; we now need to explore the overlapping loves the sonnets present in greater detail.

The remainder of this chapter will focus on some key sonnets within the sequence. Even though *Shakespeare's Sonnets* is not a drama, the sequence exhibits fluctuations of mood and changes in the narrator's attitudes towards the young man and the mistress. The reader witnesses a slow deterioration within the speaking voice, as the sequence progresses from the exuberant love depicted so memorably in poems like Sonnet 18, to the decrepit, mutually self-deluding obsessions of poems like Sonnets 138 and 144. It is this downward dynamic that we will now try to uncover through reading four sonnets. I have chosen these texts for two reasons: first, because they sharply illustrate the speaker's changing attitudes within the sequence; second, because of the poetic innovations they embody. Each poem is a departure from the conventional form or content of the Elizabethan love sonnet. I am not saying that these are the best or most important sonnets, although in Sonnets 126 and 146 I have selected two poems that occur at critical moments of tension within the sequence. Selecting from *Shakespeare's Sonnets* should not become the compilation of 'Shakespeare's Greatest Hits' – we are not following the practice of Waugh's Dennis Barlow. Rather, the close analyses below illustrate ways in which you may approach sonnets this chapter has not discussed in detail.

Read Sonnets 35, 126, 129 and 146. Using the notes in *The Norton Shakespeare* where appropriate, select one detail from each poem that strikes you as being unlike the texts you have read by Shakespeare's contemporaries.

Sonnet 35 (Figure 20) The second quatrain – which you will remember from Booth's 'farting' gloss – is a moment of extraordinary poetic self-consciousness: 'All men make faults, and even I in this, / Authorizing thy trespass with compare'. In other words, 'in the process of writing this poem – in making the comparisons I have just done to excuse your behaviour (for example, "Roses have thorns, and silver fountains mud") – I am actually colluding with your "trespass": I am corrupting myself by excusing you'. In contrast with a poem like Sonnet 18, where the poem asserts its power to preserve the young man's beauty, Sonnet 35 shows the poet–speaker turning against both his poetic craft and the object of his love.

Earlier sonneteers frequently inveigh against the cruelty of their hard-hearted mistresses – Drayton's 'As in some Countries, farre remote from hence' goes so far as to present the mistress as a vivisector – but the notion that the poet–speaker actively colludes in the pain he endures through the writing of poetry is distinctively Shakespearean. Sonnet 35 makes it impossible for the reader to divide the 'innocent' speaker from his 'guilty' beloved, by fusing the vocabulary of praise and blame. This technique is encapsulated in the final line, where the young man is 'that sweet thief which sourly robs from me': Shakespeare yokes together contradictory terms like 'sweet' and 'sour' to convey to the reader the emotional 'civil war' on which the poem turns. While the young man has 'done' something unspecified to upset the speaker, the speaker apparently does something worse by extenuating the young man in poetry.

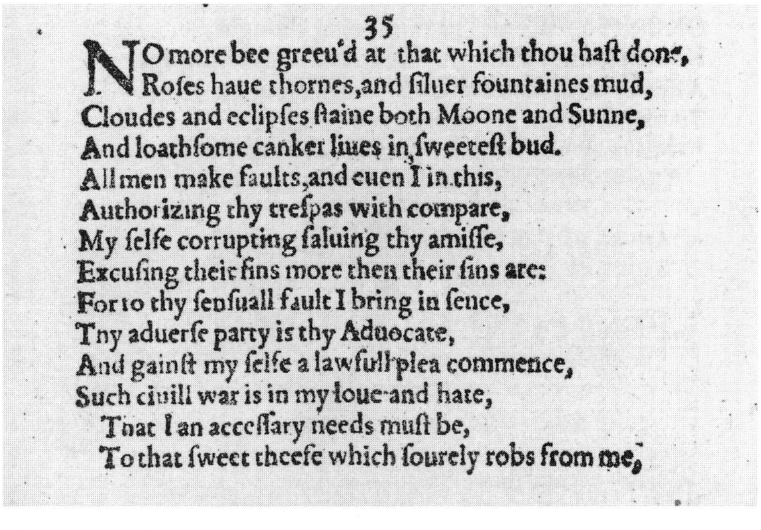

35

NO more bee greeu'd at that which thou haft done,
  Roses haue thornes,and filuer fountaines mud,
Cloudes and eclipfes ftaine both Moone and Sunne,
And loathfome canker liues in fweeteft bud.
All men make faults,and euen I in this,
Authorizing thy trefpas with compare,
My felfe corrupting faluing thy amiffe,
Excufing their fins more then their fins are:
For to thy fenfuall fault I bring in fence,
Tny aduerfe party is thy Aduocate,
And gainft my felfe a lawfull plea commence,
Such ciuill war is in my loue and hate,
    Tnat I an acceffary needs muft be,
    To that fweet theefe which fourely robs from me,

Figure 20 *Sonnet 35 in* Shake-Speares Sonnets ... , *G. Eld for T.T., London, 1609, reproduced from* Shakespeare's Sonnets; ... facsimile ... from the unrivalled original in the library of Bridgewater House ..., *Lovell Reeve, London, 1862.*

Sonnet 126 (Figure 21) This poem is remarkable both in what it says and how it says it. As *The Norton Shakespeare* indicates (p.1966), this 'sonnet' is effectively an 'envoi' to the first part of the sequence, formally demarcated from the texts surrounding it as a 12-line poem in rhyming couplets. The transgressive form of Sonnet 126 is shown graphically in the 1609 Quarto, where the final couplet is followed by a pair of italicized parentheses. Editors used to see these as printer's marks inserted to indicate that Sonnet 126 is two lines short of being a proper sonnet and, on this thinking, did not reprint them after the poem. More recently, Kerrigan, Duncan-Jones and John Lennard (1991) have suggested that the parentheses might come from Shakespeare's manuscript. If this is the case, they would illustrate the 'sense of poetic shortfall' the poem articulates (Kerrigan, 1986, p.350). Alternatively, according to Lennard, they might be grim representations of the grave the young man, like the reader, is headed for (1991, pp.41–3).

As all these different commentators indicate, in this poem form and content are strongly interconnected. The form of the sonnet is broken as Shakespeare forecasts the death of the young man at the close of the sequence of poems addressed to him. Sonneteers like Daniel and Shakespeare himself (in Sonnets 1–17) frequently use the threat of old age as an persuasive strategy: 'If you do not succumb to my charms now, you will end up old, unwanted and unfulfilled, so make the most of my offer!' Sonnet 126 is rather different, in that death is no longer postponable through love-making; as the final couplet brilliantly puts it, nature's 'audit, though delayed, answered must be, / And her quietus is to render thee'. 'Quietus' is, as *The Norton Shakespeare* explains (p.1966), a legal metaphor for the settlement of an account; to the reader of Shakespeare it also inevitably echoes Hamlet's suicidal notion that a man 'might his quietus make / With a bare bodkin' (3. 1. 77–8). In *Shakespeare's Sonnets*, death is now apparently contractually due: there are no escape clauses for either the speaker or the young man.

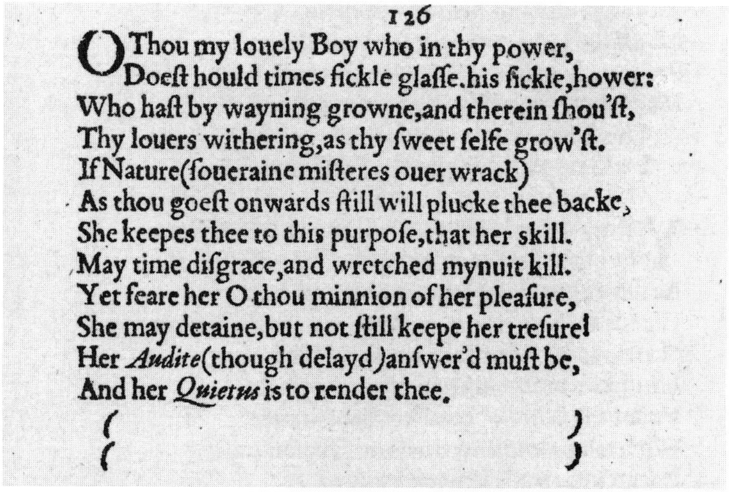

126

O Thou my louely Boy who in thy power,
Doeſt hould times fickle glaſſe,his fickle,hower:
Who haſt by wayning growne,and therein ſhou'ſt,
Thy louers withering,as thy ſweet ſelfe grow'ſt.
If Nature(ſoueraine miſteres ouer wrack)
As thou goeſt onwards ſtill will plucke thee backe,
She keepes thee to this purpoſe,that her skill.
May time diſgrace,and wretched mynuit kill.
Yet feare her O thou minnion of her pleaſure,
She may detaine,but not ſtill keepe her treſure!
Her *Audite*(though delayd)anſwer'd muſt be,
And her *Quietus* is to render thee.
(   )
(   )

Figure 21 *Sonnet 126, in* Shake-Speares Sonnets ... , *G. Eld for T.T., London, 1609, reproduced from* Shakespeare's Sonnets; ... facsimile ... from the unrivalled original in the library of Bridgewater House ..., *Lovell Reeve, London, 1862.*

Sonnet 129 (Figure 22) This is another poem where the form is as remarkable as the content. If Sonnet 20 teases the reader with the possibility of a homoerotic reading, Sonnet 129 explores male heterosexual desire with what is still a shocking frankness. (You will remember that this is the poem that an early reader scored out completely.) Although there was a thriving culture of poetic erotica in the 1590s – Shakespeare's own *Venus and Adonis* is an example of this fashion – poems about sex are rarely as explicit or as serious as Sonnet 129. Indeed, this sonnet's meditation on phallocentric desire is perhaps most readily comparable with Lear's crazed account of female genitalia: 'There's the sulphurous pit, burning, scalding, / Stench, consumption!' (*King Lear* (conflated text) 4. 6. 125–6). *The Norton Shakespeare* points out (p.1967) that the first line and a half of Sonnet 129 punningly convey the idea that sexual intercourse is the expenditure ('expense') of semen ('spirit') 'in a shameful waste' (waist). Kerrigan's paraphrase, which *The Norton Shakespeare* draws on, is even more explicit: 'lust achieving intercourse is the emission of semen (or "the ejaculation of a penis") into a shameful waist' (1986, p.357).

You may also have been struck by the tone of this poem – what Kerrigan calls its 'impersonal profundity' (p.356) – that is, while Sonnet 129 is sexually explicit, it is also markedly abstract. The narrator is not saying anything as banal as 'I slept with my mistress yesterday and thought "this whole activity is a waste of shame"'. Rather, the poem is a highly organized exposition of the addictive quality of sex. As the couplet admits, 'All this the world well knows' – the fact that sex can be maddeningly compulsive is a truism – yet what 'none knows well' is how to 'shun' the heavenly and hellish experience of sexual intercourse. Like Sonnet 118, Sonnet 129 represents interpersonal relations as simultaneously sickening *and* delightful pursuits, which the speaker therefore cannot avoid.

> **129**
>
> TH'expence of Spirit in a waste of shame
>   Is lust in action, and till action, lust
> Is periurd, murdrous, blouddy full of blame,
> Sauage, extreame, rude, cruell, not to trust,
> Inioyd no sooner but dispised straight,
> Past reason, hunted, and no sooner had
> Past reason hated as a swollowed bayt,
> On purpose layd to make the taker mad.
> Made In pursut and in possession so,
> Had, hauing, and in quest, to haue extreame,
> A blisse in proofe and proud and very wo,
> Before a ioy propofd behind a dreame,
>   All this the world well knowes yet none knowes well,
>   To shun the heauen that leads men to this hell.

Figure 22 *Sonnet 129 in* Shake-Speares Sonnets ... , *G. Eld for T.T., London, 1609, reproduced from* Shakespeare's Sonnets; ... *facsimile ...* from the unrivalled original in the library of Bridgewater House ..., *Lovell Reeve, London, 1862.*

Sonnet 146 (Figure 23) What is most immediately striking about this sonnet is that it is not really a love poem at all, or even a poem about relationships. Its focus on the dichotomy between the soul and the body is a traditional devotional image Shakespeare would have known in many different forms (Sawday, 1995, pp.16–22). So it becomes highly tempting to read it as a religious poem inadvertently placed among a series of erotic poems: at first sight, Sonnet 146 alone could justify Knights's idea that *Shakespeare's Sonnets* is a poetic miscellany. The detail I would focus on – the insistent playing on permutations of 'death' in the couplet – may help us to see that there are other ways to read this text: 'So shalt thou feed on *death*, that feeds on men, / And *death* once *dead*, there's no more *dying* then' (my emphasis). Vendler has indicated her sense of the awkwardness of these repetitions: 'The word *death*, so carefully suppressed in the body of 146 grows like a cancer in the couplet ... Aside from the estimable Pauline statement being made [St Paul's idea that death is 'the last enemy' (I Corinthians 15:26)] ... I find the proliferation of "deaths" unnervingly reiterative' (1997, p.616).

Why does Shakespeare draw attention to 'death' so repetitiously in the couplet? Why, in Vendler's terms, does he unnerve the reader? A Christian reading, of the kind both Booth and Vendler attempt to resist, would stress the poem's orthodox theology and would compare it with explicitly devotional texts like John Donne's sonnet 'Death be not proud' (first printed 1633), which similarly climaxes with the idea of the ultimate death of death: 'One short sleepe past, wee wake eternally, / And death shall be no more, death, thou shalt die' (Patrides, 1985, p.441; see Text 8). The problem with such a reading is how it explains the placement of this devotional text within a sequence concerned with the three-way relationship between the speaker, his mistress and the young man (Sonnets 144 and 147). By contrast, 'Death be not proud' is part of Donne's explicitly devotional sequence, *Holy Sonnets*.

There are other ways to read this couplet, which locate the poem more powerfully within the dynamics of the sequence as a whole. By repeating 'death' and 'dying',

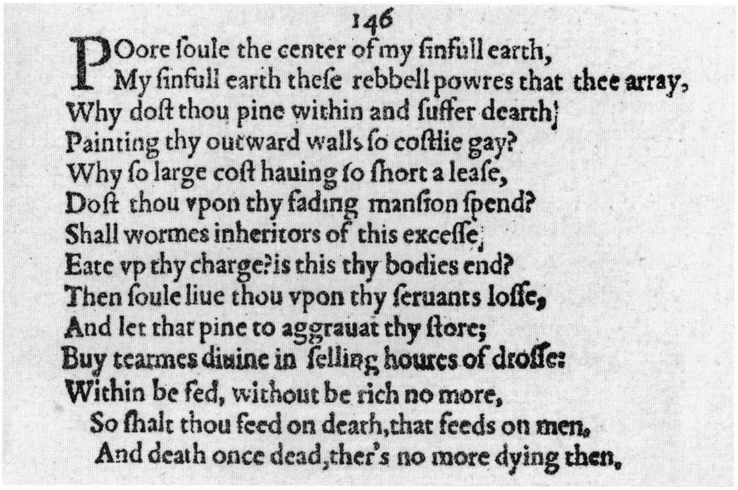
146
POore ſoule the center of my ſinfull earth,
My ſinfull earth theſe rebbell powres that thee array,
Why doſt thou pine within and ſuffer dearth
Painting thy outward walls ſo coſtlie gay?
Why ſo large coſt hauing ſo ſhort a leaſe,
Doſt thou vpon thy fading manſion ſpend?
Shall wormes inheritors of this exceſſe
Eate vp thy charge?is this thy bodies end?
Then ſoule liue thou vpon thy ſeruants loſſe,
And let that pine to aggrauat thy ſtore;
Buy tearmes diuine in ſelling houres of droſſe:
Within be fed, without be rich no more,
So ſhalt thou feed on death,that feeds on men,
And death once dead,ther's no more dying then,

Figure 23 *Sonnet 146 in* Shake-Speares Sonnets ... , *G. Eld for T.T., London, 1609, reproduced from* Shakespeare's Sonnets; ... facsimile ... from the unrivalled original in the library of Bridgewater House ..., *Lovell Reeve, London, 1862. Note the misprint: the repetition of the end of line 1 at the beginning of line 2.*

Shakespeare aggressively draws attention to the term. Vendler notes that Shakespeare suppresses 'death' in the body of Sonnet 146, but the remark also applies to the whole sequence of Sonnets 127–152: this is the first occurrence of 'death', 'dying' or 'dies' in these poems (Spevack, 1973, pp.277, 300, 336). Yet these terms were among the commonest puns in English for having an orgasm. Enobarbus's witticism about Cleopatra shows 'death' as an interchangeable term, oscillating according to context between a metonymy for sexual pleasure and for the end of life: 'I have seen her die twenty times upon far poorer moment. I do think there is mettle in death, which commits some loving act upon her, she hath such a celerity in dying' (*Antony and Cleopatra* 1. 2. 128–31). In the context of the sonnets to the mistress, it is surprising that the couplet of Sonnet 146 is the first occurrence of 'death' and related words. Sonnet 129 – a poem about orgasms – is remarkable for not using the 'death' pun. But the connection between death and sexuality is made explicit immediately after Sonnet 146 by Sonnet 147: 'I desperate now approve / Desire is death' (lines 7–8). What precisely does this mean? In his essay of this title, Jonathan Dollimore discusses the 'perverse dynamic' within Elizabethan thinking which connects desire with death (1996, p.372). His paraphrase of the lines from Sonnet 147 is helpful for understanding the couplet of Sonnet 146:

> ... it means most obviously 'I experience, I demonstrate – reluctantly, in desperation – that desire is death'; less obviously, yet just as literally it means I 'approve' that desire is death: wracked with an impossible, contradictory, self-annihilating desire, I desire death.

> (p.376)

Sexual desire, in other words, has become the desire for death. This is exactly the tone of the couplet of Sonnet 146: the narrator anticipates the death of death – which is also the death of desire – in 'self-annihilating' terms. Sonnet 147 is, like Sonnet 129, a poem explicitly concerned with the addictive quality of sex, in which death and desire become fused: for the speaker of Sonnet 129, sexual intercourse fuses hell and heaven in the same action. I would suggest that the final line of Sonnet 146 anticipates an ultimate way out for the speaker. Once death itself is dead at 'the ending doom' (55.12) of the Christian Day of Judgement, there will be no more orgasms; the hellish–heavenly compulsion that underwrites the sonnets to the mistress will be expunged. As in Sonnet 147, the speaker both sees desire as a form of death and desires death for himself. This would also explain the strange metaphors of 'feeding' in line 13: death (or sex) 'feeds on men' as an addiction, which, these poems demonstrate, ultimately 'eats up' the speaker.

So Sonnet 146 is not a conventional devotional poem, in that it verbalizes the experience of physical addiction in ways that the traditional body/soul dichotomy does not. Rather than writing as a preacher urging his audience to reject the appetite of their 'sinful earth' in favour of feeding their 'Poor soul[s]', Shakespeare here unnervingly expresses the spiritual malaise that runs through all of the sonnets. Since 'Desire is death' – since love either for the young man or the mistress seems equally to lead to the annihilation of personality – this poem suggests that the abnegation of physical desire will be spiritually enriching. While the sonnets ultimately retain a Christian perspective on time and death (there will be an end to death after the Day of Judgement), Shakespeare offers these conclusions not as consolations for human mortality but as the bitter fruit of his poet–speaker's amorous experiences.

Conclusion

Through the course of this chapter, we have charted the origins of the sonnet form, considered how *Shakespeare's Sonnets* were read by later readers, and looked at the sequence as an exploration of the speaker's conflicted relationships. Although I have made analogies between particular sonnets and passages from plays, I have also suggested that the sonnets are best understood as a sequence of lyric poems rather than as semi-dramatized offshoots from Shakespeare's work as a playwright. In this conclusion, I will briefly ask the question more directly: how can a reading of the sonnets assist our understanding of the plays?

Let's first take stock of our discoveries. From the outset, through the reading of Sonnets 18 and 65, I have argued that Shakespeare's poems are tense, meditative texts, which rely on the manipulation of complex literary contexts. We have seen that the novelty of the sonnets lies in how they alter familiar poetic tricks and idioms. Sonnet 146 recalls a traditional notion that the body and soul are at perpetual war; Sonnet 65 contributes to the ancient tradition that sees poetry as a means of perpetuating human life. In each case, Shakespeare's treatment of that tradition is idiosyncratic, and to appreciate the dynamics of that treatment, the reader has to be well-informed about the literary culture in which Shakespeare was writing.

Similarly, we have explored some of the major critical readings of the sonnets, and have seen how such interpretation is contingent on a range of extra-literary factors. It has proved difficult to read these poems as being potentially homoerotic until the final decades of the twentieth century. I have suggested that the best readings will try to combine the features of both formalist and historicist approaches; these poems are both highly charged aesthetic constructions and contributions to wider ideological debates. Intriguingly, because of their erotic content, the sonnets remain a challenge to the received view of Shakespeare as an idealized embodiment of heterosexual Englishness. Yet the texts remain focused on love and sexuality: I would argue that they are compelling precisely because they deal with emotional and sexual issues which concern most readers.

How, then, do the sonnets add to the reading of Shakespeare's plays? In many ways, the answer to this is implicit in the preceding section: while reading the sonnets in detail, we are constantly coming across passages that are reminiscent of the plays. Sonnets 127–152, for example, have often been attacked for their apparent misogyny. The speaker is hostile to and about his mistress: he claims she is false, ugly, sexually incontinent and betraying him with the young man. Yet these agendas are strikingly like the dramatic preoccupations of the Jacobean Shakespeare. As you have seen with *Cymbeline*, Shakespeare's later work returns with increasing urgency to questions of sexual identity and ownership. In this sense, the paranoiac poet– speaker of *Shakespeare's Sonnets* is very similar to the jealous husbands and fathers of plays like *King Lear*, *Othello*, *The Tempest* and *The Winter's Tale*. It would seem that in both his drama and his poetry Shakespeare, rather than being himself an obsessive misogynist, was persistently interested in the tensions within social constructions of gender and sexual desire. But where the plays dramatize complex stories with a range of different speaking parts, *Shakespeare's Sonnets* obsessively focuses on the dilemmas of one male protagonist. The sonnets depict a claustrophobic interior world, lightened only by the brilliance of Shakespeare's phrase-making. This is the other major connection that exists between the poems and the plays.

But it is not quite as simple as saying 'Shakespeare was a great playwright, therefore he was also a great poet'. What distinguishes Shakespeare's poetry from that of his contemporaries, as we have seen in our close readings of Sonnets 65, 118, 35 and 126, is his ongoing sense of the risks and shortfalls inherent within poetic language. The sonnets are almost exorbitantly self-conscious; although they repeatedly articulate the power of poetry, they are equally keen to stress its limitations. Poetic language can be deluding, facile and emotionally dangerous. As Sonnet 35 puts it 'All men make faults, and even I in this, / Authorizing thy trespass with compare'. This sense of the danger of elaborate language is one that runs through almost all of Shakespeare's plays: consider the foppish Osric with his over-conceited language in *Hamlet*. More potently, the sonnets' concern with the deceptiveness of language echoes powerfully in plays like *Measure for Measure* and *Cymbeline*, which focus on moments of verbal deceit like Angelo's proposition to Isabella (2. 5), or Giacomo's equally insinuating assault of Innogen (1. 6). Bardolators are all too ready to praise Shakespeare's language without acknowledging that one of the central concerns of his work is precisely the hollowness that can lurk within beautiful words: as Isabella puts it, there is often no way to distinguish right from wrong in the 'perilous mouths' of characters like Angelo (2. 4. 172–7). Careful reading of the sonnets reveals that it is precisely the ambivalence of poetic language that generates Shakespeare's poetry; in this sense, the doubleness of language is as addictive as doubleness of sex.

References

Auden, W.H. (1973) *Forewords and Afterwords*, London: Faber & Faber.

Barrell, J. (1988) *Poetry, Language and Politics*, Manchester: Manchester University Press.

Bate, J. (1993) *Shakespeare and Ovid*, Oxford: Clarendon Press.

Bate, J. (1997) *The Genius of Shakespeare*, London: Picador.

Booth, S. (ed.) (1977) *Shakespeare's Sonnets*, New Haven: Yale University Press.

Curtius, E.R. (1990 edn) *European Literature and the Latin Middle Ages*, trans. W.R. Trask, Princeton: Princeton University Press (first published 1953).

Dollimore, J. (1996) 'Desire is death', in *Subject and Object in Renaissance Culture*, ed. M. de Grazia, M. Quilligan and P. Stallybrass, Cambridge: Cambridge University Press, pp.369–86.

Dubrow, H. (1987) *Captive Victors: Shakespeare's Narrative Poems and Sonnets*, Ithaca: Cornell University Press.

Duncan-Jones, K. (ed.) (1997) *Shakespeare's Sonnets*, The Arden Shakespeare, Walton-on-Thames: Thomas Nelson.

Durling, R. (ed. and trans.) (1976) *Petrarch's Lyric Poems: The 'Rime Sparse' and Other Lyrics*, Cambridge, MA: Harvard University Press.

Empson, W. (1930) *Seven Types of Ambiguity*, London: Chatto & Windus.

Evans, M. (ed.) (1977) *Elizabethan Sonnets*, London: Dent.

Ferry, A. (1983) *The 'Inward' Language: Sonnets of Wyatt, Sidney, Shakespeare, Donne*, Chicago: University of Chicago Press.

Fineman, J. (1986) *Shakespeare's Perjured Eye: The Invention of Poetic Subjectivity in the Sonnets*, Berkeley: University of California Press.

Gill, S. (ed.) (1984) *William Wordsworth*, Oxford Authors Series, Oxford: Oxford University Press.

Greenblatt, S. (1980) *Renaissance Self-fashioning: From More to Shakespeare*, Chicago: University of Chicago Press.

Greenblatt, S., Cohen, W., Howard, J.E. and Maus, K.E. (eds) (1997) *The Norton Shakespeare*, New York: W.W. Norton.

Hamilton, I. (1982) *Robert Lowell: A Biography*, New York: Random House.

Herbert, T.W. (1980) 'Dramatic personae in Shakespeare's sonnets', in *Shakespeare's 'More Than Words can Witness': Essays on Visual and Nonverbal Enactments in the Plays*, ed. S. Homan, Lewisburg: Bucknell University Press, pp.77–91.

Hughes, T. (1998) *Birthday Letters*, London: Faber & Faber.

Jones, P. (ed.) (1977) *Shakespeare: The Sonnets – A Casebook*, London: Macmillan.

Kerrigan, J. (ed.) (1986) *'The Sonnets' and 'A Lover's Complaint'*, Harmondsworth: Penguin.

Kerrigan, J. (ed.) (1991) *Motives of Woe: Shakespeare and 'Female Complaint'*, Oxford: Clarendon Press.

Leishman, J.B. (1963) *Themes and Variations in Shakespeare's Sonnets*, London: Hutchinson University Library.

Lennard, J. (1991) *'But I Digress': The Exploitation of Parentheses in English Printed Verse*, Oxford: Clarendon Press.

Lowell, R. (1970) *Notebook*, London: Faber & Faber.

Marotti, A.F. (1980) '"Love is not love": Elizabethan sonnet sequences and the social order', *English Literary History*, vol.49, pp.396–428.

Martin C. (ed.) (1998) *Ovid in English*, Harmondsworth: Penguin.

Murray, I. (ed.) (1979) *The Complete Shorter Fiction of Oscar Wilde*, Oxford: Oxford University Press.

Patrides, C.A. (ed.) (1985) *The Complete English Poems of John Donne*, London: Dent.

Pequigney, J. (1985) *Such is My Love: A Study of Shakespeare's Sonnets*, Chicago: Chicago University Press.

Ringler, W.A. (ed.) (1962) *The Complete Poems of Sir Philip Sidney*, Oxford: Clarendon Press.

Sawday, J. (1995) *The Body Emblazoned: Dissection and the Human Body in Renaissance Culture*, London: Routledge.

Smith, B.R. (1994) *Homosexual Desire in Shakespeare's England: A Cultural Poetics*, Chicago: University of Chicago Press.

Spevack, M. (1973) *The Harvard Concordance to Shakespeare*, Cambridge, MA: Harvard University Press.

Vendler, H. (1997) *The Art of 'Shakespeare's Sonnets'*, Cambridge, MA: Harvard University Press.

Waugh, E. (1951 edn) *The Loved One: An Anglo-American Tragedy*, Harmondsworth: Penguin (first published London: Chapman & Hall, 1948).

SOURCES,
ANALOGUES AND
CRITICISM

Appendix 1

Text 1

Raphael Holinshed, The First Volume of Chronicles *(1587 edition)*

Shakespeare's main historical source for *Cymbeline*, the revised 1587 edition of Raphael Holinshed's *Chronicles of England, Scotland and Ireland*, offers a part-fact, part-fantasy history of early Britain. Writing under Tudor patronage, Holinshed himself drew on Julius Caesar's *De bello gallico*, the first-century historian St Bede and the twelfth-century chronicler Geoffrey of Monmouth to reconstruct the Roman invasion and occupation of Britain, as well as the subsequent expulsion of the Romans. The extracts reprinted below describe the difficulties Julius Caesar encountered in subduing the Britons (alluded to in the Queen's speech in *Cymbeline* (3. 1. 22–33)), and the relationship of 'Kymbeline or Cimbeline' to the Roman Empire.

JULIUS CAESAR IN DIFFICULTIES

[In Bk III, Ch. 10–16 Holinshed gives various accounts of Caesar's invasions of Britain. Caesar himself told of his initial difficulty in getting troops ashore and how when he had done so the Britons called for peace and gave hostages.]

[...] Peace being thus established after the fourth day of the Romans arrivall in Britaine, the 18 ships which ... were appointed to convey the horssemen over, loosed from the further haven with a soft wind. Which when they approched so neere the shore of Britaine, that the Romans which were in Cesars campe might see them, suddenlie there arose so great a tempest, that none of them was able to keepe his course, so that they were not onelie driven in sunder ... but also the other ships that lay at anchor, and had brought over the armie, were so pitifullie beaten, tossed and shaken, that a great number of them did not onelie lose their tackle, but also were carried by force of wind into the high sea; the rest being likewise so filled with water, that they were in danger by sinking to perish and to be quite lost ... There was no way for the Romans to helpe the matter: wherefore a great number of those ships were so bruised, rent and weather-beaten, that without new reparation they would serve to no use of sailing [Ch. 12].

[...][Caesar fought on and enforced a truce.] After that these things were thus ordered, Cesar, because the moneth of September was well-neare halfe spent and that winter hasted on ... determined not to staie anie longer, but having wind and weather for his purpose, got himselfe aboord with his people, and returned into Gallia.

Thus writeth Cesar touching his first journie made into Britaine. But the British historie (which *Polydor* calleth the new historie) declareth that Cesar in a pitched field was vanquished at the first encounter, and so withdrew backe into France. Beda also writeth, that Cesar ... [in] Gallia ... got togither 80 saile of great ships and row gallies, wherewith he passed over into Britaine, and there at the first being wearied with sharpe and sore fight, and after taken with a grievous tempest, he lost the greater part of his navie, with no small number of his souldiers, and almost all his horssemen: and therwith returned into Gallia, placed his souldiers in steeds to sojourne there for the winter season. Thus saith Bede. The British historie moreover maketh mention of three under-kings that aided Cassibellane in this first battell fought with Cesar ... The same historie also maketh mention of one Belinus that was generall of Cassibellanes armie, and likewise of Nenius brother to Cassibellane, who in fight happened to get Cesars swoord fastened to his shield by a blow which Cesar stroke at him. Androgeus and Tenancius were at the battell in aid of Cassibellane. But Nenius died within 15 daies after the battell of hurt received at Cesars hand [Ch. 13].

[Caesar's next landing was almost unimpeded, but again he was hindered by storm.]

[...] The next day, as he had sent foorth such as should have pursued the Britains, word came to him from Quintus Atrius, that his navie by rigour of a sore and hideous tempest was greevouslie molested, and thrown upon the shore, so that the cabels and tackle being broken and destroied with force of the unmercifull rage of the wind, the maisters and mariners were not able to helpe the matter. [He defeated the Britons however.] Cassibellane in the end was forced to fall to a composition in covenanting to paie a yearelie tribute of three thousand pounds ...

[...] The reverend father Bede writing of this matter, saith thus: After that Cesar [had] returned into Gallia ... he caused ships to be made readie, to the number of 600, with the which repassing into Britaine, whilest he marched foorth with a mightie armie against the enimies, his ships that lay at anchor being taken with a sore tempest, were either beaten one against another, or else cast upon the flats and sands, and so broken; so that fortie of them were utterlie perished, and the residue with great difficultie were repaired. The horssemen of the Romans at the first encounter were put to the worsse, and Labienus the tribune slaine. In the second conflict he vanquished the Britains, not without great danger of his people ... the strong citie of Troinovant with hir duke Androgeus delivering fortie hostages, yeelded unto Caesar ... Thus much touching the war which Julius Cesar made against the Britains, in bringing them under tribute to the Romans. But this tributarie subjection was hardlie mainteined for a season [Ch. 16].

CYMBELINE AND GUIDERIUS [Ch. 18]

After the death of Cassibellane, Theomantius or Tenantius the yoongest son of Lud was made king of Britaine in the yeere of the world 3921, after the building of Rome 706, and before the comming of Christ 45 ... Theomantius ruled the land in good quiet, and paid the tribute to the Romans which Cassibellane had granted, and finallie departed this life after he had reigned 22 yeares, and was buried at London.

Kymbeline or Cimbeline the sonne of Theomantius was of the Britains made king after the deceasse of his father ... This man (as some write) was brought up at Rome, and there made knight by Augustus Cesar, under whome he served in the warres, and was in such favour with him, that he was at libertie to pay his tribute or not. Little other mention is made of his dooings, except that during his reigne, the Saviour of the world of our Lord Jesus Christ the onelie sonne of God was borne of a virgine, about the 23 yeare of the reigne of this Kymbeline ... some writers doo varie, but the best approved affirme, that he reigned 35 years and then died, and was buried at London, leaving behind him two sonnes, Guiderius and Arviragus.

But here is to be noted, that although our histories doo affirme, that as well this Kymbeline, as also his father Theomantius, lived in quiet with the Romans, and continuallie to them paied the tributes which the Britains had covenanted with Julius Cesar to pay, yet we find in the Romane writers, that after Julius Cesars death, when Augustus had taken upon him the rule of the empire, the Britains refused to paie that tribute: whereat as Cornelius Tacitus reporteth, Augustus (being otherwise occupied) was contented to winke; howbeit, through earnest calling upon to recover his right by such as were desirous to see the uttermost of the British kingdome; at length, to wit, in the tenth yeare after the death of Julius Cesar, which was about the thirteenth yeare of the said Theomantius, Augustus made provision to passe with an armie over into Britaine, and was come forward upon his journie into Gallia Celtica: or as we maie saie, into these hither parts of France.

But here receiving advertisements that the Pannonians, which inhabited the countrie now called Hungarie, and the Dalmatians whome now we call Slavons had rebelled, he thought it best first to subdue those rebells neere home, rather than to seeke new countries, and leave such in hazard whereof he had present possession, and so turning his power against the Pannonians and Dalmatians, he left off for a time the warres of Britaine. [Twice more Augustus was prevented thus from crossing to Britain] ... But whether this controversie which appeareth to fall forth betwixt the Britains and Augustus, was occasioned by Kymbeline, or some other prince of the Britains, I have not to avouch: for that by our writers it is reported that Kymbeline, being brought up in Rome, and knighted in the court of Augustus, ever shewed himselfe a friend to the Romans, and chieflie was loth to breake with them, because the youth of the Britaine nation should not be deprived of the benefit to be trained and brought up among the Romans, whereby they might learne both to behave themselves like civill men, and to atteine to the knowledge of feates of warre.

[...] Guiderius the first sonne of Kymbeline ... began his reigne in the seventeenth yeere after th'incarnation of Christ. This Guiderius being a man of stout courage, gave occasion of breach of peace betwixt the Britains and Romans, denieing to paie them tribute, and procuring the people to new insurrections, which by one meane or other made open rebellion, as Gyldas saith. Whereupon the emperour Caligula (as some thinke) tooke occasion to leavie a power, and ... he ment not onlie to reduce the Iland unto the former subjection, but also to search out the uttermost bounds thereof, to the behoofe of himselfe, and of the Romane monarchie [Ch. 19]. [All he did however was to gather cockle shells ('the spoile of the Ocean') from the seashore.]

[...] There be that write, how Claudius subdued and added to the Romane empire, the Iles of Orknie situate in the north Ocean beyond Britaine: which might well be accomplished either by Plautius, or some other his lieutenant. [Gyldas wrote of the Britons at this time as spiritless cowards] so a common proverbe followeth thereof, to wit, That the Britains were neither valiant in warre, nor faithfull in peace ...

In the British historie we find other report as thus, that Claudius at his comming aland at Porchester, beseiged that towne, to the rescue whereof came Guiderius, and giving battell to the Romans, put them to the woorse, till at length one Hamo, being on the Romans side, changed his shield and armour, apparelling himselfe like a Britaine, and so entring into the thickest prease of the British host, came at length where the king was, and there slue him. But Arviragus perceiving this mischiefe, to the end the Britains should not be discouraged therewith, caused himselfe to be adorned with the kings cote-armour and other abiliments, and so as king continued the fight with such manhood, that the Romans were put to flight. Claudius retired back to his ships, and Hamo to the next woods, whom Arviragus pursued, and at length drove him unto the sea side, and there slue him yer he could take the haven which was there at hand; so that the same tooke name of him and was called a long time after, Hamons haven [i.e. Southampton] ... Thus have you heard how Guiderius or Guinderius ... came to his end, which chanced (as some write) in the 28 yeere of his reigne [Bk IV. Ch. 2].

[In Ch. 3 Holinshed tells how Arviragus succeeded his brother and 'bare himselfe right manfullie against Claudius and his Romans'.]

[...] Whereupon Claudius doubting the sequele of the thing, sent messengers unto Arviragus to treat of concord, and so by composition the matter was taken up, with condition that Claudius should give his daughter Genissa in marriage unto Arviragus, and Arviragus should acknowledge to hold his kingdome of the Romans ... [But apparently Claudius had no daughter named Genissa.]

And heere to speake my fansie also what I thinke of this Arviragus, and the other kings ... I will not denie but such persons there were, and the same happilie bearing verie great rule in the land ... [But he is doubtful about when and where.] For my part therefore, sith this order of the British kinglie succession in this place is more easie to be flatly denied and utterlie reprooved, than either wiselie defended or trulie amended, I will referre the reforming thereof unto those that have perhaps seene more than I have, or more deepelie considered the thing, to trie out an undoubted truth.

[In Ch. 4 Holinshed gives (with some scepticism) the British account telling how Arviragus later refused tribute and fought an indecisive battle against Vespasian.]

On the morrow after queene Genissa made them friends, and so the warres ceassed for that time, by hir good mediation.

(From Geoffrey Bullough (1975) *Narrative and Dramatic Sources of Shakespeare*, Volume VIII, London: Routledge & Kegan Paul, pp.41–6)

Text 2

Giovanni Boccaccio, The Decameron, *anonymously translated (1620)*

The wager story in *Cymbeline* closely resembles the ninth tale of the second day of Giovanni Boccaccio's *Decameron*, written in 1349–51. Although no English translation of *The Decameron* from earlier than 1620 survives, the closeness of *Cymbeline* to Boccacico's tale suggests that Shakespeare must have read either a translation that has been lost, or one of the many Italian originals or French translations that would have been available to him. The extract from the anonymous 1620 translation of the ninth tale reprinted below is in two parts. The first recounts the wager between Bernado (the Posthumus figure) and Ambrogiuolo (the Giacomo figure), as well as the chest scene and Ambrogiuolo's triumphant return to claim victory in the wager. The second presents the conclusion of the tale, with Genevra (the Innogen figure) revealing her masculine disguise (as Sicurano) and exposing Ambrogiuolo's villainy, and Ambrogiuolo (unlike Giacomo) coming to an extremely violent end.

The Second Day: The ninth Novell.

Bernardo, a Merchant of Geneway, being deceived by another Merchant, named Ambrogiuolo, lost a great part of his goods. And commanding his innocent Wife to be murthered, she escaped, and (in the habite of a man) became servant to the Soldane. The deceiver being found at last, shee compassed such meanes, that her husband Bernardo came into Alexandria, and, there, after due punishment inflicted on the false deceiver, she resumed the garments againe of a woman, and returned home with her Husband to Geneway.

[1]

Madam Eliza having ended her compassionate discourse, which indeede had moved all the rest to sighing; the Queene, who was faire, comely of stature, and carrying a very majesticall countenance, smiling more familiarly then the other, spake to them thus: ... Many times among vulgar people, it hath passed as a common Proverbe: That the deceiver is often trampled on, by such as he hath deceived. And this cannot shew it selfe (by any reason) to be true, except such accidents as awaite on treachery, doe really make a just discovery thereof. And therefore according to the course of this day observed, I am the woman that must make good what I have saide for the approbation of that Proverbe: no way (I hope) distastfull to you in the hearing, but advantageable to preserve you from any such beguiling.

There was a faire and goodly Inne in Paris, much frequented by many great Italian Merchants, according to such variety of occasions and businesse, as urged their often resorting thither. One night among many other, having had a merry Supper together, they began to discourse on divers matters, and falling from one relation to another; they communed in very friendly manner, concerning their wives, lefte at home in their houses. Quoth the first, I cannot well imagine what my wife is now doing, but I am able to say for my selfe, that if a pretty female should fall into my company: I could easily forget my love to my wife, and make use of such an advantage offered.

A second replyed; And trust me, I should do no lesse, because I am perswaded, that if my wife be willing to wander, the law is in her owne hand, and I am farre enough from home: dumbe walles blab no tales, and offences unknowne are sildome or never called in question. A third man unapt in censure, with his former fellowes of the Jury; and it plainely appeared, that all the rest were of the same opinion, condemning their wives over-rashly, and alledging, that when husbands strayed so far from home, their wives had wit enough to make use of their time.

Onely one man among them all, named Bernardo Lomellino, and dwelling in Geneway, maintained the contrary; boldly avouching, that by the especiall favour of Fortune, he had a wife so perfectly compleate in all graces and vertues, as any Lady in the world possibly could be, and that Italy scarsely contained her equall. But, she was goodly of person, and yet very young, quicke, quaint, milde, and courteous, and not any thing appertaining to the office of a wife, either for domesticke affayres, or any other imployment whatsoever, but in woman-hoode shee went beyond all other. No Lord, Knight, Esquire, or Gentleman, could be better served at his Table, then himselfe dayly was, with more wisedome, modesty and discretion. After all this, hee praised her for riding, hawking, hunting, fishing, fowling, reading, writing, enditing, and most absolute keeping his Bookes of accounts, that neither himselfe, or any other Merchant could therein excell her. After infinite other commendations, he came to the former point of their argument, concerning the easie falling of women into wantonnesse, maintaining (with a solemne oath) that no woman possibly could be more chaste and honest than she: in which respect, he was verily perswaded, that if he stayed from her ten years space (yes all his life time) out of his house; yet never would shee falsifie her faith to him, or be lewdly allured by any other man.

Amongst these Merchants thus communing together, there was a young proper man, named Ambrogiuolo of Placentia, who began to laugh at the last prayses which Bernardo had used of his Wife, and seeming to make a mockerie thereof, demaunded, if the Emperour had given him this priviledge, above all other married men? Bernardo being somewhat offended, answered: No Emperour hath done it, but the especiall blessing of heaven, exceeding all the Emperours on the earth in grace, and thereby have I received this favour; whereto Ambrogiuolo presently thus replyed. Bernardo, without all question to the contrary, I beleeve that what thou hast said, is true; but (for ought I can perceive) thou hast slender judgement in the Nature of things: because, if thou diddst observe them well, though couldst not be of so grosse understanding. For, by comprehending matters in their true kinde and nature, thou wouldst speake of them more correctly then thou doest. And to the end, thou mayest not imagine, that we who have spoken of our Wives, doe thinke any otherwise of them, then as well and honestly as thou canst of thine, nor that any thing else did urge these speeches of them, or falling into this kinde of discourse, but onely by a naturell instinct and admonition, I will proceede familiarly, a little further with thee, uppon the matter alreadie propounded.

I have evermore understoode, that man was the most noble creature, formed by God to live in this World, and woman in the next degree to him: but man, as generally is beleeved, and as is discerned by apparent effects is the most perfect of both. Having then the most perfection in him, without all doubt, he must be so much the more firme and constant. So in like manner, it hath beene, and is universally graunted, that Woman is more various and mutable, and the reason thereof may be approved by many naturall circumstances, which were needless now to make any mention of. If a man then be possessed of the greater stability, and yet cannot containe himselfe from condiscending, I say not to one that entreates him, but to desire any other that may please him; and beside, to covet the enjoying of his owne pleasing contentment (a thing not chancing to him once in a moneth, but infinite times in a dayes space). What can you then conceive of a fraile Woman, subject (by nature) to entreaties, flatteries, giftes, perswasions, and a thousand other inticing meanes, which a man (that is affected to her) can use? Doest thou thinke then that she hath any power to containe? Assuredly, though thou shouldest rest so resolved, yet cannot I be of the same opinion. For I am sure thou beleevest, and must needes confesse it, that thy wife is a Woman, made of flesh and blood, as other women are: if it be so, she cannot bee without the same desires, and the weaknesse or strength as other women have, to resist naturall appetites as her owne are. In regard whereof, it is meerely impossible (although she be most honest) but she must needs doe that which other Women doe: for there is nothing else possible, either to be denied or affirmed to the contrary, as thou most unadvisedly hast done.

Bernardo answered in this manner. I am a Merchant, and no Philosopher, and like a Merchant I meane to answer thee. I am not to learne, that these accidents by thee related, may happen to fooles, who are voide of understanding or shame: but such as are wise, and endued with vertue, have alwayes such a precious esteeme of their honour, that they wil containe those principles of constancie, which men are meerely carelesse of, and I justifie my wife to be one of them. Beleeve me Bernado, replyed Ambrogiuolo, if so often as thy wives minde is addicted to wanton folly, a badge of scorne should arise on thy forehead, to render testimony of hir female frailty, I beleeve the number of them would be more, then willingly you would wish them to be. And among all married men in every degree, the notes are so secret of their wives imperfections, that the sharpest sight is not able to discerne them: and the wiser sort of men are willing not to know them; because shame and losse of honour is never imposed, but in cases evident and apparent.

Perswade thy selfe then Bernado, that what women may accomplish in secret, they will rarely fail to doe: or if they abstaine, it is through feare and folly. Wherefore, hold it for a certain rule, that that woman is onely chaste, that never was solicited personally, or if she endured any such suite, either shee answered yea, or no. And albeit I know this to be true, by many infallible and naturall reasons, yet could I not speak so exactly as I doe, if I had not tried experimentally, the humours and affections of divers Women. Yea, and let me tell thee more Bernardo, were I in private company with thy wife, howsoever thou presumest to thinke her to bee, I should account it a matter of no impossibility, to finde in her the selfsame frailty.

Bernadoes blood now began to boyle, and patience being a little put downe by choller, thus he replyed. A combat of words requires over-long continuance; for I maintaine the matter which thou deniest, and all this sorts to nothing in the end. But seeing thou presumest, that all women are so apt and tractable, and thy selfe so confident of thine owne power: I willingly yeeld (for the better assurance of my wifes constant loyalty) to have my head smitten off, if thou canst winne her to any such dishonest act, by any meanes whatsoever thou canst use unto her; which if thou canst not doe, thou shalt onely loose a thousand duckets of Gold. Now began Ambrogiuolo to be heated with these words, answering thus. Bernardo, if I had won the wager, I know not what I should doe with thy head; but if thou be willing to stand upon the proofe, pawne downe five thousand Duckets of gold, (a matter of much lesse value than thy head) against a thousand Duckets of mine, granting me a lawfull limited time, which I require to be no more than the space of three moneths, after the day of my departing hence. I will stand bound to goe for Geneway, and there winne such kinde consent of thy Wife, as shall be to mine owne content. In witnesse whereof, I will bring backe with me such private and especiall tokens, as thou thy selfe shalt confesse that I have not failed. Provided, that thou doe first promise upon thy faith, to absent thy selfe thence during my limitted time, and be no hinderance to me by thy Letters, concerning the attempt by me undertaken.

Bernardo saide, Be it a bargaine, I am the man that will make good my five thousand Duckets; and albeit the other Merchants then present, earnestly laboured to breake the wager, knowing great harme must needs ensue thereon: yet both the parties were so hot and fiery, as all the other men spake to no effect, but writings was made, sealed, and delivered under either of their hands, Bernardo remaining at Paris, and Ambrogiuolo departing for Geneway. There he remained some few dayes, to learne the streetes name where Bernardo dwelt, as also the conditions and qualities of his Wife, which scarcely pleased him when he heard them; because they were farre beyond her Husbands relation, and shee reputed to be the onely wonder of women; whereby he plainely perceived, that he had undertaken a very idle enterprise, yet would he not give it over so, but proceeded therein a little further.

He wrought such meanes, that he came acquainted with a poore woman, who often frequented Bernadoes house, and was greatly in favour with his wife; upon whose poverty he so prevailed, by earnest perswasions, but much more by large gifts of money, that he won her to further him in this manner following. A faire and artificiall Chest he caused to be purposely made wherein himselfe might be aptly contained, and so conveyed into the House of Bernadoes Wife, under colour of a formall excuse; that the poore woman should be absent from the City for two or three dayes, and shee must keepe it safe till she returne. The Gentlewoman suspecting no guile, but that the Chest was the receptacle of all the womans wealth; would trust it in no other roome, then her owne Bed-chamber, which was the place where Ambrogiuolo most desired to bee.

Being thus conveyed into the Chamber, the night going on apace, and the Gentlewoman fast asleepe in her bed, a lighted Taper stood burning on the Table by her, as in her Husbands absence shee ever used to have: Ambrogiuolo softly opened the Chest, according as cunningly hee had contrived it, and stepping forth in his sockes made of cloath, observed the scituation of the Chamber, the paintings, pictures, and beautifull hangings, with all things else that were remarkable, which perfectly he committed to his memory. Going neere to the bed, he saw her lie there sweetly sleeping, an her young Daughter in like manner by her, she seeming then as compleate and pleasing a creature, as when shee was attired in her best bravery. No especiall note or marke could hee descrie, whereof he might make credible report, but onely a small wart upon her left pappe, with some few haires growing thereon, appearing to be as yellow as gold.

Sufficient had he seene, and durst presume no further; but taking one of her Rings, which lay upon the Table, a purse of hers, hanging by on the wall, a light wearing Robe of silke, and her girdle, all which he put into the Chest; and being in himselfe, closed it fast as it was before, so continuing there in the Chamber two severall nights, the Gentlewoman neither mistrusting or missing any thing. The third day being come, the poore woman, according as formerly was concluded, came to have home her Chest againe, and brought it safely into her owne house; where Ambrogiuolo comming forth of it, satisfied the poore woman to her owne liking, returning (with all the forenamed things) so fast as conveniently he could to Paris.

Being arrived there long before his limmitted time, he called the Merchants together, who were present at the passed words and wager; avouching before Bernardo, that he had won his five thousand Duckets, and performed the taske he undertooke. To make good his protestation, first he described the forme of the Chamber, the curious pictures hanging about it, in what manner the bed stood, and every circumstance else beside. Next he shewed the severall things, which he brought away thence with him, affirming that he had received them of her selfe. Bernardo confessed, that his description of the Chamber was true, and acknowledged moreover, that these other things did belong to his Wife: But (quoth he) this may be gotten, by corrupting some servant of mine, both for intelligence of the Chamber, as also of the Ring, Purse, and what else is beside; all which suffice not to win the wager, without some other more apparent and pregnant token. In troth, answered Ambrogiuolo, me thinkes these should serve for sufficient proofes; but seeing thou art so desirous to know more: I plainely tell thee, that faire Genevra thy Wife, hath a small round wart upon her left pappe, and some few little golden haires growing thereon.

When Bernardo heard these words, they were as so many stabs to his heart, yea, beyond all compasse of patient sufferance, and by the changing of his colour, it was noted manifestly, (being unable to utter one word) that Ambrogiuolo had spoken nothing but the truth. Within a while after, he saide; Gentlemen, that which Ambrogiuolo hath saide, is very true, wherefore let him come when he will, and he shall be paide; which accordingly he performed on the very next day, even to the utmost penny, departing then from Paris towards Geneway, with a most malicious intention to his Wife. Being come neere to the City, he would not enter it, but rode to a Country house of his, standing about tenne miles distant thence. Being there arrived, he called a servant, in whom hee reposed especial trust, sending him to

Geneway with two Horses, writing to his Wife, that he was returned, and shee should come thither to see him. But secretly he charged his servant, that so soone as he had brought her to a convenient place, he should there kill her, without any pitty or compassion, and then returne to him againe.

[2]

Great Soldane, I am the miserable and unfortunate Genevra, that for the space of six whole yeeres, have wandered through the world, in the habite of a man, falsely and most maliciously slaundered, by the villainous traytor Ambrogiuolo, and by this unkinde cruell husband, betraied to his servant to be slaine, and left to be devoured by savage beasts. Afterward, desiring such garments as better fitted for her, and shewing her breasts, she made it apparent before the Soldane and his assistants, that shee was the very same woman indeede. Then turning her selfe to Ambrogiuolo, with more then manly courage, she demanded of him, when, and where it was, that he lay with her, as (villainously) he was not ashamed to make his vaunt? But hee, having alreadie acknowledged the contrarie, being stricken dumbe with shamefull disgrace, was not able to utter one word.

The Soldane, who had always reputed Sicurano to be a man, having heard and seene so admirable an accident; was so amazed in his minde, that many times he was very doubtfull, whether this was a dreame, or an absolute relation of trueth. But, after hee had more seriously considered thereon, and found it to be reall and infallible: with extraordinary gracious praises, he commended the life, constancy, condition and virtues of Genevra, whom (til that time) he had always called Sicurano. So committing her to the company of honourable Ladies, to be changed from her manly habite; he pardoned Bernardo her husband (according to her request formerly made) although hee had more justly deserved death: which likewise himselfe confessed, and falling at the feet of Genevra, desired her (in teares) to forgive his rash transgression, which most lovingly she did, kissing and embracing him a thousand times.

Then the Soldane strictly commaunded, that on some high and eminent place of the Citie, Ambrogiuolo should be bound and impaled on a stake, having his naked body nointed all over with honey, and never to bee taken off, untill (of it selfe) it fell in peeces, which, according to the sentence, was presently performed. Next, he gave expresse charge, that all his mony and goods should be given to Genevra, which valued above ten thousand double Duckets. Forthwith a solemne Feast was prepared, wherein much honor was done to Bernardo, being the husband of Genevra: and to her, as to a most worthy woman, and matchlesse wife, he gave in costly Jewels, as also vessels of gold and silver plate, so much as did amount to above ten thousand double Duckets more.

When the feasting was finished, he caused a Ship to be furnished for them, graunting them license to depart from Geneway when they pleased; whither they returned most richly and joyfully, being welcomed home with great honour, especially Madam Genevra, whom every one supposed to be dead; and alwayes after, so long as she lived, shee was most famous for her manifold vertues. But as for Ambrogiuolo, the verie same day that hee was impaled on the stake, annointed with honey, and fixed in the place appointed, to his no meane torment: he not onely died, but likewise was devoured to the bare bones, by Flies, Waspes, and Hornets, whereof the Countrey notoriously aboundeth. And his bones, in full forme and fashion, remained strangely blacke for a long time after, knit together by the sinewes; as a witnesse to many thousands of people, which afterward beheld the

Carkasse of his wickednesse against so good and vertuous a Woman, that had not so much as a thought of any evill towards him. And thus was the Proverbe truly verified, that shame succeedeth after ugly sinne, and the deceiver is trampled and trod, by such as himselfe hath deceived.

(From Geoffrey Bullough (1975) *Narrative and Dramatic Sources of Shakespeare*, Volume VIII, London: Routledge & Kegan Paul, pp.50–6, 61–3)

Text 3

Michael Shapiro, 'Chronological list of plays with heroines in male disguise' from Gender in Play on the Shakespearean Stage: Boy Heroines and Female Pages

That Innogen's strategy of disguising herself as a boy (the page Fidele) was not unusual in Elizabethan and Jacobean drama is demonstrated by the length of the list of plays in which heroines donned male apparel. In fact, between 1608 and 1611, when *Cymbeline* was first being performed, there were no fewer than twelve other plays with women characters (played by boys) disguising themselves as men. The first date given is that of performance, and the bracketed date is that of first publication. Blank spaces in the relevant columns indicate that the author or acting company are unknown.

	[Play]	[Author]	[Acting company]
1570–83 [1599]	*Clyomon and Clamydes*		
1576–80? [1594]	*The Wars of Cyrus*	Farrant	Chapel?
c. 1578 [1578]	*Promos and Cassandra*	Whetstone	unacted?
1583–85 [1592]	*Gallathea*	Lyly	Paul's
c. 1589 [1592?]	*Soliman and Perseda*	Kyd?	
c. 1590 [1598]	*James the Fourth*	Greene	Queen's?
1592–94 [1615]	*The Four Prentices of London*	Heywood	Admiral's
c. 1593 [1623]	*The Two Gentlemen of Verona*	Shakespeare	Chamberlain's
1593–94 [1599]	*George a Greene*		Sussex's
1596–98 [1600]	*The Merchant of Venice*	Shakespeare	Chamberlain's
1598 [1616]	*Englishmen for My Money*	Haughton	Admiral's
1599–1600 [1602]	*Antonio and Mellida*	Marston	Paul's
c. 1600 [1601]	*Cynthia's Revels*	Jonson	Chapel
1600 [1623]	*As You Like It*	Shakespeare	Chamberlain's
c. 1600 [1600]	*The Maid's Metamorphosis*		Paul's
1601–2 [1623]	*Twelfth Night*	Shakespeare	Chamberlain's
1601–2 [1611]	*May Day*	Chapman	Chapel

c. 1602 [1602]	*How a Man May Choose a Good Wife from a Bad*		Worcester's
c. 1602 [1631]	*The Fair Maid of the West, I*	Heywood	
1603? [1603]	*Philotus*		unacted?
1603–5 [1638]	*The Wise Woman of Hogsden*	Heywood	Queen Anne's
1604 [1608]	*The Honest Whore, I*	Dekker, Middleton	Prince Henry's
1604 [1605]	*The Fair Maid of Bristow*		King's
1604–7 [1608?]	*Your Five Gallants*	Middleton	Chapel?
1605–13? [1647]	*Love's Cure*	Fletcher	King's
1605–6 [1607]	*The Fleire*	Sharpham	Queen's Revels
1607–8 [1611]	*Ram Alley*	Barry	King's Revels
1608 [1608]	*The Dumb Knight*	Markham	King's Revels
1608? [1615]	*Cupid's Revenge*	Beaumont, Fletcher	Queen's Revels
1608–09 [1647]	*Wit at Several Weapons*	Beaumont, Fletcher	
1608–9 [1623]	*Cymbeline*	Shakespeare	King's
c. 1609 [1620]	*Philaster*	Fletcher	King's
1610 [1613]	*The Revenge of Bussy D'Ambois*	Chapman	Queen's Revels
1610 [1619]	*The Maid's Tragedy*	Fletcher	King's
c. 1610 [1612]	*A Christian Turned Turk*	Daborne	
1611? [1640]	*The Night Walker*	Fletcher	Queen's Revels?
1611 [1611]	*The Roaring Girl*	Dekker, Middleton	Prince Henry's
c. 1611 [1618]	*Amends for Ladies*	Field	Queen's Revels
c. 1611 [1657]	*No Wit, No Help Like a Woman's*	Middleton	Lady Elizabeth's?
c. 1613 [1614]	*The Hogge Hath Lost His Pearl*	Tailor	"apprentices"
1613? [1647]	*The Honest Man's Fortune*	Fletcher	Lady Elizabeth's
1614 [MS]	*Hymen's Triumph*	Daniel	
c. 1616 [1647]	*Love's Pilgrimage*	Fletcher	King's
c. 1616 [1652]	*The Widow*	Middleton	King's
1619 [1662]	*Anything for a Quiet Life*	Middleton	King's
1619? [1657]	*More Dissemblers Besides Women*	Middleton	King's?
1620 [1622]	*The Heir*	May	Red Bull troupe
1620–30 [MS]	*The Partial Law*		
c. 1621 [1647]	*The Pilgrim*	Fletcher	King's

1621 [1621]	*The Witch of Edmonton*	Dekker, Ford, Rowley	King's
1621? [S. R. 1660]	*The Faithful Friends*	Fletcher?	
c. 1622 [1623]	*The Duke of Milan*	Massinger	King's
1623 [1647]	*The Maid in the Mill*	Fletcher, Rowley	King's
1625 [1631]	*The School of Compliment, or Love Tricks*	Shirley	Lady Elizabeth's
1626 [1629]	*The Wedding*	Shirley	Queen Henrietta's
c. 1626 [1629]	*The Maid's Revenge*	Shirley	Queen Henrietta's
1628 [1629]	*The Lover's Melancholy*	Ford	King's
1629? [1629]	*The Deserving Favorite*	Carlell	King's
1629 [1631]	*The New Inn*	Jonson	King's
1629 [1630]	*The Grateful Servant*	Shirley	Queen Henrietta's
c. 1631 [1632]	*The Rival Friends*	Hausted	Cambridge
1631 [MS]	*The Swisser*	Wilson	King's
c. 1632 [1632]	*The Changes, or Love in a Maze*	Shirley	King's Revels
c. 1633 [1636]	*The Challenge for Beauty*	Heywood	King's
c. 1635 [1641]	*The Antiquary*	Marmion	Queen Henrietta's
1636 [1640]	*Hollander*	Glapthorne	Queen Henrietta's
1637? [1651]	*The Lady Errant*	Cartwright	privately
1636 [1655]	*The Bashful Lover*	Massinger	King's
1636? [1653]	*A Mad Couple Well Matched*	Brome	Beeston's Boys?
1637? [1658]	*The English Moor*	Brome	Queen Henrietta's
1637? [1653]	*The Damoiselle*	Brome	Beeston's Boys?
1637? [1640]	*The Prisoners*	Killegrew	Queen Henrietta's
1638? [1639]	*Argalus and Parthenia*	Glapthorne	Beeston's Boys
c. 1638 [1640]	*Sicily and Naples*	Harding	Oxford
c. 1638 [1652]	*The Doubtful Heir*	Shirley	King's
c. 1639 [1657]	*The Obstinate Lady*	Cockayne	
1639? [1673]	*The Distresses, or the Spanish Lovers*	Davenant	King's
1640 [1652]	*The Imposture*	Shirley	King's
1642 [1652]	*The Sisters*	Shirley	King's

(From Michael Shapiro (1994) *Gender in Play on the Shakespearean Stage: Boy Heroines and Female Pages*, Ann Arbor: University of Michigan Press, pp. 221–3)

Text 4

Francis Beaumont and John Fletcher, Philaster, or Love Lies a-Bleeding, *Act 2, Scene 2*

Francis Beaumont and John Fletcher, who were youthful contemporaries and rivals of Shakespeare, saw their play *Philaster, or Love Lies a-Bleeding* first performed in 1609 by the King's Men. *Philaster* bears more than a passing resemblance to *Cymbeline*. In the extract reprinted below, Pharamond (the Giacomo figure) first unsuccessfully tries to seduce Galatea (the virtuous Innogen figure), and then with enthusiastic encouragement seduces Megra. Galatea's virtue is rewarded in the course of the play, whereas both Pharamond and Megra suffer for failing to curb their sexual appetites.

Enter Pharamond.

PHARAMOND.

Why should these ladies stay so long? They must come this way. I know the queen employs 'em not, for the reverend mother sent me word they would all be for the garden. If they should all prove honest now, I were in a fair taking. I was never so long without sport in my life, and in my conscience 'tis not my fault. Oh, for our country ladies!

Enter Galatea.

Here's one bolted; I'll hound at her. Madam!

GALATEA.

Your grace.

PHARAMOND.

Shall I not be a trouble?

GALATEA.

Not to me, sir.

PHARAMOND.

Nay, nay, you are too quick. By this sweet hand –

GALATEA.

You'll be forsworn, sir. 'Tis but an old glove. If you will talk at distance, I am for you. But, good prince, be not bawdy nor do not brag. These two I bar, and then I think I shall have sense enough to answer all the weighty apothegms your royal blood shall manage.

PHARAMOND.

Dear lady, can you love?

GALATEA.

Dear prince, how dear? I ne'er cost you a coach yet nor put you to the dear repentance of a banquet. Here's no scarlet, sir, to blush the sin out it was given for. This wire mine own hair covers, and this face has been so far from being dear to any that it ne'er cost penny painting. And for the rest of my poor wardrobe, such as you see, it leaves no hand behind it to make the jealous mercer's wife curse our good doings.

PHARAMOND.

You mistake me, lady.

GALATEA.

Lord, I do so. Would you or I could help it!

PHARAMOND.

Do ladies of this country use to give no more respect to men of my full being?

GALATEA.

Full being? I understand you not, unless you grace means growing to fatness, and then your only remedy, upon my knowledge, prince, is in a morning a cup of neat white wine brew'd with carduus, then fast till supper. About eight you may eat. Use exercise and keep a sparrow hawk; you can shoot in a tiller. But of all your grave must fly phlebotomy, fresh pork, conger, and clarified whey. They are all dullers of the vital spirits.

PHARAMOND.

Lady, you talk of nothing all this while.

GALATEA.

'Tis very true, sir; I talk of you.

PHARAMOND.

This is a crafty wench. I like her wit well; 'twill be rare to stir up a leaden appetite. She's a Danaë and must be courted in a shower of gold. Madam, look here. All these and more than –

GALATEA.

What have you there, my lord? Gold? Now, as I live, 'tis fair gold. You would have silver for it to play with the pages. You could not have taken me in a worse time, but if you have present use, my lord, I'll send my man with silver and keep your gold for you.

PHARAMOND.

Lady, lady!

GALATEA.

She's coming, sir, behind will take white money. Yet for all this I'll match ye. *Exit* Galatea *behind the hangings.*

PHARAMOND.

If there be but two such more in the kingdom and near the court, we may even hang up our harps. Ten such camphor constitutions as this would call the golden age again in question, and teach the old way for every ill-fac'd husband to get his own children. And what a mischief that will breed, let all consider.

Enter Megra.

Here's another. If she be of the same last, the devil shall pluck her on. Many fair mornings, lady!

MEGRA.

As many mornings bring as many days
Fair, sweet, and hopeful to your grace.

PHARAMOND [*aside*].
> She gives good words yet. Sure this wench is free. –
> If your more serious business do not call you,
> Let me hold quarter with you. We'll talk an hour
> Out quickly.

MEGRA.
> What would your grace talk of?

PHARAMOND.
> Of some such pretty subject as yourself.
> I'll go no further than your eye or lip.
> There's theme enough for one man for an age.

MEGRA.
> Sir, they stand right, and my lips are yet even,
> Smooth, young enough, ripe enough, and red enough,
> Or my glass wrongs me.

PHARAMOND.
> Oh, they are two twinn'd cherries dyed in blushes
> Which those fair suns above with their bright beams
> Reflect upon and ripen. Sweetest beauty,
> Bow down those branches that the longing taste
> Of the faint looker-on may meet those blessings
> And taste and live.

MEGRA [*aside*].
> Oh, delicate sweet prince,
> She that hath snow enough about her heart
> To take the wanton spring of ten such lines off
> May be a nun without probation. –
> Sir, you have in such neat poetry gather'd a kiss
> That if I had but five lines of that number,
> Such pretty begging blanks, I should commend
> Your forehead or your cheeks and kiss you, too.

PHARAMOND.
> Do it in prose. You cannot miss it, madam.

MEGRA.
> I shall, I shall.

PHARAMOND.
> By my life, you shall not.
> I'll prompt you first. [*Kisses her.*] Can you do it now?

MEGRA.
> Methinks 'tis easy now I ha' done't before,
> But yet I should stick at it.

PHARAMOND.
> Stick till tomorrow;
> I'll ne'er part you, sweetest. But we lose time.
> Can you love me?

MEGRA.

Love you, my lord? How would you have me love you?

PHARAMOND.

I'll teach you in a short sentence 'cause I will not load your memory. This is all: love me and lie with me.

MEGRA.

Was it lie with you that you said? 'Tis impossible.

PHARAMOND.

Not to a willing mind that will endeavor. If I do not teach you to do it easily in one night as you'll go to bed, I'll lose my royal blood for't.

MEGRA.

Why, prince, you have a lady of your own that yet wants teaching.

PHARAMOND.

I'll sooner teach a mare the old measures than teach her anything belonging to the function. She's afraid to lie with herself if she have but any masculine imaginations about her. I know when we are married I must ravish her.

MEGRA.

By mine honor, that's a foul fault indeed, but time and your good help will wear it out, sir.

PHARAMOND.

And for any other I see, excepting your dear self, dearest lady, I had rather be Sir Tim the schoolmaster and leap a dairy maid. Madam!

MEGRA.

Has your grace seen the court star, Galatea?

PHARAMOND.

Out upon her! She's as cold of her favor as an apoplex.
She sail'd by but now.

MEGRA.

And how do you hold her wit, sir?

PHARAMOND.

I hold her wit? The strength of all the guard cannot hold it, if they were tied to it; she would blow 'em out of the kingdom. They talk of Jupiter; he's but a squib-cracker to her. Look well about you and you may find a tongue bolt. But speak, sweet lady; shall I be freely welcome?

MEGRA.

Whither?

PHARAMOND.

To your bed. If you mistrust my faith, you do me the unnoblest wrong.

MEGRA.

I dare not, prince, I dare not.

PHARAMOND.

Make your own conditions, my purse shall seal 'em; and what you dare imagine you can want. I'll furnish you withal. Give two hours to your thoughts every morning about it. Come, I know you are bashful. Speak in my ear. Will you be mine? Keep this, and with it me. Soon I will visit you.

MEGRA.

My lord, my chamber's most unsafe, but when 'tis night I'll find some means to slip into your lodging; till when –

PHARAMOND.

Till when, this and my heart go with thee. *Exuent.*

Enter Galatea *from behind the hangings.*

GALATEA.

Oh, thou pernicious petticoat prince, are these your virtues? Well, if I do not lay a train to blow your sport up, I am no woman. And, Lady Towsabell, I'll fit you for't. *Exit* Galatea.

(From Francis Beaumont and John Fletcher (1975) *Philaster*, ed. Dora Jean Ashe, London: Edward Arnold, pp.30–7)

Text 5

George Bernard Shaw, 'Foreword' from Cymbeline Refinished: A Variation on Shakespear's Ending

In 1936, George Bernard Shaw rewrote the final act of *Cymbeline* in order to correct what he took to be tedious and dramatically implausible contortions in the original. Comparing his labours with Shakespeare's *Cymbeline* to those of Mozart in adding to the score of Handel's *Messiah*, in a Foreword, reprinted below, Shaw sets out his objections to the play and his sympathetic attitude towards tampering with 'the classics'.

Foreword

The practice of improving Shakespear's plays, more especially in the matter of supplying them with what are called happy endings, is an old established one which has always been accepted without protest by British audiences. When Mr Harley Granville-Barker, following up some desperate experiments by the late William Poel, introduced the startling innovation of performing the plays in the West End of London as exactly as Shakespear wrote them, there was indeed some demur; but it was expressed outside the theatre and led to no rioting. And it set on foot a new theory of Shakespearean representation. Up to that time it had been assumed as a matter of course that everyone behind the scenes in a theatre must know much better than Shakespear how plays should be written, exactly as it is believed in the Hollywood studios today that everyone in a film studio knows better than any professional playwright how a play should be filmed. But the pleasure given by Mr Granville-Barker's productions shook that conviction in the theatre; and the superstition that Shakespear's plays as written by him are impossible on the stage, which had produced a happy ending to King Lear, Cibber's Richard III, a love scene in the tomb of the Capulets between Romeo and Juliet before the poison takes effect, and had culminated in the crude literary butcheries successfully imposed on the public and the critics as Shakespear's plays by Henry Irving and Augustin Daly at the end of the last century, is for the moment heavily discredited. It may be asked then why I, who always fought fiercely against that superstition in the days when I was a journalist–critic, should perpetrate a spurious fifth act to Cymbeline, and do it too, not wholly as a literary *jeu d'esprit*, but in response to an actual emergency in the theatre when it was proposed to revive Cymbeline at no less sacred a place than the Shakespear Memorial Theatre at Stratford-upon-Avon.

Cymbeline, though one of the finest of Shakespear's later plays now on the stage, goes to pieces in the last act. In fact I mooted the point myself by thoughtlessly saying that the revival would be all right if I wrote a last act for it. To my surprise this blasphemy was received with acclamation; and as the applause, like the proposal, was not wholly jocular, the fancy began to haunt me, and persisted until I exorcised it by writing the pages which ensue.

I had a second surprise when I began by reading the authentic last act carefully through. I had not done so for many years, and had the common impression about it that it was a cobbled-up affair by several hands, including a vision in prison accompanied by scraps of quite ridiculous doggerel.

For this estimate I found absolutely no justification nor excuse. I must have got it from the last revival of the play at the old Lyceum theatre, when Irving, as Iachimo, a statue of romantic melancholy, stood dumb on the stage for hours (as it seemed) whilst the others toiled through a series of *dénouements* of crushing tedium, in which the characters lost all their vitality and individuality, and had nothing to do but identify themselves by moles on their necks, or explain why they were not dead. The vision and the verses were cut out as a matter of course; and I ignorantly thanked Heaven for it.

When I read the act as aforesaid I found that my notion that it is a cobbled-up *pasticcio* by other hands was an unpardonable stupidity. The act is genuine Shakespear to the last full stop, and late phase Shakespear in point of verbal workmanship.

The doggerel is not doggerel: it is a versified masque, in Shakespear's careless woodnotes wild, complete with Jupiter as *deus ex machina*, eagle and all, introduced, like the Ceres scene in The Tempest, to please King Jamie, or else because an irresistible fashion had set in, just as at all the great continental opera houses a ballet used to be *de rigueur*. Gounod had to introduce one into his Faust, and Wagner into his Tannhäuser, before they could be staged at the Grand Opera in Paris. So, I take it, had Shakespear to stick a masque into Cymbeline. Performed as such, with suitable music and enough pictorial splendor, it is not only entertaining on the stage, but, with the very Shakespearean feature of a comic jailor which precedes it, just the thing to save the last act.

Without it the act is a tedious string of unsurprising *dénouements* sugared with insincere sentimentality after a ludicrous stage battle. With one exception the characters have vanished and left nothing but dolls being moved about like the glass balls in the game of solitaire until they are all got rid of but one. The exception is the hero, or rather the husband of the heroine, Leonatus Posthumus. The late Charles Charrington, who with his wife Janet Achurch broke the ice for Ibsen in England, used to cite Posthumus as Shakespear's anticipation of his Norwegian rival. Certainly, after being theatrically conventional to the extent of ordering his wife to be murdered, he begins to criticize, quite on the lines of Mrs Alving in Ghosts, the slavery to an inhuman ideal of marital fidelity which led him to this villainous extremity. One may say that he is the only character left really alive in the last act; and as I cannot change him for the better I have left most of his part untouched. I make no apology for my attempt to bring the others back to dramatic activity and individuality.

I should like to have retained Cornelius as the exponent of Shakespear's sensible and scientific detestation of vivisection. But as he has nothing to say except that the Queen is dead, and nobody can possibly care a rap whether she is alive or dead, I have left him with her in the box of puppets that are done with.

I have ruthlessly cut out the surprises that no longer surprise anybody. I really could not keep my countenance over the identification of Guiderius by the mole on his neck. That device was killed by Maddison Morton, once a famous farce writer, now forgotten by everyone save Mr Gordon Craig and myself. In Morton's masterpiece, Box and Cox, Box asks Cox whether he has a strawberry mark on his left arm. "No" says Cox. "Then you are my long lost brother" says Box as they fall into one another's arms and end the farce happily. One could wish that Guiderius had anticipated Cox.

Plot has always been the curse of serious drama, and indeed of serious literature of any kind. It is so out-of-place there that Shakespear never could invent one. Unfortunately, instead of taking Nature's hint and discarding plots, he borrowed them all over the place and got into trouble through having to unravel them in the last act, especially in The Two Gentlemen of Verona and Cymbeline. The more childish spectators may find some delight in the revelation that Polydore and Cadwal are Imogen's long lost brothers and Cymbeline's long lost sons; that Iachimo is now an occupant of the penitent form and very unlike his old self; and that Imogen is so dutiful that she accepts her husband's attempt to have her murdered with affectionate docility. I cannot share these infantile joys. Having become interested in Iachimo, in Imogen, and even in the two long lost princes, I wanted to know how their characters would react to the *éclaircissement* which follows the battle. The only way to satisfy this curiosity was to rewrite the act as Shakespear might have written it if he had been post-Ibsen and post-Shaw instead of post-Marlowe.

In doing so I had to follow the Shakespearean verse pattern to match the 89 lines of Shakespear's text which I retained. This came very easily to me. It happened when I was a child that one of the books I delighted in was an illustrated Shakespear, with a picture and two or three lines of text underneath it on every third or fourth page. Ever since, Shakespearean blank verse has been to me as natural a form of literary expression as the Augustan English to which I was brought up in Dublin, or the latest London fashion in dialogue. It is so easy that if it were possible to kill it it would have been burlesqued to death by Tom Thumb, Chrononhotonthologos, and Bombastes Furioso. But Shakespear will survive any possible extremity of caricature.

I shall not deprecate the most violent discussion as to the propriety of meddling with masterpieces. All I can say is that the temptation to do it, and sometimes the circumstances which demand it, are irresistible. The results are very various. When a mediocre artist tries to improve on a great artist's work the effect is ridiculous or merely contemptible. When the alteration damages the original, as when a bad painter repaints a Velasquez or a Rembrandt, he commits a crime. When the changed work is sold or exhibited as the original, the fraud is indictable. But when it comes to complete forgery, as in the case of Ireland's Vortigern, which was much admired and at last actually performed as a play by Shakespear, the affair passes beyond the sphere of crime and becomes an instructive joke.

But what of the many successful and avowed variations? What about the additions made by Mozart to the score of Handel's Messiah? Elgar, who adored Handel, and had an unbounded contempt for all the lesser meddlers, loved Mozart's variations, and dismissed all purist criticism of them by maintaining that Handel must have extemporized equivalents to them on the organ at his concerts. When Spontini found on his visit to Dresden that Wagner had added trombone parts to his choruses, he appropriated them very gratefully. Volumes of variations on the tunes of other composers were published as such by Mozart and Beethoven, to say nothing of Bach and Handel, who played Old Harry with any air that amused them. Would anyone now remember Diabelli's vulgar waltz but for Beethoven's amazing variations, one of which is also a variation on an air from Don Giovanni?

And now consider the practice of Shakespear himself. Tolstoy declared that the original Lear is superior to Shakespear's rehandling, which he abhorred as immoral. Nobody has ever agreed with him. Will it be contended that Shakespear had no right to refashion Hamlet? If he had spoiled both plays, that would be a reason for reviving them without Shakespear's transfigurations, but not for challenging Shakespear's right to remake them.

Accordingly, I feel no qualm of conscience and have no apology to make for indulging in a variation on the last act of Cymbeline. I stand in the same time relation to Shakespear as Mozart to Handel, or Wagner to Beethoven. Like Mozart, I have not confined myself to the journeyman's job of writing "additional accompaniments": I have luxuriated in variations. Like Wagner dealing with Gluck's overture to *Iphigenia in Aulis* I have made a new ending for its own sake. Beethoven's Ninth Symphony towers among the classic masterpieces; but if Wagner had been old enough in his Dresden days not only to rescore the first and greatest movement as he did, but to supply the whole work with a more singable ending I should not have discouraged him; for I must agree with Verdi that the present ending, from the change to six-four onward, though intensely Beethovenish, is in performance usually a screaming voice destroying orgy.

I may be asked why all my instances are musical instead of literary. Is it a plot to take the literary critics out of their depth? Well, it may have that good effect; but I am not aiming at it. It is, I suppose, because music has succeeded to the heroic rank taken by literature in the sixteenth century. I cannot pretend to care much about what Nat Lee did in his attempts to impart Restoration gentility to Shakespear, or about Thomas Corneille's bowdlerization of Molière's *Festin de Pierre*, or any of the other literary precedents, though I am a little ashamed of being found in the company of their perpetrators. But I do care a good deal about what Mozart did to Handel, and Wagner to Gluck; and it seems to me that to discuss the artistic morality of my alternative ending without reference to them would be waste of time. Anyhow, what I have done I have done; and at that I must leave it.

I shall not press my version on managers producing Cymbeline if they have the courage and good sense to present the original word-for-word as Shakespear left it, and the means to do justice to the masque. But if they are halfhearted about it, and inclined to compromise by leaving out the masque and the comic jailor and mutilating the rest, as their manner is, I unhesitatingly recommend my version. The audience will not know the difference; and the few critics who have read Cymbeline will be too grateful for my shortening of the last act to complain.

G. B. S.

AYOT SAINT LAWRENCE, *December 1945*

(From George Bernard Shaw (1974) *The Bodley Head Bernard Shaw Collected Plays with their Prefaces*, Volume VII, London: The Bodley Head, pp.179–86)

Text 6

Janet Adelman, 'Masculine authority and the maternal body: the return to origins in Cymbeline', *from* Suffocating Mothers: Fantasies of Maternal Origin in Shakespeare's Plays, 'Hamlet' to 'The Tempest'

Janet Adelman's discussion is a good example of recent feminist criticism of *Cymbeline*. It draws attention to the contradictory and contested dramatization of gender roles and the function of the patriarchal family in the play. Adelman also notes the incoherence of the two main plot lines – the wager story and the conflict between Rome and Britain – but concludes that ultimately 'both plots enact the recuperation of male power over the female'.

Cymbeline has seemed to many a radically incoherent play. Despite the deliberate bravura of the recognition scene, in which all the plots are yoked violently together, the play does not cohere: the final scene, in which the emotional force of one recognition is constantly being interrupted by another, is diagnostic of the play as a whole, in which the focus of our attention continually shifts, in which we are hard-pressed to decide on the play's dominant action or even its dominant characters. The title leads us to expect that Cymbeline will be at the play's center; and yet, despite his structural importance in the last scene, he is for the most part conspicuously marginal. He is of course literally absent for a great many scenes, especially the most memorable scenes; and though his literal absence might not count for much – Henry IV is absent throughout his name-plays, and yet his role is genuinely central to them – this king is not memorable even when he is on stage. Marginal to the actions that most nearly concern him – the actions of Cloten, the lost sons, and the Roman invasion – he remains a pasteboard figure even when he becomes structurally central in the last scene; and the flatness of his character extends to the characters of those most intimately connected with him: his sons, his queen, her son. For the interest provided by psychological realism, we look to Imogen, Posthumus, and to some extent Iachimo; despite Cymbeline's titular status, the disrupted marriage is at the center of the play for most audiences, and, at least in the beginning, Cymbeline seems to matter chiefly as the initial blocking agent to that marriage. But the marriage plot provides only a very uncertain center: the plot that is virtually the play's only concern for the first two acts is literally marginalized, displaced from the center, nearly disappearing in acts 3 and 4, replaced by the question of the tribute due Rome, by Cloten's various attempts on Imogen, and by the wilderness education of Cymbeline's lost sons. This structural displacement is moreover reiterated in the last scene, where our anticipated pleasure in the reunion of husband and wife is first interrupted by another long account of the wicked

Queen's wickedness [5. 6. 244–59] – an interruption that must be very difficult to stage – and finally displaced altogether by Cymbeline's regaining of his sons and by the business of Rome.

Cymbeline is conspicuously without a center; and its centerlessness seems to me related in ways not merely structural to the absence of Cymbeline himself as a compelling male figure. His absence in the play is so prominent, I think, because he strikes us as absent even when present, absent to himself: as the first scene with Lucius [3. 1] makes comically evident, he has simply been taken over by his wicked queen and her son. And the failure of male autonomy portrayed grotesquely in him is the psychological starting point of the play as well as the determinant of its structural weaknesses; despite the prominence of the marriage plot, the repair of that failure is the play's chief business. But this goal is ultimately disastrous for its emotional coherence, and not only because the characters of the marriage plot are far more engaging than the relatively pasteboard characters of the Cymbeline plot: in *Cymbeline*, a plot ostensibly about the recovery of trust in a woman and the renewal of marriage is circumscribed by a plot in which distrust of woman is the great lesson to be learned and in which male autonomy depends on the dissolution of marriage. Moreover, the effect of the Imogen–Posthumus plot is everywhere qualified by the effect of the Cymbeline plot, and the two plots seem to be emotionally at cross-purposes: if one moves toward the resumption of heterosexual bonds in marriage, the other moves toward the renewed formation of male bonds as Cymbeline regains both his sons and his earlier alliance with an all-male Rome, the alliance functionally disrupted by his wife. Hence the emotional incoherence of the last scene: the resolution of each plot interrupts the other, leaving neither satisfactorily resolved.

The degree to which the two plots are apparently at cross-purposes – the degree to which their different psychological goals disturb the coherence of the play – is registered in the play's extraordinarily problematic representation of Rome. For the Cymbeline plot, Rome is the ancient seat of honor, the place of the heroic father Caesar who knighted Cymbeline in his youth; for the marriage plot, Rome is the seat of a distinctly Renaissance and Italianate corruption, home to Iachimo's "Italian brain" [5. 6. 196], the place of a fashionable cynicism about the attemptability of all women. Fifteen centuries separate these places: hence our surprise at finding Lucius and Iachimo in the same army. But they are even further apart psychologically than chronologically. Both Romes represent a male refuge from women: Posthumus's Rome of adolescent male competition over women serves as a defense against women as surely as Cymbeline's adopted fatherland does. But Posthumus must leave his Rome – psychologically as well as literally – before he can find Imogen; Cymbeline must in effect return to his as the sign that he has broken the bond with his wife, and his return will be part of his triumph. And as with the other plot elements, the differences here are not brought into dialogue; they are simply set side by side and ignored.

The different valuations of Rome required by the Cymbeline plot and the marriage plot are, I think, diagnostic of the apparently different valuations of women that govern the two plots. These different valuations recur strikingly in the play's contradictory articulations of the parthenogenesis fantasy that is at its core. Embodied in a variety of ways throughout the play, the fantasy of parthenogenesis is overtly articulated twice: once in Posthumus's wish for an alternative means of generation in which women need not be half-workers [2. 5. 1–2]; and again in

Cymbeline's response to the regaining of his children ("O, what am I? / A mother to the birth of three?" [5. 6. 369–70]). Posthumus's fantasy, I shall argue, is part of his brutal rage at Imogen's power to betray him, to redefine him as his mother could redefine him through her apparent act of infidelity; it is in effect the moment when he discovers that he has a mother and that his identity is radically contingent upon her sexuality. As such, it is the impediment to the happy ending of the marriage plot; it must apparently be discarded before Posthumus can recover Imogen and his harmonious sense of family. But for Cymbeline, the parthenogenesis fantasy *is* the happy ending. By suggesting that Cymbeline has produced these children all by himself, the fantasy here – after the death of his wife – makes the regaining of his children into a reward for his renewed male autonomy: having finally separated from the wicked stepmother of the play, he is allowed to take on the power of the mothers and to produce a family in which women are not half-workers. The fantasy apparently rejected in the marriage plot is thus enshrined in the Cymbeline plot; to a striking degree, I shall argue, its fulfillment determines the shape of that plot.

The parthenogenesis fantasy is central to the Cymbeline plot because it so perfectly answers the needs of that plot. The Cymbeline plot takes as its psychological starting point Cymbeline's failure of authority and his need to separate himself from the woman he trusts over-much. But insofar as Shakespeare characterizes that woman repeatedly as mother and stepmother, he infuses the play with the deep anxiety of the mother–infant bond; Cymbeline's failure of autonomy here is thus associated with the infant's failure to separate from the overwhelming mother. And insofar as she inhibits male autonomy, this mother is by definition evil; the play asks us to blame all Cymbeline's evil on her control over him. Hence the extent to which everything in his kingdom – and in Cymbeline himself – rights itself once she is dead and her wickedness is exposed. She becomes the scapegoat for Cymbeline's misjudgment and tyranny: her death magically restores what we are presumably supposed to think of as his original goodness at the same time that it restores his autonomy; her magical death in fact construes his new moral stature as his renewed autonomy. Moreover, Cymbeline's recovered autonomy is instantly rewarded by his recovery of his family; and as if to consolidate his new separation from her, that renewed family is strikingly male. For despite our own interest in Imogen, despite the expectations produced by *King Lear, Pericles,* and *The Winter's Tale,* even despite Cymbeline's last-minute protestation of his love for Imogen [4. 3. 5] and his instantaneous affection for her as Fidele [5. 6. 92–9], little in the play defines either her loss or her recovery as central to him; the final and most deeply felt recovery is of his sons, not his daughter. It is in fact striking that Cymbeline expresses much more immediate affection for his daughter when she is disguised as the boy Fidele than he has ever expressed for her as a girl; he accepts her more readily as a surrogate son than as a daughter ("Boy, / Thou hast look'd thyself into my grace, / And art mine own" [5. 6. 93–5]). That even Imogen is recovered first as a son underscores the extent to which the renewed family of the last scene is male. The final moments of the play in fact enact Cymbeline's recovery of three generations of all-male relation: the recovery not only of his lost sons, but also of the wronged Belarius as his "brother" [5. 6. 400], and of his psychic father, the Roman Octavian who had knighted him in his youth [3. 1. 67–8]. Insofar as these recoveries are the consequence of his separation from his wicked queen, his triumphant articulation of the parthenogenesis fantasy as he recovers his children is perfectly appropriate: for that fantasy seeks to rob women of their fearful power by imagining sexual generation without mothers. In effect, Cymbeline celebrates his triumphant separation from the mother's power by appropriating that power for himself, consolidating his own power by claiming to absorb hers.

Cymbeline's recovery of his sons can serve as the sign of his separation from his queen and hence his renewed masculine autonomy partly because the sons function in the plot to literalize the transference of power from female to male: Imogen, heir to the kingdom at the beginning of the play [1. 1. 4], is displaced by them at the end. [5. 6. 374]. These sons are particularly fitting agents of this displacement: throughout the play, they have served to define a realm decidedly in opposition to the female, a realm in which they preserve their father's royal masculinity more successfully than he can. Belarius steals the princes long before the wicked queen comes on the scene; nonetheless, these two actions seem causally related in the psychological if not the literal plot. Cymbeline's readiness to believe the worst of Belarius – whom he loved [3. 3. 58] – signals the breaking of a crucial male bond; and the vacuum caused by the breach of this bond – the loss both of Belarius and of his sons – in effect enables the intrusion of the queen and the implicit substitution of her son for his own. In their absence, the court becomes the site of female corruption, while the pastoral to which Belarius flees enables the continuation of the male bond *in absentia* in a landscape of idealized masculinity. Despite Belarius's brief invocation of "thou goddess, / Thou divine Nature" [4. 2. 170–1], that is, this is a relentlessly male pastoral, sufficiently hostile to the female that the princes' nurse-mother dies, and Imogen, who can enter its landscape only in male disguise, also dies to them. For female nature in this play is dangerous, its poisonous flowers the province of the wicked stepmother; but here, the princes need fear no poison [3. 3. 77]. Belarius's pastoral is thus constructed as a safe site for masculinity uncontaminated by women; and in this landscape, the masculinity weakened in Cymbeline can thrive. Belarius's rather fatuous and too often repeated assertions that Cymbeline's kingly blood flies out in the extreme martial masculinity of his hidden sons [3. 3. 79–98; 4. 4. 53–4] make a claim about Cymbeline's masculinity that we never see verified by the action; the effect is to make us feel that they are purer vials of their father's blood than Cymbeline himself is.

The sons can function as the sign of Cymbeline's recuperated masculine autonomy at the end of the play because they have functioned throughout as a split-off and hence protected portion of his masculinity. The familiar romance plot of the lost children here literalizes this psychic splitting: removed from their father and his susceptibility to corruption by the queen, the boys are raised in an all-male world, virtually uncontaminated by women and hence able to maintain Cymbeline's masculinity pure even while he himself is corrupted. The twice-repeated phrase with which Belarius re-introduces them to their father – "First pay me for the nursing of thy sons" [5. 6. 323, 325] – confirms their purely male lineage and suggests the extent to which that purity depends on Belarius's appropriation of the female, his capacity to take on female roles and so dispense with women. Given this psychic configuration, it seems to me significant that the princes do not enter the stage for the first time until after Posthumus has ascribed all evil to the woman's part and has wished for a birth exempt from woman. Their mother virtually unmentioned, their nurse dead, reared by a male substitute for her, the princes come close to realizing a safe version of Posthumus's parthenogenesis fantasy; hence the appropriateness of Cymbeline's articulation of his own version of the fantasy – "O, what am I? A mother to the birth of three?" – when they return to him.

The Belarius who nursed Cymbeline's children and thus became the repository of his masculine lineage and his masculine selfhood is welcomed back in language that suggests the renewal of permanent male bonds: "Thou art my brother; so we'll hold thee ever" [5. 6. 400]. Functionally, these bonds can be renewed only in the absence of the queen: Belarius's return (and hence the return of Cymbeline's sons) depends not on Cymbeline's revoking the initial charges of treason against Belarius (these are mentioned only to be ignored by Cymbeline [5. 6. 334–6]) but on her death. And that death itself is complexly portrayed as the consequence of an encounter that anticipates and ensures Cymbeline's resumption of triumphant masculinity and true masculine lineage. Cymbeline tells us that the queen has "A fever with the absence of her son; / A madness, of which her life's in danger" [4. 3. 2–3]; we first hear of her illness immediately after we have seen Guiderius kill Cloten. In effect, this encounter causes the death of the queen; and in itself it prefigures Cymbeline's own resumption of autonomous masculinity.

Guiderius clearly sees the contest as the test of his own masculinity ("Have not I / An arm as big as thine? a heart as big?" [4. 2. 78–9]); and – taking his cue from Cloten's own introduction of himself as "son to th' queen" [4. 2. 95] – he constructs Cloten's beheading as his return to the maternal matrix: "I have sent Cloten's clotpoll down the stream, / In embassy to his mother" [4. 2. 185–6]. This return moreover follows out the logic of parentage in these two sons: if the princes are an experiment in male parthenogenesis, a portion of Cymbeline's own masculinity split off and preserved from the taint of women, Cloten is an experiment in female parthenogenesis – he is apparently made without a father, the product of his mother's will alone. The struggle between Guiderius and Cloten thus becomes emblematically a struggle between the mother's son and the father's, the false heir and the true. By his triumph over Cloten, Guiderius not only proves his own masculinity but begins the process of regaining his full identity, replacing Cloten as his father's heir, emblematically asserting the rights of the father's son here even as his return will later enact the return of power from female heir to male. But at the same time, the encounter between Guiderius and Cloten epitomizes the struggle within Cymbeline: as Cymbeline's potential heir, Cloten is the sign of his damaged masculinity, the sign of his subjection to female power; and Guiderius is the heir of Cymbeline's true masculine selfhood. The triumph of the true heir causes the queeen's death because it signals the dissolution of her power; the princes' next act as the bearers of triumphant masculinity will be the literal rescue of their father. And this rescue simultaneously confirms their masculinity and his. Initially sexually ambiguous, "with faces fit for masks" [5. 5. 21], the princes are marked as decisively masculine by their military heroics: as Posthumus reports, they "could have turn'd / A distaff to a lance" [5. 5. 33–4]. When we next see them, Cymbeline is asking them to stand by his side [5. 6. 1], in the place of his dead queen.

In a strategy characteristic of this play's displacements of conflict away from its main characters, Cymbeline's own magical regaining of male autonomy is thus figured through his sons: their participation in an all-male realm and their triumph over the mother's son enact the heroic masculinity that will rescue Cymbeline himself; and through them, the king's own masculine autonomy, preserved apart from the taint of woman, is returned to him. Cymbeline's last-minute decision to renew the payment of tribute to Rome at first seems a deflection from this action; but like the recovery of Belarius and his sons, it serves to ratify Cymbeline's autonomous masculinity by ratifying male bonds. His decision is first of all, an undoing of his queen's will and hence the sign of his new separation from her:

> My peace we will begin: and Caius Lucius,
> Although the victor, we submit to Caesar,
> And to the Roman empire; promising
> To pay our wonted tribute, from the which
> We were dissuaded by our wicked queen,
> Whom heavens in justice both on her, and hers,
> Have laid most heavy hand.

[5. 6. 459–65]

Heaven's justice to the queen in effect guarantees the rightness of his decision to resume the male bond disrupted by her wickedness. Cymbeline has already suggested the value of this bond when he tells Lucius, "Thy Caesar knighted me; my youth I spent / Much under him; of him I gather'd honour" [3. 1. 67–8]. Having recovered his sons, and through them his own masculinity, Cymbeline now moves to recover the basis of that masculinity in the past, in the father-figure who enables and is the sign of separation from the overwhelming mother: through union with the imperial Caesar, Cymbeline reconstitutes his bond with that father. This is the bond functionally disrupted by the play's wicked stepmother: hence the need to insist on her wickedness – yet again – as a precondition of reunion.

But as Shakespeare surely knew, he was on tricky ground here, and not just because the Rome with which Cymbeline reunites is sometimes disturbingly *Italiante*. In the history plays, belief in the fierce independence of England – and autonomy behind its protective sea-barrier – had always been the sign of heroic masculine virtue; and even in this play, belief in patriotic self-sufficiency and hardihood is articulated not only by the villainous queen and her son, but also by Posthumus [2. 4. 15–26]. English concern about lost autonomy is to some extent assuaged by Cymbeline's military victory over Lucius, but – despite the religious resonance of Augustus's Rome or the political resonance of James I's foreign policy and his self-promotion as Augustus – it is not easy to construe reunion with the Rome of this play as an unmitigated triumph for England or for Cymbeline's authority. The troublesome reunion with Rome in fact suggests the conflicted desire for merger even at the root of the desire for autonomy. The soothsayer's words as he responds to Cymbeline – words given prominence by their position very close to the end of the play – suggest what is at stake in this psychologically complex moment:

> The fingers of the powers above do tune
> The harmony of this peace. The vision,
> Which I made known to Lucius ere the stroke
> Of yet this scarce-cold battle, at this instant
> Is full accomplish'd. For the Roman eagle,
> From south to west on wing soaring aloft,
> Lessen'd herself and in the beams o' the sun
> So vanished; which foreshadow'd our princely eagle,
> Th'imperial Caesar, should again unite
> His favor with the radiant Cymbeline,
> Which shines here in the west.

[5. 6. 466–76]

Cymbeline demonstrates his autonomy – his independence from the will of his queen – by his submission to Caesar, his merger with a male will larger than his own. As at the end of *Hamlet*, the soothsayer registers the presence of a fantasy in which dangerous merger with the female is replaced by a benign and sanctified merger with the male. And the safe merger becomes the foundation of a triumphant male authority: Cymbeline submits to Caesar; but the imperial Caesar vanishes into Cymbeline. Submission to the father rather than the mother miraculously turns out to be the way to increase the son's power and radiance, as the father lends his own radiance to his sun/son: hence the fantasy registered in the soothsayer's words, the fantasy that reinterprets the son's submission to the father as the father's vanishing into the beams of the son.

The Cymbeline plot celebrates the return of male authority only by destroying the wicked mother and her son, clearing an imaginative space for an all-male family and hence for reunion with the father's Rome; in each of its elements, it realizes Cymbeline's parthenogenetic fantasy. The marriage plot ostensibly moves in the opposite direction, turning Posthumus away from the similar fantasy with which he responds to Imogen's apparent betrayal of him. If Cymbeline moves toward the resumption of male identity and male bonds only by destroying the heterosexual family based in the mother's body, Posthumus moves toward the resumption of that family as the basis for his own male identity, fully conferred on him by his vision in prison. Trust in woman is the key term in both plots, but the two plots differ radically in their valuation of that term: if Cymbeline must learn to distrust – and hence to separate himself from – his wife, Posthumus must learn the trust that enables reunion with his. Not long before Cymbeline naively claims that it would have been vicious to have mistrusted his wife [5. 6. 65–6], Posthumus gives voice to his renewed trust in one of the most extraordinary moments in Shakespeare: extraordinary because Posthumus recovers his sense of Imogen's worth not – like Othello or Claudio or Leontes – after he has become convinced of her chastity, but before. For once, the fundamental human worth of a woman has become disengaged from the question of her chastity; in the face of his own guilt in ordering her dead, her supposed adultery has become "wrying but a little" [5. 1. 5].

This extraordinary moment suggests that the reunion of Posthumus and Imogen is contingent psychologically on Posthumus's learning the lesson Imogen teaches Iachimo – "the wide difference / 'Twixt amorous and villainous" [5. 6. 194–5] – and hence accepting her sexuality as part of her goodness. Partly because such acceptance is rare among Shakespearean heroes – only Antony seems to achieve it, and then only intermittently – it is tempting to see Posthumus's new valuation of Imogen as the culmination of the marriage plot, and hence to see the marriage plot as radically opposed to the Cymbeline plot, as I have thus far argued. But how radical is their opposition in fact? Despite their apparently opposed goals, the marriage plot seems to me to participate strikingly in the conditions of the Cymbeline plot, conditions that insist on the subjugation of female power and the return of authority to the male; like the Cymbeline plot, it takes as its psychic premise the anxieties expressed through the parthenogenesis fantasy, anxieties about male identity and female power to define the male. These anxieties – manifest in Cymbeline's subjection to his queen – are initially encoded in the marriage plot through Posthumus's situation as Imogen's unacknowledged husband. Deprived at birth of the familial identifiers that would locate him, psychologically and socially, Posthumus defines himself and is defined for others largely by Imogen's choice of him. She is "that which makes him both without and within" [1. 4. 8]: "his virtue / By her election may be truly read" [1. 1. 52–3]; "he must be weighed rather by her value than his own" [1. 4. 12]. She can make or unmake him: radically deprived of family, dependent on her love for his position, he has no secure self; he cannot return any gift that is worth what he has received [1. 1. 120–1].

The marriage plot rejoins husband and wife; but it does so only through an action designed to reverse their initial positions. Posthumus begins the play radically placeless, radically subject to definition by his wife and queen; he ends the play an exemplar of heroic masculinity, upholder of the kingdom, rescuer of the king. The Imogen he leaves behind is a powerful and powerfully passionate woman, the only heir to a king; the Imogen he returns to is the faithful page of a defeated soldier, about to lose her kingdom to her brother. The structural chiasmus creates the suspicion that, as in the Cymbeline plot, Posthumus's gain requires Imogen's loss. Posthumus's return to Imogen is in fact thoroughly mediated by her victimization, as though that victimization were its precondition: he returns to her in imagination only when he thinks her dead, only when he is given safe passage by the bloody cloth that ambiguously signifies both her wounded sexuality and his punishment of her. And his act of violence toward her immediately before they are united disturbingly underscores this precondition: he strikes her, punishing her as the upstart he might initially have been mistaken for ("Thou scornful page, / There lie thy part" [5. 6. 228–9]). His violence here literally enables their reunion – Pisanio reveals Imogen's identity only because he thinks Posthumus may have killed her – and it suggests Posthumus's need to dominate Imogen physically, as he has dominated her psychologically, before that reunion can take place. Imogen's masochistic response – "Think that you are upon a rock, and now / Throw me again" [5. 6. 262–3] – moreover does little to qualify his domination: in fact the whole play has brought her to this moment of submission.

Initially, Imogen is a wonderfully vivid presence, shrewd, impetuous, passionate, and very much the proprietress of her own will. Unlike the Posthumus who allows himself to be defined by events – including the event of his marriage – Imogen is extraordinarily forceful in defining herself and her relation to father and husband. Her initial election of Posthumus against her father's will, her contempt at his various attempts to bully her, her easy penetration of Iachimo's attempts at seduction, her initial anger when she hears Posthumus's charges against her [3. 4. 39–43]: all demonstrate her extraordinary self-possession; though as fiercely loving and loyal as any of Shakespeare's idealized women, her self-determination is a far cry from their characteristic self-abnegation. But their self-abnegation is precisely what the play brings her to. The crucial moment in this process seems to me her turn from anger to a masochistic self-sacrifice in her response to Posthumus's accusation. As she moves from the righteous indignation of "False to his bed? What is it to be false?" [3. 4. 39] to "When thou see'st him, / A little witness my obedience. Look, / I draw the sword myself" [3. 4. 64–6], she charts the trajectory of her submission; a moment later, she will proclaim her heart "obedient as the scabbard" [3. 4. 79] to receive the sword. Newly practicing a masochistic self-abnegation phrased as obedience to male will, she bizarrely redefines even the grounds for her anger at Posthumus: now she chides him not for betraying her love but for having caused her "disobedience 'gainst the king my father" [3. 4. 87–8]. Given her new emphasis on obedience to male authority, the action Imogen is about to undergo takes on the configuration of a punishment for her initial act of self-definition: her willingness now to obey Posthumus's sword becomes in effect the righting of her first disobedience of her father, the righting of the very vividness of selfhood that had attracted us to her in the first place.

In asking her to give up the habits of a princess as he counsels her to take on male disguise, Pisanio summarizes the process of submission: "You must forget to be a woman; change / Command into obedience" [3. 4. 154–5]. Because she has commanded as a woman, Imogen must simultaneously give up her command and her femaleness, as though her male disguise were the sign of her penitential obedience to male power. And it is: by the end of the scene, her female selfhood has undergone a process of radical constriction. Helpless, she accepts Pisanio's plan to make herself into Lucius's page, doubly putting herself under male management; when we next see her, her femaleness itself will be submerged in her disguise. The degree to which similar disguises serve to enable the selfhood of the earlier women in the comedies emphasizes the reduction of Imogen's power here: far more than any of Shakespeare's other transvestite women, she will feel her own inadequacy as a man; the disguise reveals her not as a powerfully self-directing woman but as a hopelessly inadequate man. As she takes on the disguise, she gives up command with a vengeance, becoming uncharacteristically directionless, the nearly passive recipient of her brother's kindness, Cloten's sexual fantasy, and the queen's poison. The masculine disguise that initially seemed a way for her to find Posthumus and hence perhaps regain him [3. 4. 150] – as her predecessors in the source stories do – becomes instead the sign of her passivity, her willingness to allow events to define her. Settling into helpless androgyny, she gives up her own powerful femininity, entering willingly into the realm from which women have been displaced, into the plot that has displaced her own: "I'd change my sex to be companion with them, / Since Leonatus' false" [3. 6. 85–6]. From this point on, she will no longer generate the action through her own will; that role increasingly passes from her to Posthumus, as his repentance, his vision, and his heroism become the focus and motivator of the action.

Imogen begins the play as a primary defining figure, defining herself, her husband, and the dramatic focus for the audience; by the end, she has learned her place. She virtually disappears between 4. 2 and 5. 6, displaced by the husband she had initially defined, the father she had initially defied. In its treatment of her, that is, the play enacts a revenge that in its own way parallels Posthumus's revenge, scourging her sexual body even while insisting that he repent of his violence. Her turn toward masochism may be psychologically plausible when read within the boundaries of her own subjectivity; but it is nonetheless accompanied by something like the play's sadism toward her: robbed of her own powerful selfhood, put entirely under male command, she becomes imaginatively the victim not only of Posthumus's revenge and Cloten's rape fantasy but also of her author's cruelty. During the play's penitential middle section, the woman who easily penetrated Iachimo's deceit cannot tell the body of Cloten from her husband's; the woman who had directed our perceptions becomes the object of our pity precisely for her helpless inability to see what we already know. Harried, degraded, she gives up command with a vengeance, becoming entirely subject to those around her. And despite the happy ending of the marriage plot, there is no sign that she will be allowed to regain her own powerful selfhood; indeed, the happy ending is radically contingent on her self-loss, on the ascendancy of male authority and the circumscription of the female. The tapestries of Imogen's bedchamber tell the story of "proud Cleopatra, when she met her Roman, / And Cydnus swell'd above the banks" [2. 4. 70–1]; but *Cymbeline* is the undoing of that story, the unmaking of female authority, the curtailing of female pride, as much for Imogen as for the wicked queen.

In veiled form, then, both plots enact the recuperation of male power over the female. In this recuperation, the marriage plot oddly replicates the conditions governing Cymbeline's parthenogenetic fantasy: insofar as the play successfully turns Posthumus away from his rage at Imogen and redirects him toward heterosexual reunion, it does so only by first unmaking woman's power to form or deform man. And in this unmaking, it answers the conditions of Posthumus's own parthenogenesis fantasy: the radical uncertainty about male identity central to both plots is in fact distilled in his "woman's part" speech; and even while it is ostensibly the marker of the psychic place Posthumus must leave, that speech dictates the terms of his return. For Posthumus recovers his marriage at the end only through a series of defensive strategies designed to excise the woman's part in him: his fantasized revenge against Imogen, her harrying by events beyond her control, and the scapegoating of Iachimo and especially Cloten all serve to preserve his manhood intact, enabling his return by first confirming his pure masculine identity.

The woman's part speech cuts to the heart of anxiety about male identity and female power, associating both with the mother's capacity to unmake the son's identity through her sexual fault:

> Is there no way for men to be, but women
> Must be half-workers? We are all bastards,
> And that most venerable man, which I
> Did call my father, was I know not where
> When I was stamp'd. Some coiner with his tools
> Made me a counterfeit: yet my mother seem'd
> The Dian of that time: so doth my wife
> The nonpareil of this.

[2. 5. 1–8]

Posthumus's logic takes as its starting point a rational uncertainty about male lineage and hence abut the patriarchal structures on which identity is based: insofar as Posthumus's identity depends on his status as his father's son, his mother's infidelity would make him counterfeit. So far, so good: but the parthenogenesis fantasy of the opening lines makes bastardy contingent not on the mother's infidelity but on her mere participation in the act of procreation. The gap between the opening question – "Is there no way for men to be, but women / Must be half workers?" – and the answer – "We are all bastards" – contains a submerged *if*: if there is no way for men to come into being without the half-work of women, then we are all bastards. As in *King Lear*, bastardy is the sign of the mother's presence in the child: only the pure lineage of the father, uncontaminated by the mother, would guarantee legitimacy. The rational concern with patriarchal lineage thus covers a fantasy in which maternal sexuality *per se* is always infidelity, always a displacement of the father and a corresponding contamination of the son; in effect, through her participation in the procreative act, the mother makes the son in her own image. Hence Posthumus's hysterical desire to unmake her part in him:

> Could I find out
> The woman's part in me – for there's no motion
> That tends to vice in man, but I affirm
> It is the woman's part.

[2. 5. 19–22]

But why should the supposed infidelity of his wife return Posthumus to his mother and hence to the woman's part in him? And what is this woman's part? The association of the beloved's sexual fault with the mother's is of course familiar from *Troilus and Cressida*, but here it functions less as a marker for the soiling of the idealized mother than as shorthand for the covert equation that makes female sexuality – legitimate or illegitimate – responsible for the sexual fault in man: as though Imogen's sexuality evoked the woman's part in Posthumus, making him acknowledge himself (for the first time) as born of woman. Posthumus will go on to associate the woman's part with all vices great and small, "all faults that name, nay, that hell knows" [2. 5. 27]; but in his first articulation, it is associated specifically with the sexual fault, the "motion" that tends to "vice" in man. In this formulation, sexuality itself is – familiarly – the inheritance from the woman's part in procreation; and as Posthumus recoils from that part in himself, the "part" takes on a specifically anatomical tinge, as though Posthumus – like Lear – catches a terrifying glimpse of the "mother" within.

[...]

In the "woman's part" speech, Imogen's "rosy pudency" had threatened to turn Posthumus into a Cloten, registering the woman's part in him through his own sexual desire; her sexuality, like his mother's, would in effect mark him as a mother's son, no longer his father's legitimate heir. Without Cloten to take on the burden of his sexuality, Posthumus himself would collapse into Cloten, and the distinction on which the marriage – and the play – depends would be undone. But the play rescues Posthumus, displacing the male sexual body – the derivative of the woman's part – from him and relocating it in Cloten; and then it visits on Cloten the punishment deflected from Posthumus. Cloten's psychological function in relation to Posthumus thus takes as its starting point the same parthenogenesis fantasy that governs the Cymbeline plot: if Cloten's death serves in the Cymbeline plot as the point at which father's son triumphs over mother's, and hence as the point of origin for Cymbeline's restored masculinity, it serves in the marriage plot to liberate Posthumus from the woman's part by proxy. With Cloten's death, Posthumus is free to reenter the stage and begin his reconstruction as father's son; and as father's son, he can safely regain an Imogen who is powerless, an Imogen from whom there is no longer anything to fear.

This reconstruction is the business of the last act. Posthumus's decision to fight in disguise against the part he comes with is initially defined as one of his rites of penitence [5. 1. 24–6]; but the disguise itself is designed to show him forth as one of the Leonati, worthy through his manliness to be his father's son ("Let me make men know / More valour in me than my habits show. / Gods, put the strength o' th' Leonati in me!" [5. 1. 29–31]). Fighting unknown, he can establish a secure masculine identity in no way indebted to Imogen's choice of him, dependent rather on his status as heroic warrior and his alliance with a series of patriarchal families: after easily defeating Iachimo, whose "manhood" has been "taken off" by his sexual guilt [5. 2. 1–2], his next action is to ally himself with the lost princes in rescuing the father from whom they are all estranged. And after this rescue, he is rewarded by a vision of the renewed patriarchal family, a vision that systematically undoes the horror of the woman's part speech:

> *Solemn music. Enter (as in an apparition)* Sicilius Leonatus, *father to* Posthumus, *an old man, attired like a warrior, leading in his hand an ancient matron (his wife, and mother to Posthumus) with music before them. Then,*

after other music, follow the two young Leonati *(brothers to Posthumus) with wounds as they died in the wars. They circle Posthumus round as he lies sleeping.*

[5. 5. 123, 1–8]

The woman's part speech had recorded the loss of both his chaste mother and his venerable father as ideal images through the action of an uncontrolled female sexuality; now – in the family asexually begotten by a "grandsire," Sleep [5. 5. 217] – that sexuality is firmly under control. Posthumus's father – dressed in the garb that epitomizes his successful masculinity – now leads his mother by the hand; reconstructed as a matron, her sexuality is now in the service of the patriarchal family, producing warrior sons as the sign of male lineage. This righting of hierarchy is ratified by Jupiter's appearance: as the play's ultimate strong father, he reassures us that events have been under his control all along. Under the double guidance of two asexual fathers – grandsire Sleep and the Jupiter who "coin'd" Posthumus's life [5. 5. 117] – Posthumus undoes the horrific vision of the "coiner with his tools" who made him counterfeit [2. 5. 5], establishing his new identity as father's son by establishing a pure male lineage, subduing the woman's part in his family and in himself.

The vision is troubling not only because of the oft-debated quality of its verse and the somewhat tacked-on quality of Jupiter's reassurances, but also because it condenses and hence makes visible the contrary impulses that govern the play. Posthumus falls asleep crying out for renewed intimacy with Imogen ("O Imogen, / I'll speak to thee in silence" [5. 5. 122–3]); when the audience hears the solemn music announcing the presence of the supernatural, surely the expectation is that Posthumus will be given what he has asked for, some form of communion with or reassurance about Imogen. Instead, he is given a graphic representation of the successfully patriarchal family. This shift epitomizes both the displacement of the marriage plot by the Cymbeline plot and the conditions that enable Imogen's return: by the end, according to Jupiter's prophecy, Imogen's sexual body has been unmade and she has been reduced to a "piece of tender air" [5. 6. 446], while Posthumus has been enlarged to a young lion.

The fragile recoveries of the marriage plot thus rest on a series of accommodations that radically reduce Imogen's power, displace both sexuality and its appropriate punishment away from Posthumus, and celebrate his renewed status as father's son; they rest, that is, on a thorough undoing of the fantasy of contamination by the "woman's part." If the Cymbeline plot magically does away with the problematic female body and achieves a family and a masculine identity founded exclusively on male bonds, the marriage plot manages somewhat less magically to achieve the same ends: in their very different styles, both enact versions of a world in which women need not be half-workers. Despite their ostensibly opposed goals, the plots interlock and are driven by the same anxieties: Posthumus's "woman's part" speech is apparently disowned by the play, and yet its terms generate the Cymbeline plot. Behind Posthumus's response to Imogen's imagined infidelity looms the figure of the father weakened or displaced by the overwhelming wife/mother: looms precisely Cymbeline and his queen. The son lost there – made counterfeit through the father's loss of authority – is epitomized by Cloten, who is the embodiment of the mother's son Posthumus fears in himself. And the pure father's son Posthumus wishes to be is localized in Guiderius and Arviragus, in alliance with whom Posthumus recovers his manhood. The elements of the Cymbeline plot thus function as two-dimensional projections of the fears condensed in the "woman's part" speech; the marriage plot is interrupted by the Cymbeline plot because the Cymbeline plot enacts in exaggerated form the fears about masculine identity and contamination by the female that disrupt marriage.

In the end, despite the violent yoking together of opposites in the romances as a whole: the plot that would recover trust in the female is frustrated and baffled by the plot that would recover masculine authority; the two remain incompatible. And yet this very incompatibility allows the two plots to protect one another: the recovery of Imogen conceals the extent to which the Cymbeline plot grounds its masculine authority on the excision of the female; the Cymbeline plot provides the context in which Imogen can safely return. For the Cymbeline plot fulfills the conditions of her return, enabling the marriage by shielding the marriage plot from the responsibility for those conditions: as the shadowy projections of the Cymbeline plot serve to protect Posthumus, exorcising the woman's part in him and enabling his pure manhood, they serve to chasten Imogen, punishing her for her sexuality and remaking her in boy's clothes, the woman's part in her utterly subdued.

> (From Janet Adelman (1992) *Suffocating Mothers: Fantasies of Maternal Origin in Shakespeare's Plays, 'Hamlet' to 'The Tempest'*, London and New York: Routledge, pp.200–13, 216–19)

Text 7

Jodi Mikalachki, 'The masculine romance of Roman Britain: Cymbeline *and early modern English nationalism'*

By paying detailed attention to Jacobean understandings of nationalism, Jodi Mikalachki argues in the spirit of the new historicists that *Cymbeline* dramatizes the major political and sexual anxieties of it age. Close analysis of the Welsh aspects of the play and the character of the Queen convinces Mikalachki that *Cymbeline* contributes to the ideological production of 'a civil masculine foundation for early modern English nationalism'.

> The birth of the English nation was not the birth of a nation;
> it was the birth of the nations, the birth of nationalism.
>
> Nations have no clearly identifiable births.

It is somewhat misleading to put the above quotations together, since the first describes the birth of nationalism in England at a specific historical moment (the sixteenth century), while the second invokes the (usually imagined to be) ancient origins of something that has come to be called a nation. I juxtapose them here not simply to imply a wide divergence of scholarly opinion but also to suggest that any discussion of nationalism and early modern England necessarily involves both ways that these quotations read the phenomenon they describe: one places the origins of English nationalism (and perhaps of nationalism more generally) in the early modern period; the other recognizes early modern England's own perception of its national origins in antiquity. The quotations do nevertheless represent opposite poles in theories of nationalism. The first introduces Liah Greenfeld's recent study of early modern England as the world's first nation; assuming the causal primacy of ideas, Greenfeld argues for the idea of the nation as the constituitive element of modernity. The second quotation virtually concludes the last appendix to Benedict Anderson's influential *Imagined Communities*, a study that famously rejects ideological definitions of nationalism, considering it instead alongside anthropological terms like *kinship* or *religion*, and arguing strongly for its emergence in the eighteenth-century Americas. Both works participate in the new social, political, and historical interest in nationalism that developed during the 1980s, just as its subject seemed about to become obsolete.

My own approach emphasizes the interplay between historical obsolescence and continuity with the past in the recovery of national origins. I am less concerned to establish whether nationalism did indeed originate in sixteenth-century England (believing, as I do, that nationalism, too, has no clearly identifiable birth) than I am to explore the complexitites of early modern attempts to recover English national origins. The tensions of this sixteenth-century project of recovery – its drive, on one hand, to establish historical precedent and continuity and, on the other, to exorcise a primitive savagery it wished to declare obsolete – inform virtually all expressions of early modern English nationalism. These tensions derive from the period's broader social tensions about order, manifested most acutely in anxiety over the nature of familial relations and the status of the family as a model for the order of the state. The centrality of the family and the church to early modern English articulations of the nation suggests that Anderson's anthropological focus might be particularly appropriate to the study of English nationalism in this period. His understanding of nationalism as aligned "not with self-consciously held political ideologies, but with the large cultural systems that preceded it, out of which – as well as against which – it came into being," informs my own understanding and guides my consideration of how perceptions of national origins reflected and shaped early modern concepts of the English nation.

Greenfeld's intellectual history is not without interest, however, particularly given the prominent role of early modern intellectuals – scholars, poets, visual artists – in developing nationalist icons and narratives in England. One of the great intellectual stumbling blocks to the recovery of national origins in sixteenth-century England was the absence of a native classical past on which to found the glories of the modern nation. Worse yet, the primitive British savagery that purportedly preceded Roman conquest proved antithetical to a fundamental principle of hierarchy in early modern England, for the Britons made no distinction of sex in government. Powerful females loomed large in early modern visions of national origins, from the universal gendering of the topographical and historical "Britannia" as feminine to the troubling eruptions of ancient queens in the process of civilization by Rome. Like the unruly women who challenged the patriarchal order of early modern England, these powerful and rebellious females in native historiography threatened the establishment of a stable, masculine identity for the early modern nation.

Recent work on the mutually informing constructs of nationalism and sexuality has defined the former as a virile fraternity perpetuated by its rejection of overt male homosexuality and its relegation of women to a position of marginalized respectability. I would argue that this gendering and sexualizing of the nation, generally presented as having emerged in the eighteenth century, had become current by the early seventeenth century in England and involved both an exclusion of originary female savagery and a masculine embrace of the civility of empire. Jacobean dramas set in Roman Britain often conclude with a masculine embrace, staged literally or invoked rhetorically as a figure for the new relation between Rome and Britain. These concluding embraces depend on the prior death of the female character who has advocated or led the British resistance to Rome. The exorcism of this female resistance, constructed as savage, grounds the stable hybrid that crowns these plays with a promise of peace for Britain and wider membership in the Roman world of civilization. And yet it is precisely the savage females banished from the conclusions of these dramas – ancient queens like Fletcher's Bonduca or the wicked Queen of Shakespeare's *Cymbeline* – who articulate British nationalism and patriotism.

In the following account I shall read Shakespeare's romance of Roman Britain in terms of these issues of gender and sexuality, taking both as constitutive of the nationalism the play articulates. In doing so, I hope not only to revise twentieth-century readings of *Cymbeline* as a nationalist drama but also to explore Renaissance anxiety about native origins and the corresponding difficulty of forging a historically based national identity in early modern England.

I

The Queen's great patriotic speech in 3. 1 has long been a stumbling block in interpretations of *Cymbeline*. Combining appeals to native topography, history, and legendary origins, it recalls the highest moments of Elizabethan nationalism:

> ... Remember, sir, my liege,
> The kings your ancestors, together with
> The natural bravery of your isle, which stands
> As Neptune's park, ribb'd and pal'd in
> With rocks unscaleable and roaring waters,
> With sands that will not bear your enemies' boats,
> But suck them up to th' topmast. A kind of conquest
> Caesar made here, but made not here his brag
> Of "Came, and saw, and overcame:" with shame
> (The first that ever touch'd him) he was carried
> From off our coast, twice beaten: and his shipping
> (Poor ignorant baubles!) on our terrible seas,
> Like egg-shells mov'd upon their surges, crack'd
> As easily 'gainst our rocks. For joy whereof
> The fam'd Cassibelan, who was once at point
> (O giglot fortune!) to master Caesar's sword,
> Made Lud's town with rejoicing-fires bright,
> And Britons strut with courage.

> [3. 1. 17–34]

The Queen's opening command to remember invokes the restitutive drive of early modern English nationalism. The nation's glorious past – its resistance to the great Julius Caesar, its ancient line of kings, and the antiquity of its capital – depends paratactically on this command, emerging in the incantatory power of names like "Lud's town" and Cassibelan and in the powerful icon of native topography. Moved by this nationalist appeal, Cymbeline refuses to pay the tribute demanded by the Roman emissaries, thus setting Britain and Rome at war.

As the last of the play's many reversals, however, Cymbeline agrees to pay the tribute and announces his submission to the Roman emperor. In place of the bonfires of victory remembered by his queen, he commands that "A Roman, and a British ensign wave / Friendly together" as both armies march through Lud's town [5. 6. 480–1]. This volte-face is the more remarkable in that the Britons have just defeated the Romans in battle. Honor, not force, dictates Cymbeline's decision, as he invokes the promise made by his uncle Cassibelan to Julius Caesar, from which, he recalls, "We were dissuaded by our wicked queen" [1. 463]. Despite everything else the Queen does to earn this epithet, Cymbeline accords it here in the context of her opposition to the Roman tribute, her disruption of the masculine network of kinship, promises, and honor that binds Cymbeline to Rome. In this final assessment of the political plot, the king's full censure falls on the radical nationalism articulated by "our wicked queen."

Critics who wish to read *Cymbeline* as a straightforward celebration of national identity dismiss the Queen's motivation as mere self-interest. By doing so, they fail to interrogate the corporate self-interest that animates nationalism. They further marginalize the Queen by focusing on the oafish Cloten as the main proponent of an objectionable patriotism, thus avoiding the problem of how to interpret her delivery of one of the great nationalist speeches in Shakespeare. Even those who do acknowledge the interpretive difficulties of this scene find ultimately that the patriotic voices of the Queen and Cloten must be rejected in order to effect the play's romance conclusion. G. Wilson Knight's masterful account of Shakespeare's use of Roman and British historiography remains the most instructive in this regard. Knight casts Cymbeline's refusal to pay the tribute, the pivotal national action in the play as a "question of Britain's islanded integrity." While noting Posthumus's early description of British virtue in his reference to Julius Caesar's respect for British courage [2. 4. 20–6], Knight nevertheless recognizes that the Queen expresses it much more satisfyingly in 3. 1. He argues, however, that the Queen and Cloten are types Britain must ultimately reject in order to recognize freely her Roman obligation and inheritance. Writing shortly after the Second World War, Knight comments that the national situation in *Cymbeline* serves, "as often in real life, to render violent instincts respectable."

George L. Mosse's argument about nationalism and sexuality, which culminates in an analysis of Nazi Germany, also rests on the term *respectable*. Indeed, in Mosse's analysis an alliance between nationalism and respectability is crucial to the formulation and dissemination of both. He traces naturalized concepts of respectability to the eighteenth century, when modern nationalism was emerging, and finds both to be informed by ideals of fraternity for men and domesticity for women. Men were to engage actively with one another in a spirit of brotherhood, while women were to remain passively within the domestic sphere, exercising a biological maternal function that in no way challenged the spiritual bonding of adult males. "Woman as a national symbol was the guardian of the continuity and immutability of the nation, the embodiment of its respectability," Mosse observes, adding that the more respectable nationalist movements become, the more respectable their feminine icons look. When Knight notes in 1947 how the national situation in *Cymbeline* serves "to render violent instincts respectable," he intuits the naturalized alliance between nationalism and respectability that Mosse theorizes forty years later.

Cymbeline's Queen is hardly a figure of national respectability. Even her maternal devotion to Cloten can be censured, and the rest of her career as evil stepmother, would-be poisoner, and finally suicide fully earns Cymbeline's concluding appro-bation of the "heavens [who] in justice both on her, and hers, / Have laid most heavy hand" [5. 6. 464–5]. Yet Cymbeline's insistence on her political intervention as the mark of her wickedness per se suggests a critique of the nationalism she articulates. This convergence of national and personal wickedness indicates the difficulty of forging national identity before the eighteenth-century alliance of nationalism and respectability. Indeed, the complex and somewhat clumsily resolved romance of *Cymbeline* dramatizes the immediate prehistory of that alliance and its constitutive elements. Early modern England certainly had an ideal of respectable womanhood, one that (as in the eighteenth century) rested on the chastity and subordination of women within the patriarchal household. Susan Amussen has demonstrated, however, that the terms of this ideal were not so clear nor so universally accepted in the seventeenth century as has often been suggested. Definitions of wifely obedience in particular were contested by seventeenth-century Englishwomen, despite their general acquiescence to the principle of female subordination. Only by the late seventeenth and early eighteenth centuries are these challenges muted, suggesting that the naturalized ideal of feminine respectability Mosse invokes as an element of nationalism had been fully internalized by women. The difficulties of constructing and ensuring this sexual ideal in the early seventeenth century reveal themselves in the complex formation of a national identity in *Cymbeline*.

If respectable nationalism depends in part on respectable womanhood, someone other than the wicked Queen must embody it. Imogen, so beloved of the Victorians for her wifely devotion and forbearance, might figure as the wicked Queen's respectable double, and she does indeed come to represent an alternative nationalism. Her progress through a series of disguised identities and alliances, not all of them British, indicates the amount of work needed to construct a national icon of feminine respectability, just as the messages from and about the Queen in the final scene assert the impossibility of resolving the drama without invoking her feminine wickedness. This duality of feminine respectability and wickedness reveals how fraught early modern English nationalism was with fears of the unrespectable, or, in the language of the period, the uncivil or barbaric. It also indicates how important gender was as a category for working out these fears. Work that applies Mosse's analysis of nationalism and sexuality to the early modern period notes the identification of the feminine with the barbaric in nationalist discourse. Jonathan Goldberg's reading of *Plimoth Plantation* as the inaugural text of a national American literature notes its persistent alignment of Anglo women with Indians. Although not precisely identical, he argues, they must both "be effaced in order for history to move forward as the exclusive preserve of white men."

The collapse of the categories of "woman" and "savage" also informs *Cymbeline*. Anxiety about gender, given a nationalist inflection, haunts the drama, emerging particularly in contests over Roman–British relations. If it is most apparent in the caricature of feminine wickedness represented by the Queen, who tries to come between Britain and Rome, it also informs masculine characters in all-male settings. After the Queen's intervention in 3. 1, British articulation and enactment of male bonding become increasingly important, from Belarius's reconstitution of an all-male family in the Welsh cave to the princes' further bonding with Posthumus on the battle field and the ultimate reconciliation of Rome and Britain in the final scene. Although Imogen appears in all these settings, she does so only in boy's dress, a costume she retains to the play's conclusion. I shall discuss the implications of her disguise more fully below but would point out here that it shifts not only her gender but also her status and age from married adult to single youth. These shifts make more apparent the exclusion of adult women, particularly mothers, from the scenes of male bonding in *Cymbeline*. An historiographical concern over originary females seems to be enacted here in familiar terms. The construction of the Queen as a figure of savage excess, even if not especially with regard to her maternity, recalls Goldberg's formulation of the necessary effacement of women and savages "in order for history to move forward as the exclusive preserve of white men." In the context of *Cymbeline*, one might alter his last words to read "civilized" or perhaps "Romanized men." All roads of male bonding lead to Rome in this play and, correspondingly, to a place in the exclusive preserve of Roman history.

Critics reading *Cymbeline* from the perspective of early modern historiography are divided on the question of Rome's role. Those who identify the play's romance resolution with the Romans cite the importance of Rome in British chronicle history and Jacobean enthusiasm for Augustan analogies. Others argue that in *Cymbeline* Shakespeare exorcises his fascination with Roman history in favor of a more humane British national ethic. Early modern responses were not so one-sided. In their attempts to reconcile ancient British patriotism and a civilized union with Rome, English historians acknowledged and developed a hybrid nationalist response to the Roman Conquest. Violently patriotic queens played an important role in negotiating this hybrid. The hierarchial binarism of gender, fundamental to the construction of early modern society, also governed that period's construction of the ancient British relation to Rome. In the section that follows, I shall examine this phenomenon through the early modern historiography of two ancient Britons, Boadicea and Caractacus. Although separately historically by almost twenty years, these two figures of ancient British patriotism appear side by side in early modern accounts of Roman Britain. Their dramatic juxtaposition reveals much about the gendering and sexualizing of national origins and identity in early modern England.

II

Cymbeline's Queen has no direct source in Holinshed's reign of Kymbeline. She bears a striking resemblance, however, to Voadicia, or Boadicea, who appears in Holinshed's narrative of Roman Britain roughly sixty years after the events depicted in Shakespeare's play. Like Cymbeline's Queen, Boadicea opposed the Roman conquerors but ultimately failed to free Britain of the imperial yoke, taking her own life (or dying of "a natural infirmity") after a conclusive battle. Also like the wicked Queen, she was famous for her nationalist stance, especially her great speech on British freedom and resistance to tyranny, where she opposed the payment of tribute to Rome and invoked the same topoi of the island's natural strengths and the glorious history of Britain's people and kings. Ultimately, Boadicea, too, suffered condemnation for her ruthless defense of this position. Although Holinshed acknowledges the legitimacy of her initial grievance (the Romans had seized her late husband's kingdom, raped her daughters, and had her flogged), he finds that her female savagery carried her too far in revenge. Showing no mercy, Boadicea led the "dreadful examples of the Britons' cruelty" until her undisciplined army of women and men finally met defeat at the hands of a smaller, well-organized band of Romans under the leadership of Suetonius. The editorial summary of her revolt makes explicit both the cause of her failure and the reason for her condemnation: "the chief cause of the Britons insurging against the Romans, they admitted as well women as men to public government."

Caractacus, on the other hand, wins unqualified historiographical praise for both his initial resistance and his eventual submission to Rome. In 43 AD he led the western tribe of the Silurians in revolt against Rome. Although he, like Boadicea, was defeated, he did not end his life but was taken to Rome to be led as a captive in the Emperor Claudius's triumphal procession. There he so distinguished himself by the dignity of his speech and bearing that he won freedom and commendation of his manly courage from Claudius himself. Caractacus's manliness, his Roman *virtus*, is the focus of early modern accounts of his uprising. The patriotic oration Caractacus delivers before Claudius is never condemned. On the contrary, the 1587 Holinshed cites it as both laudable and successful, calling it the "manly speech to the Emperor Claudius, whereby he and his obtain mercy and pardon." The term *manly* draws an implicit contrast with the earlier condemnation of Boadicea's revolt as an example of feminine government.

The distinction between Caractacus's manly *romanitas* and Boadicea's female savagery became a standard feature of early modern accounts of Roman Britain. Camden begins his collection of "Grave Speeches and Wittie Apothegmes of woorthie Personages of this Realme in former times" with a thirteen-line citation of the "manly speech" of Caractacus before Claudius. He follows this with a three-line speech from Boadicea, after which, he reports, she lets a hare out of her lap as a token of the Romans' timidity. This superstitious piece of barbarism meets with the fate it deserves, for "the successe of the battell prooved otherwise." As late as Milton's *History of Britain* in 1671, the distinction was maintained. Milton cites in full Caractacus's manly speech and offers him as a classic exemplum of masculine virtue. When he comes to Boadicea's rebellion, however, he refuses to include her oration, saying that he does not believe in set speeches in a history and that he has cited Caractacus only because his words demonstrate "magnanimitie, soberness, and martial skill." In fact Milton accuses his classical sources of having put words into Boadicea's mouth "out of a vanity, hoping to embellish and set out thir Historie with the strangeness of our manners, not caring in the meanwhile to brand us with the rankest note of Barbarism, as if in *Britain* Woemen were Men, and Men Woemen." In this standard pairing of the male and female British rebels against Rome, then, Boadicea represented "the rankest note of Barbarism," that state in which gender distinctions are collapsed. Caractacus, on the other hand, was a figure of exemplary manliness, invoked to counterbalance the overwhelming female savagery of Boadicea and to reestablish British masculinity.

Fletcher seems to have followed this pattern in composing his drama *Bonduca*. Although he derived most of his historical information from classical sources and Holinshed's *Chronicles*, he also included a character named Caratach, Bonduca's cousin and general of the Britons. Caratach conducts the war by Roman rules, for which he expresses great admiration. He even chastises Bonduca for her extravagant speeches against the Romans, thus anticipating Milton's rejection of her feminine oratory. Because she defied Caratach's order to return to her spinning wheel and instead meddled in the affairs of men, Bonduca is made to bear full responsibility for the Britons' eventual defeat. Despite her eponymous role in the drama, she dies in Act 4, leaving the "Romophile" Caratach to represent Britain in the last act. During that act he earns the further admiration of the Roman soldiers, who publicly honor and praise him for his Roman virtues. The play ends with his embrace by the Roman commander Suetonius and the latter's words: "Ye shew a friends soul. / March on, and through the Camp in every tongue, / The Vertues of great *Caratach* be sung."

Other plays of the period which deal with British rebellion against Rome end with the same masculine embrace. In *The Valiant Welshman*, a dramatization of Caractacus's rebellion, the character "Caradoc" is betrayed into Roman hands by the duplicitous British queen Cartamanda and brought before the Emperor Claudius. Claudius then recalls Caradoc's valor in battle, lifts him up from his kneeling posture, and celebrates his valiant name. In William Rowley's *A Shoemaker, a Gentleman*, a disguised British prince twice saves the life of the Emperor Dioclesian and rescues the imperial battle standard in successive clashes with Vandals and Goths. On resigning his trophies to Dioclesian in the next scene with the words "Now to the Royall hand of Caesar I resigne / The high Imperiall Ensigne of Great Rome," the prince is bidden by the emperor to "Kneele downe, / And rise a Brittaine Knight" (3. 5. 17–19). *Fuimus Troes, or the True Trojans*, a play about Julius Caesar's conquest, ends in a metaphorical embrace of the empire, with the words "The world's fourth empire Britain doth embrace." With the exception of Rowley's *Shoemaker*, these plays work toward a reconciliation between Rome and Britain that is exclusively masculine. Any women who might have figured in the action (and they usually do so in invented love plots) have been killed off, leaving the stage free for men to conclude matters of true historic import. With the exclusion of women from the action, the stage of Roman Britain becomes the "exclusive preserve" of men, both British and Roman. The triumph of exclusion is figured in the masculine embrace that is the dominant trope of these final scenes, invoked as a metaphor of empire and embodied in the stage embraces of male Britons by Roman commanders and in the symbolic merging of their national emblems.

If the masculine romance of Roman Britain delivers Britain from the self-destructive violence of the wicked Queen, however, it also defines the province of Britannia as the passive object of Roman desire. Mosse emphasizes the fear of male homosexuality that haunts the fraternal bonding of nationalism. Goldberg expands on this idea in his analysis of *Plimoth Plantation*, citing William Bradford's need to separate the pervasive homosociality of his founding American fantasy of all-male relations "by drawing the line – lethally – between its own sexual energies and those it calls sodomitical." Commenting on Bradford's reluctant inclusion of "'a case of buggery'" because "'the truth of the history requires it,'" Goldberg sets the unrealizable desire to distinguish the ordinary male bonding from sodomy at the heart of Bradford's history: "The truth of the history, as I am reading it, is the entanglement of the 'ancient members' with and the desire to separate from the figure of the sodomite who represents at once the negation of the ideal and its literalization." Fear of homosexuality is neither so clear nor so lethal in early modern constructions of Roman Britain, where female savagery is the primary object of revulsion. When Fletcher and Shakespeare attempt the literalization of this masculine ideal in terms of a purely British nationalism, however, they produce scenes of male bonding characterized by feminine and domestic behavior.

[...]

The experiment in an all-male British world is more developed in *Cymbeline*. In the middle of Act 3, after ties with Rome have been broken, Shakespeare introduces the Welsh retreat of Belarius, Guiderius, and Arviragus. This idyll represents as full a return to unmitigated Britishness as the wicked Queen's opposition to the payment of tribute. Just as her resistance to Rome fails, causing (in Cymbeline's view) her own death and that of her son, so, too, does the primitive fantasy of the Welsh cave fail to stave off the ultimate embrace with Rome. In the latter case it is not the death of the British heirs that ends this hope but rather their fear that they will lack a historical afterlife. When Belarius praises the purity of their Welsh retreat, contrasting it with the tales he has told the boys "Of courts, of princes; of the tricks in war" [3. 3. 15], the elder son responds: "Out of your proof you speak: we poor unfledg'd, / Have never wing'd from view o' th' nest; nor know not / What air's from home" [ll. 27–9]. He concedes that the quiet life of their retreat may be sweeter to Belarius than the court but asserts that "unto us it is / A cell of ignorance" [ll. 32–3]. His younger brother then adds:

> What should we speak of
> When we are old as you? When we shall hear
> The rain and wind beat dark December? How
> In this our pinching cave shall we discourse
> The freezing hours away? We have seen nothing:
> We are beastly.

[ll. 35–40]

What the brothers protest is their exclusion from history. They have seen nothing; they are barbaric. Confined to their pinching cave in Wales, they have, quite literally, no history to speak of. This conflict between the princes and their presumed father comes to a head when the brothers want to enter the battle against the Romans. Belarius takes their zeal as an irrepressible sign of their royal blood, which longs to "fly out and show them princes born" [4. 4. 54]. It is equally, however, a sign of their desire to enter the world of history. Belarius's own sense of having been painfully shaped by a wider experience only fuels this desire. "O boys, this story / The world may read in me: my body's mark'd / With Roman swords," he claims [3. 3. 55–7], as though his body were a literalization of the Roman writing of ancient British history. Without fighting the Romans, the princes will have no such marks to read by the winter fire when they are old. The masculine rite of passage such scars represent for them personally is a version of the national entry into history by means of the Roman invasion. For early modern historiographers Britain, too, would have remained outside history had she never entered into a battle with the Romans.

This convergence of the personal and the national in the forging of masculine identity offers the possibility of reconciling two of the most important interpretive traditions of *Cymbeline*: the psychoanalytic and the historicist. Where historicists find the battle and its aftermath puzzling and inconclusive in terms of the play's treatment of Roman–British relations, psychoanalytic critics focus on the battle as the play's central masculine rite of passage, interpreting it in archetypal terms that ignore its historiographical complexity. The approach I have been advocating, developed from Mosse's insight about the interrelatedness of nationalism and sexuality, historicizes the development of sexual and national identities as it demonstrates their interdependence. Janet Adelman, while recognizing the historiographical complexity of Cymbeline's submission to Rome, interprets it in psychoanalytic terms as a result of "the conflicted desire for merger even at the root of the desire for autonomy." In historiographical terms, I would argue that in early modern England an originary engagement with Rome was necessary for the formation of an autonomous national identity. Roman Britain came to play a foundational role in the recovery of native origins not only because it provided a context for the male bonding that characterizes modern nationalism but also because it enabled exorcism of the female savagery that challenged both autonomy and the respectability of nationalism.

Engagement with Rome also brought Britain into the masculine preserve of Roman historiography. It is battle with the Romans that affords Cymbeline's sons, the male Britons of the next generation, that historical identity they lacked in their pastoral retreat. In the dramatization of this episode, they achieve historical status instantly, not because they rewrite Roman history, or win a lasting victory, but rather because that victory is immediately described and preserved in historiographical forms. As soon as the princes' stand with Belarius has been presented dramatically, Posthumus recapitulates it as a historical battle narrative, complete with citations of brave speeches and descriptions of the terrain and deployment of troops [5. 5. 1–51]. His interlocutor responds by producing an aphorism to commemorate their action, "A narrow lane, an old man, and two boys" [l. 52], which Posthumus improves into a rhymed proverb: "Two boys, an old man twice a boy, a lane, / Preserved the Britons, was the Romans' bane" [ll. 57–8]. The transformation of the dramatic stand in 5. 2 into narrative, aphorism, and the proverb in 5. 3 represents instant historicization. This making of history issues directly from engagement with the Romans, which also leads to the princes' restoration as Cymbeline's male heirs. Both the continuance of the masculine British line and the entrance of its youngest branches into written history require abandonment of the purely British romance of the cave of Wales.

III

[...] I would like to close with a word about the relative roles of homophobia and misogyny in early modern constructions of national origins. In Mosse's formulation the greatest threat to the male bonding of nationalism is overt male homosexuality, an anxiety Goldberg discovers as early as the 1630s in *Plimoth Plantation*. Both theorists emphasize the interrelatedness of homphobia and misogyny in the formation of masculine national identity. In the masculine romance of Roman Britain, fears of effeminacy and of women are also intertwined. It strikes me, however, that the latter are much more explicit than the former. A fear of originary female savagery consistently drove early modern historians and dramatists of ancient Britain to find refuge in the Roman embrace. The complexities of Britain's position in this embrace certainly raise issues of sexuality, but these seem to me to be subordinated to an overriding concern about the gender of national origins. British origins in all these works emerge as unavoidably feminine, either in the savagery of a wicked queen or in the feminized domesticity and submission of the British male to the Roman embrace. I take the violence with which early modern dramtists and historians rejected the figure of the ancient British queen as an indication of how thoroughly their failure to transform the femininity of national origins disturbed them. Their attempts to avoid this originary femininity led them ultimately to embrace a subordinate status in the Roman empire. While this new status also consigned Britain to a feminized role, it avoided the savagery of the purely British nationalism articulated by ancient queens. It also allowed for a historical afterlife for Britian. In contrast to the ancient queen's savage refusal of empire, the masculine embrace of Roman Britain became the truly generative interaction, producing a civil masculine foundation for early modern English nationalism.

(From Jodi Mikalachki (1995) 'The masculine romance of Roman Britain: *Cymbeline* and early modern English nationalism,' *Shakespeare Quarterly*, vol. 46, no. 3, pp.301–16, 321–2)

Appendix 2

Text 1

Ovid, Epilogue from The Metamorphoses, *trans. Arthur Golding*

The *Metamorphoses*, a long Roman poem in 15 books by Ovid (43 BCE–*c.* CE 17), was one of Shakespeare's favourite texts; it was a source he frequently drew on in both drama and poetry (see, for example, the 1593 narrative poem *Venus and Adonis*). The *Metamorphoses* is a witty and digressive redaction of a great range of classical myths, unified by its concern with stories in which people change from one state or body to another. Although he would have been able to read the Latin original, Shakespeare also drew on an accurate translation of 1567 by Arthur Golding (1536–1606).

> Now have I brought a woork to end which neither *Joves* feerce wrath,
> Nor swoord, nor fyre, nor freating age with all the force it hath
> Are able too abolish quyght. Let comme that fatall howre
> Which (saving of this brittle flesh) hath over mee no powre,
> And at his pleasure make an end of myne uncerteyne tyme.
> Yit shall the better part of mee assured bee to clyme
> Aloft above the starry skye. And all the world shall never
> Be able for to quench my name. For looke how farre so ever
> The Romane Empyre by the ryght of conquest shall extend,
> So farre shall all folke reade this woork. And tyme without all end
> (If Poets as by prophesie about the truth may ame)
> My lyfe shall everlastingly bee lengthened still by fame.

(From Christopher Martin (1998) *Ovid in English*, Harmondsworth: Penguin, p.75)

Text 2

Edmund Spenser, Sonnet 75 from Amoretti and Epithalamion

Edmund Spenser (*c.*1552–99) was one of the most influential Elizabethan poets. As well as being the author of the national epic, *The Faerie Queene* (1590, 1596), Spenser published important works in most poetic genres from 1579 to 1599 and so shaped much later poetry. His sonnet sequence *Amoretti and Epithalamion* (1595) is a typically accomplished and idiosyncratic adaptation of this fashionable poetic mode, ending – rather than with protracted erotic frustration – with the marriage of the poet–speaker and his lady.

> One day I wrote her name upon the strand,
>   but came the waves and washed it away:
>   agayne I wrote it with a second hand,
>   but came the tyde, and made my paynes his pray.
> 'Vayne man', sayd she, 'that doest in vaine assay
>   a mortall thing so to immortalize,
>   for I my selve shall lyke to this decay,
>   and eek my name bee wyped out lykewize.'

'Not so', (quod I) 'let baser things devize
   to dry in dust, but you shall live by fame:
   my verse your vertues rare shall eternize,
   and in the hevens wryte your glorious name:
Where, whenas death shall all the world subdew,
   our love shall live, and later life renew.'

(From Maurice Evans (ed.) (1977) *Elizabethan Sonnets*, London: Dent, p.146)

Text 3

Petrarch, 'Pace non trovo' from Rime sparse, *trans. Robert Durling*

Rime sparse (*Scattered Rhymes*) by Franceso Petrarch (1304–74) inaugurated the European fashion for sequences of love sonnets.

Peace I do not find, and I have no wish to make war; and I fear and hope, and burn and am of ice; and I fly above the heavens and lie on the ground; and I grasp nothing and embrace all the world.

One has me in prison who neither opens nor locks, neither keeps me for his own nor unties the bonds; and Love does not kill and does not unchain me, he neither wishes me alive nor frees me from the tangle.

I see without eyes, and I have no tongue and yet cry out; and I wish to perish and I ask for help; and I hate myself and love another.

I feed on pain, weeping I laugh; equally displeasing to me are death and life. In this state am I, Lady, on account of you.

(From Robert M. Durling (ed. and trans.) (1976) *Petrarch's Lyric Poems: The 'Rime Sparse' and Other Lyrics*, Cambridge, MA: Harvard University Press, p.272)

Text 4

Petrarch, 'Pace non trovo' from Rime sparse, *trans. Sir Thomas Wyatt*

Sir Thomas Wyatt (*c.*1503–42) adapted and translated several of Petrarch's poems into English.

I find no peace and all my war is done.
I fear and hope, I burn and freeze like ice.
I fly above the wind yet can I not arise.
And naught I have and all the world I seize on.
That looseth nor locketh, holdeth me in prison
And holdeth me not, yet can I scape no wise;
Nor letteth me live nor die at my device
And yet of death it giveth me occasion.
Without eyen I see and without tongue I plain.
I desire to perish and yet I ask health.

I love another and thus I hate myself.
I feed me in sorrow and laugh in all my pain.
Likewise displeaseth me both death and life,
And my delight is causer of this strife.

(From R.A. Rebholz (ed.) (1978) *Sir Thomas Wyatt: The Complete Poems*,
Harmondsworth: Penguin, p.80)

Text 5

Sir Philip Sidney, Sonnet 1 from Astrophel and Stella

Sir Philip Sidney (1552–86) was one of the most powerful Elizabethans. As a
politician and courtier, he held an influential place at court; as a writer and patron of
literature he exerted a considerable influence on literary style and fashion. *Astrophel
and Stella*, first published in 1591, but probably written between 1581 and 1582,
began the boom in sonnet sequences. It constitutes a semi-fictionalized account of
Sidney's relationship with Penelope Devereux, sister of Robert Devereux, second
Earl of Essex.

Loving in truth, and faine in verse my love to show,
That she (deare she) might take some pleasure of my paine;
Pleasure might cause her reade, reading might make her know,
Knowledge might pitie winne, and pitie grace obtaine,
I sought fit words to paint the blackest face of woe,
Studying inventions fine her wits to entertaine;
Oft turning others' leaves, to see if thence would flow
Some fresh and fruitfull showers upon my sunne-burn'd braine.
    But words came halting forth, wanting Invention's stay;
Invention, Nature's child, fled step-dame Studie's blowes,
And others' feete still seem'd but strangers in my way.
Thus great with child to speake, and helplesse in my throwes,
    Biting my trewand pen, beating my selfe for spite,
    'Foole,' said my Muse to me, 'looke in thy heart and write.'

(From Maurice Evans (ed.) (1977) *Elizabethan Sonnets*, London: Dent, p.2)

Text 6

Michael Drayton, Sonnet 50 from Idea

Michael Drayton (1563–1631) was a lifelong professional poet who published
important works in all of the major poetic genres. His *Poems* of 1619 is a collected
edition of his work, which includes his sonnet sequence *Idea*, first published as *Ideas
Mirrour* in 1594.

As in some Countries, farre remote from hence,
The wretched Creature destined to die,
Having the Judgement due to his Offence,
By Surgeons beg'd, their Art on him to trie,

Which on the Living worke without remorse,
First make incision on each mast'ring Veine,
Then stanch the bleeding, then trans-pierce the Coarse,
And with the Balmes recure the Wounds againe;
Then Poyson, and with Physike him restore:
Not that they feare the hope-lesse Man to kill,
But their Experience to increase the more:
Ev'n so my Mistres workes upon my Ill,
   By curing me and killing me each How'r,
   Onely to shew her Beautie's Sov'raigne Pow'r.

(From Maurice Evans (ed.) (1977) *Elizabethan Sonnets*, London: Dent, p.108)

Text 7

Edmund Spenser, Sonnet 50 from Amoretti and Epithalamion

See the headnote to Text 2.

Long languishing in double malady
   of my hart's wound and of my bodie's greife,
   there came to me a leach that would apply
   fit medicines for my bodie's best reliefe.
'Vayne man' (quod I) 'that hast but little priefe,
   in deep discovery of the mynd's disease,
   is not the hart of all the body chiefe,
   and rules the members as it selfe doth please?
Then with some cordialls seeke first to appease
   the inward languour of my wounded hart,
   and then my body shall have shortly ease:
   but such sweet cordialls passe Physition's art.
Then, my lyfe's Leach, doe you your skill reveale,
   and with one salve both hart and body heale.'

(From Maurice Evans (ed.) (1977) *Elizabethan Sonnets*, London: Dent, p.135)

Text 8

John Donne, 'Death be not proud' from Holy Sonnets

Unlike Michael Drayton, John Donne (1572–1631) was not a professional poet. He wrote in a wide range of styles throughout his life, but his poems were only published after his death. His sonnets reflect his religious concerns, and are focused on the speaker's relationship with God rather than with a lover.

Death be not proud, though some have called thee
Mighty and dreadfull, for, thou are not soe,
For, those, whom thou think'st, thou dost overthrow,
Die not, poore death, nor yet canst thou kill mee;

From rest and sleepe, which but thy pictures bee,
Much pleasure, then from thee, much more must flow,
And soonest our best men with thee doe goe,
Rest of their bones, and soules deliverie.
Thou art slave to Fate, chance, kings, and desperate men,
And dost with poyson, warre, and sicknesse dwell,
And poppie, or charmes can make us sleepe as well,
And better then thy stroake; why swell'st thou then?
One short sleepe past, wee wake eternally,
And death shall be no more, death, thou shalt die.

(From C.A. Patrides (ed.) (1985) *The Complete English Poems of John Donne*, London:
Dent, pp.440–1)

Text 9

John Barrell, 'Editing out: the discourse of patronage and Shakespeare's twenty-ninth sonnet' from Poetry, Language and Politics

John Barrell's essay exemplifies the move in literary studies since the 1980s to historicize the study of literature more systematically. Barrell considers Stephen Booth's 1977 edition of *Shakespeare's Sonnets* and argues that Booth's modernization of spelling and punctuation 'edits out' much of the historical specificity of Sonnet 29 in terms of its concern with issues of patronage.

I

The only edition of Shakespeare's sonnets to be published in his lifetime is the quarto volume of 1609, printed by George Eld for Thomas Thorpe. In his own, enormous edition of the sonnets, first published in 1977, Stephen Booth prints a facsimile of each poem as it appears in the quarto, and on the opposite page a repunctuated version of the poem, with the spelling modernised (*Shakespeare's Sonnets*, edited with analytic commentary by Stephen Booth (New Haven and London: Yale University Press, 1977); page numbers in brackets in this essay refer to the third edition, 1980). His purpose in producing his own versions of the sonnets is explained at length in the course of his preface and commentary, and I will consider what he has to say about this in some detail later in this essay. For the moment I shall quote only a few of the remarks he offers by way of explanation. 'My primary purpose', he writes, '... is to provide a text that will give a modern reader as much as I can resurrect of a Renaissance reader's experience of the 1609 Quarto; it is, after all, the sonnets we have and not some hypothetical originals that we value.' For 'the effects of almost four centuries are such that a modern reader faced with the Quarto text sees something that is effectively very different from what a seventeenth-century reader saw' (ix). As Booth points out, 'the spelling and punctuation of the 1609 Quarto are not necessarily or even probably Shakespeare's own', but 'probably result from a printer's whims, errors, or idiosyncrasies' (xiii–xv). And even if they were Shakespeare's, Booth argues, 'it would not matter much', for to modern readers, at least if they are not in the habit of reading renaissance texts in renaissance editions or in facsimiles, the original spelling may have a misleading quaintness, Furthermore, the function of punctuation, and the value of punctuation marks, have changed considerably since 1609, so that 'modern readers, accustomed to logically ... directive punctuation' may well be 'inclined to misinterpret' poems if they are not aware of this (ix).

Booth also attempts, in his commentary, to provide a full gloss on all the words in the sonnets which seem to him ambiguous or which in the Renaissance had meanings now unfamiliar to the modern reader. For 'once an editor has told him about the connotative and denotative significance of some of Shakespeare's words and phrases, a modern reader can read Shakespeare's sonnets and respond to them very much as a seventeenth-century reader would. He enjoys them and, I think, misses very little, if any, of their greatness and beauty' (xii). Booth's purpose in doing this is not to enable us to arrive at a more correct *interpretation* of the poems. On the contrary, one of his purposes in writing his commentary, he explains, is 'to advertise a criticism that does not try to say how a work should be read or should have been read in the past but instead concerns itself with how the work is read, how it probably *was* read, and why'. He believes that 'every impression that a poem evokes in the majority of its modern readers and can be demonstrated as a probable response in the majority of the poet's contemporaries is and was a part of that poem and cannot be argued away' (508). The aim of the glosses is to reopen poems that have been prematurely closed by interpretation, and by treating impressions of meaning which are surplus to that interpretation as disposable.

Booth's hostility to the idea that poems have correct interpretations is a part of his desire 'to recommend an unmediated analysis of works of art': by 'unmediated' he seems to mean '*ideologically* unmediated' (515, 513; my emphasis). But when he invites us to regard it as a matter of fact that the sonnets are characterised by 'greatness and beauty'; when we read that 'all of us were brought up on the idea that what poets say is sublime – takes us beyond reason', and that Booth's commentary 'tries to describe the physics by which we get there' (x); and when we are told that it is the complexity which gives the sonnets their 'magic' (xiii) – when we are told all this, we are forcibly reminded that what is ideology to one person is nature to another. We may suspect that Booth's confidence, that he can offer something near to an unmediated account of the sonnets, proceeds from an equal confidence that a belief 'all of us were brought up on' is outside the realm of ideology – is simply *true*.

It seems from Booth's explanation of his commentary that impressions of meaning available to a modern reader, but not (by reason of changes in the meanings of words) to a renaissance reader, are not as much a part of the poem as the impressions available to them both. I agree with him; though it seems to me that in doing so I am indulging what he might call an 'ideological' predisposition to try to understand poems in relation to the historical moment of their production. It is less clear whether Booth believes that the opposite of his contention would also be true: that impressions available to the renaissance reader, but no longer to the modern reader, are equally less valid than those perceptible to both. Booth would no doubt argue that the completeness of his commentary is an attempt to ensure that this issue doesn't arise: the glosses try to give the modern reader access to all the meanings a renaissance reader might have experienced. But meaning, of course, is not just a function of semantics – it is a product also (as Booth himself is at pains to point out) of syntax; and if the punctuation of a poem is amended so as to make that poem more accessible to the modern reader, there is evidently a risk that the syntax of the poem will be amended as well, and that meanings available in the quarto will disappear from the modern text. And this is all the more likely to happen if the editor who sets about repunctuating the sonnets holds certain truths, about their greatness, magic, and complexity, to be self-evident, for he will certainly not believe that all poems are great, magical, and complex – only some poems, only a certain kind of poem can be all those things. And it may then happen that the process of repunctuating a poem will become a process of representing it as just that certain kind of poem.

II

What kind of poem Booth finds great, magical, and complex I will try to consider at the end of this essay. But it seems unlikely that this poem would qualify:

> When in disgrace with Fortune and mens eyes,
> I all alone beweepe my out cast state,
> And trouble deafe heaven with my bootlesse cries,
> And looke upon my selfe and curse my fate.
> Wishing me like to one more rich in hope,
> Featur'd like him, like him with friends possest,
> Desiring this man's art, and that man's skope,
> With what I must injoy contented least,
> Yet in these thoughts my selfe almost despising,
> Haplye I thinke on thee, and then my state,
> (Like to the Larke at breake of daye arising)
> From sullen earth sings himns at Heavens gate,
> For thy sweet love remembered such welth brings,
> That then I skorne to change my state with Kings.

This is the version of Shakespeare's 29th sonnet as it appeared in the 1609 quarto, except that I have substituted the short 's' for the long throughout, changed a few 'u's into 'v's, and the second 'i' in 'inioy' to 'j', and have replaced the 'VV' – the 'double u' – of the opening word with 'W'. Now I am probably no less suspicious than Booth of the notion that we can arrive at 'correct' interpretations of poems, though I think for a different reason, for I cannot imagine an interpretation of a poem which would not proceed from a specific reading position, and would not be mediated by ideology. But I see no reason to believe that we should not therefore attempt to produce readings of poems which, however much we may dislike the word 'interpretation', inevitably do 'interpret' them in the sense that they foreground some meanings and push others into the background. In fact I do not see what use we could make of poems if we did not do this. That said, I want to offer a reading of this poem of a kind that will certainly violate its beauty and complexity, for I want to offer that reading in the form of a paraphrase and a commentary on my paraphrase. The point of the exercise is to show that one way of understanding this poem would involve giving a very specific gloss to numerous of the words and phrases it uses – words and phrases like 'bootless cries', 'rich in hope', 'friends', 'art', 'scope', even 'love'.

These words and phrases, taken by themselves, or in relation to the particular sense-units in which they occur, seem capable of a wide, in some cases a very wide, range of meanings; but that range will be narrowed considerably when we consider them in the context of each other, and perceive that they can be seen to signal in the poem the presence of a specific discourse, in terms of which they cohere and co-operate to define the historical moment of their utterance, and to specify, within that moment, the social position of the narrator who utters them. That discourse is the discourse of patronage, and, more particularly, that discourse as it is represented in complaints about the *lack* of patronage; this is a discourse we encounter repeatedly in the poetry and non fictional prose of the late Elizabethan and early Jacobean period. Its general characteristic, like that of all discourses, is to privilege one particular meaning of the various potential meanings of the words it employs, in such a way as to make them, almost, technical terms, but in such a way also to suggest that those privileged and special meanings are the meanings the words 'normally', they 'naturally' have.

The discourse of patronage, however, is represented in complaints about the lack or the withdrawal of patronage in such a way as seems at once to accept and to challenge that the 'normal' meanings of words are also their 'natural', their right meanings. For among the characteristics of the discourse of patronage, I want to suggest, are that it represents personal relations as economic relations (or it is, at least, unwilling to consider how there might be a distinction between the two); and that it represents personal reputation as something to be measured in terms not of moral worth or worthlessness, but in terms of honour and shame and their equivalents, which it estimates in terms of material success – or at least, once again, it is unwilling to focus on the distinction between moral and material worth and worthlessness. When this discourse comes to be used in utterances which complain of the lack of patronage, its failure to make such distinctions is apparently made an object of censure, as it must be if the complainant is to base a demand for patronage on the fact that he – for it is men we are speaking of – is morally worthy to receive it; but that censure cannot be pressed to the point where it would appear that to be in receipt of patronage is dishonourable, for the complaint is also a request, and one unlikely to succeed if the petitioner represents patrons and patronised alike merely as complicit in an agreement to distort the language of true value.

My paraphrase is long and clumsy, because it attempts to offer a gloss on a number of the words and phrases in the poem – especially those I have already picked out – at the same time as it tries to produce a continuity of meaning. But I will apologise for it at greater length in a moment:

> When I am out of favour with the fickle goddess of prosperity, and shamed in the eyes of men, all alone I weep for my condition as a social outcast, and I pester heaven with my complaints, but heaven is deaf, so that my complaints bring me no profit, and I look on myself from outside, as others see me, and I curse my lot in life. Wishing that I was like someone with better expectations of advancement – as good looking as this man, as well supplied with rich and influential friends as that man – envying the ingratiating arts of the one, and the other's range of career opportunities, contented least of all with the advantages I *do* possess, and still almost despising myself for thinking this way – it may happen that I think of you; and then my condition, like the lark arising at break of day, no longer complains to heaven but sings hymns at heaven's gate, though, unlike the lark, my condition remains on the dull and melancholy earth. For when I am reminded of the deep affectionate regard you have for my interests, I am in possession of such spiritual wealth, that I would think it a disgrace to change my condition with that which kings enjoy.

Let me offer some criticisms of that paraphrase – a random selection of them – before I make an attempt to justify some of the meanings which it sets out to privilege. For all its length, the paraphrase is particularly inept whenever it encounters some very salient moments of ambiguity. Let's look, for example, at the line 'Yet in these thoughts my selfe almost despising'. It's impossible to decide, and only a paraphrase obliges us to decide, whether the narrator's self-contempt is a part of his despair, or whether it is part of what enables him to transcend it, or whether, because we can't decide which it is, we simply have to say that it is both. The problem turns on the ambiguity of the word 'yet', which embodies a similar ambiguity as is nowadays embodied in the word 'still': that is, 'yet' can indicate that at the moment when the thought of 'thee' enters the narrator's mind, he is still in that state of self-contempt described in the first eight lines of the poem; or it can indicate that he despises himself for despising himself, and that to some degreee this reversal makes a passage for the thought of 'thee' to enter his mind; in which case 'yet' will have the force of 'but'. I have chosen to privilege the first of these meanings only because Booth's version, which we will look at later, puts a semi-colon at the end of line 8, and so may privilege the second, especially if we read the sonnet with the expectation that the sestet will somehow counter the drift of the meaning in the octet.

Or consider the word 'at' in line 12. It is essential to my contention that we can read this poem as at once critical of, and complicit with, the discourse of patronage, that though the poet's state, and the lark, both sing hymns at heaven's gate, the 'state' is primarily to be pictured as still on the earth, while the lark is in the air. As applied to the action of the lark, 'at' indicates where the lark is, where it does its singing; as applied to the action of the state, 'at' indicates the direction, the object at which the state projects its hymns – we hear this second meaning in such a sentence as 'the dog is baying at the moon', or indeed in such a line as Drayton's 'Like to the Dog that barketh at the Moone'. But there is nothing my paraphrase can do to indicate a double function in the word.

Thirdly among this random set of criticisms, I have chosen to give salience to one particular meaning of the word 'love', which emphasises its status as a term in the discourse of patronage, when even within that discourse itself the word is thoroughly ambiguous, and when it is crucial to its status as part of that discourse that it is ambiguous. By substituting for the word 'love' the words 'deep and affectionate regard you have for my interests', I have tried to defamiliarise the word – to specify out of all its possible and various and compound meanings one which most clearly represents it as a part of the discourse of patronage, and most clearly removes it from the meanings we most readily attach to the word today. Thus, among the meanings my paraphrase pushes away is the one by which we indicate the kind of feeling which, we may imagine, can properly be described as love when it is entertained exclusively for one person: I mean the meaning by which I might say 'I love Tom', and you might reply, 'Oh, I thought you loved Harry'. My paraphrase, on the contrary, refers to an emotion, perhaps more a concern, which someone, and a patron in particular, may feel or entertain towards a *number* of people; and to the degree to which we read Shakespeare's sonnets as love-poems, in the conventional sense, to that degree we will find the meaning offered by my paraphrase a misrepresentation of the narrator's meaning. My rather brutally materialistic phrase makes the narrator's idea of love, we could say, seem *cheap*.

But then again, among the meanings of the word 'love' which do not indicate the kind of attachment which the *OED* defines as 'based upon difference of sex' and 'the normal basis of marriage' – among those meanings is the love of God; and if the narrator's thoughts of 'thee' lead him to sing hymns to heaven, then to exclude that meaning, as I have done, will certainly be to limit the range of meanings, or the complex of meanings, in the word. These two objections to my paraphrase take on even more weight if we put them together; it is a frequent device of Elizabethan love-poetry deliberately to blur the distinction between the exclusive love for another person, and love for God, a blurring whose effect is to insist not just on the profundity but also on the purity of an exclusive attachment of 'love'; and to insist also on the ideal perfection of the beloved. Taken together, these meanings – this compound meaning – of an exclusive and divine love may certainly seem to reveal the inadequacy, even the inappropriateness, of my paraphrase of the word.

Its inadequacy I admit, and I will elaborate upon it; but its inappropriateness is another matter. In defence of my paraphrase of the word 'love', I have said that of all the meanings that I believe to be partially appropriate here, I have chosen to foreground the one least likely to occur to modern readers; and the one which most clearly connects the word with the other terms from the discourse of patronage which the poem deploys, and which I shall look at in a minute. For in the period when the poem was written, the word 'love' is frequently to be found describing the relations of patron and patronised, or the emotion which for example a petitioner for patronage claims to feel for a potential patron. A late Elizabethan poet who professes 'love' for a rich aristocrat, and who gives expression to that 'love' by dedicating a play to him, will not say that his love is cheapened – he will say indeed that his love is properly requited if in return for that expression of love he is offered a couple of pounds, which was the going rate. A patron whose love for a poet was more abundant, whose pocket was longer, or whose desire or need for praise and honour was greater, might believe it to be an expedient, or even – for I do not intend to be merely cynical – an appropriate acknowledgement of the poet's 'love', to up the rate, even to as much as a fiver. Best of all, he might put himself out to secure the petitioner some position, some job – whether a sinecure, or one to which substantial duties were attached – which would guarantee him a more steady income, and so guarantee a continuation of the poet's love, which otherwise, though claimed to be undying, would fizzle out if the next dedication went unrewarded, or the poet was lucky enough to find a more generous patron.

Now as I say, I do not want to be merely cynical about this situation, and there is no reason to doubt that there were relations between poet and patron which were relations of such mutual regard as to make it seem appropriate to us that they should be described by the word 'love', in some such sense as we might attribute to the word now. But they remained economic relations – relations of patronage – whatever else they might also have been: relations in which the patron's love was expressed by money, however it was also expressed. So while we can say that the economic dependence of the poet upon his patron was sanitised, and as it were treated as incidental, by the description of the relation as one of love, we must also say that the patron's love was at least in part *represented* by his gift of money or position. But if this was the situation in what we can think of as the best possible case – and where we can imagine a genuine and affectionate regard between poet and patron – then of course it had to be claimed to be the situation in *all* cases of patronage. For the more the language of love was played down, the more a relation of patronage would be exposed as one in which the patron was exchanging money for reputation. Furthermore, if, one way or another, it was necessary to represent relations of patronage in terms of relations of love – and, on the poet's part, as a relation of exclusive love – and if one function of that representation was to purify and idealise what was always of course an economic transaction, it is not surprising that the distinction between love for another and love for God should be blurred in the discourse of patronage, just as it was in love poems which seem concerned with relationships conceived of as non-economic.

III

All this may serve to justify my point that the word 'love' had a specific function within the discourse of patronage, but all this does not, of course, justify my paraphrase – it does nothing to support my claim that in this poem the word is being used as part of that discourse. That claim is based on an argument which, like all such arguments, is necessarily circular. What I am claiming, in short, is that each of the words and phrases such as 'disgrace', 'fortune', 'bootless', 'rich in hope', 'with friends possest', 'art', 'scope', 'injoy' – that each of these can carry the specific significance ascribed to it by the discourse of patronage, only because all the others can; that each of them has a meaning defined for it by all the others, in such a way as to foreground that meaning, to put it in front of all the other meanings which, individually, each word or phrase can bear. Let's start by taking the phrase 'more rich in hope', which, within the context of the line in which it occurs, seems to offer itself, perhaps, as defining a wish that the narrator were, simply, a more optimistic sort of chap.

'Hope' is a term frequently used in the discourse of patronage: let me take an example from what is probably the most famous pamphlet written by Thomas Nashe, *Pierce Penniless his Supplication to the Devil*, a work in which disappointment at the absence or withdrawal of patronage seems to be less a feeling of temporary loss of advantage than a permanent condition of life; and which, on that basis, assumes a licence to disambiguate, to undress, if I can put it that way, the terms of the discourse which, for reasons I have already suggested, it was usually necessary to keep muffled. This is not the case, however, when Pierce comes to a consideration of the virtues of the dead Philip Sidney:

> Gentle *Sir Philip Sidney*, thou knewst what belonged to a Scholler, thou
> knewst what paines, what toyle, what travel, conduct to perfection: wel
> couldst thou give every Vertue his encouragement, every Art his due,
> every writer his desert.

This sentence of course leaves it open, leaves it ambiguous what it is that 'belongs' to a scholar; what kind of encouragement Sidney thought appropriate to virtue, what it was he thought 'due' to art, or what it was that a writer 'deserved'. If we say, in each case, that it's money that is being spoken of, we will seem to cheapen, here too, the very special kind of 'love' that Sidney apparently evinced towards men of parts. But the next sentence puts it in no doubt: it is money that's being spoken of, but somehow money as transfigured, money as guaranteeing a regard which it cannot of course wholly represent. For Pierce continues:

> But thou art dead in thy grave, and hast left too few successors of thy
> glory, too few to cherish the Sons of the Muses, or water those budding
> hopes with their plenty, which thy bounty erst planted.

It is, then, money that belongs to a scholar; but which belongs to him only by the same natural law as water belongs to, because it is necessary to, a tree or a flowering shrub.

Or here is Spenser, dedicating 'The Ruines of Time' to Sidney's sister the Countess of Pembroke, and lamenting the death of her brother:

> ... God hath disdeigned the world of that most noble Spirit, which was
> the hope of all learned men, and the Patron of my young *Muses*;
> togeather with him both their hope of anie further fruit was cut off: and
> also the tender delight of those their first blossoms nipped and quite
> dead.

And here is the Fox in Spenser's 'Mother Hubberds Tale' complaining that the service he has done his country has got him nowhere:

> And still I hoped to be up advanced,
> For my good parts; but still it hath mischaunced.
> Now therefore that no lenger hope I see ...
> I meane to turne the next leafe of the booke.

Or we could take an example from Drayton's revised version of his eclogues, in which, in the voice of the shepherd Rowland, he complains of his inability to attract lucrative patronage while appearing to complain of some more specifically pastoral persecution:

> To those fat Pastures, which flocks healthfull keepe,
> Malice denyes me entrance with my Sheepe.

Therefore, says Rowland, 'my hopes are fruitlesse'.

These examples seem to summon 'more rich in hope', in Shakespeare's poem, within the orbit of the discourse of patronage. Once there, the phrase summons a word like 'bootless' within the same orbit: it weakens further the weak senses of the word ('useless' or 'unavailing', as Booth has it, 180), and foregrounds the sense 'bringing in no booty', no profit – no 'fruit', as the common euphemism would have it. It suggests that the 'friends' in line 6, represented as they are as a possession of whoever it is the narrator envies, are precisely the kind of rich and influential friends whose love is represented by the disbursement of money or the offer of a salaried position. It focuses the word 'Fortune', not as mere chance but as fortuitous prosperity, or as the deity who now extends and withholds the prosperity which, to many writers in renaissance Britain, could come only from patronage: as the Fox again complains:

> Thus manie yeares I now have spent and worne,
> In meane regard, and basest fortunes scorne.

Within the discourse of patronage, in 'disgrace with ... men's eyes' comes to mean to be shamed by one's poverty, and to be held 'in meane regard'. 'Art' comes to refer to that kind of skill in social address which, whatever one's worth as an artist, will secure lucrative patronage; as Spenser's Colin Clout complains, success at court is to be won by those who have

> A filed toung furnisht with tearmes of art,
> No art of schoole, but Courtiers schoolery.
> For arts of schoole have there small countenance.

'Scope' comes to mean neither the subject-matter available to a writer (180), nor imaginative or intellectual range: the second meaning was probably not firmly attached to the word for another two centuries – at least, the only example of that meaning offered by the *OED* prior to 1775 is the instance we are now considering, in this poem, where the word seems rather to mean, within the discourse we are identifying, the freedom of opportunity which money and position can offer.

The presence in the poem of that discourse also suggests that the narrator does not wish to be more good looking simply so that, in the general course of life, he will be more attractive to other people, but because, as Pierce Penniless points out, 'comliness' may persuade a patron to look favourably upon a petitioner. It suggests that when the narrator curses his fate, he is doing something akin to what Pierce does when he 'curses' his 'birth', the meaness of which obliges him to become a petitioner. And most crucial of all, it suggests that the 'outcast state' that the narrator beweeps is not his state of mind, his 'downcast spirits', his subjective sense of himself as an outsider, of such a kind as may change to a mood of elation in the right circumstances. It suggests rather that it is his state 'in regard to welfare or prosperity', as the *OED* puts it, or his social condition, something akin to his 'estate', with a sense of social and economic disadvantage combined: the 'estate' which Pierce also bemoans, and attempts to relieve, and which he imagines must be relieved by money, if he is to cease to be a social and economic outcast. This is not something which can be relieved by a decision to think positive and look on the bright side, and this point will come to be of importance when we come to examine Booth's version of the poem.

We do not, of course, have to start the process of identifying the discourse of patronage by starting as I have, with the phrase 'more rich in hope'; we could start with almost any of the words and phrases I have referred to, and, having identified its meaning within that discourse, we could observe how it attracts the others into the same discourse. My point is that each word and phrase offers to define the others; and it is together, each supporting the other, that they produce the discourse within the poem.

Let us return now to the word 'love', and to the nature of the relation it suggests between the narrator and 'thee'. Now if we came across this poem in isolation from the sonnets that surround it, we might find ourselves believing – and reasonably enough – that 'thee' is God. The poem would then make a single and coherent statement, that when the narrator is depressed about his economic and social disadvantages in the competition for patronage, he thinks of God, whose love brings such spiritual wealth as to pluck him out of the slough of despair and envy, and make him aware that the love of God offers him rewards and consolations far more worth having than anything to be won in that demeaning struggle. But if we read this poem as one of a run of Shakespeare's sonnets, which continually address a 'thee' who is clearly human, and male, we are unlikely to plump for that solution; in which case we are left with a puzzle, which, by the very nature of the discourse of patronage, cannot be solved.

The puzzle is this: is the relationship of love between the narrator and 'thee' to be understood not as a relationship of poet to patron, but as an exclusive attachment of deep affection, entirely uninvolved in economic considerations of the kind that appear to infect the friendship spoken of earlier in the poem? If it is, then the love that 'thee' has for the narrator seems to work more of less as the love of God would work, in releasing him from the degrading circle of envy and interest. Or is the love of the kind that a patron may be supposed to have for a petitioner? We cannot tell, because if it is the second kind of love, then its effects will still have to be described in spiritual rather than material terms, so as to represent that economic relation as so sanitised, so purified, so much a marriage of true minds, that the material wealth the relationship may bring to the narrator is not to be mentioned alongside the spiritual refreshment and encouragement it brings him. When I say 'is not to be mentioned', I intend both senses of the phrase: it is not worthy of mention, and it must not be mentioned – it is unmentionable.

I can put the point best this way. The poem may say, and this we could call the best possible case, that the special and exclusive love of 'thee' for 'I' is like the love of God, and makes all the economic worries that the speaker has been prey to entirely beneath consideration. Or, at the other extreme, the poem may be actively concealing a less beautiful and magical meaning, a meaning that runs like this: 'when I'm pushed for money, with all the degradation that poverty involves, I sometimes remember you, and you're always good for a couple of quid'. But whatever is being said or not said here, the discourse of patronage invoked earlier in the poem refuses to allow us to decide, precisely because, as I have argued, it is the nature of that discourse that it represents the economic relations of patron and petitioner in terms that must be indistinguishable from other kinds of purer, more ideal relationships of love.

The fact that we cannot find a solution to this puzzle does not make it a waste of time to attempt to define its terms; for to do so enables us to do something to situate the poem at the historical moment of its production: a moment, for example, at which the commercial market for writing was not so developed as to enable a writer to be a professional writer in the sense that he could hope to be supported by his sales, and be exempt from the need for patronage; but a moment, also, when the growth of literacy and learning, and other more purely economic factors, meant that there were far more petitioners for patronage than the potential patrons were able or willing to patronise. To attempt to define the terms of the puzzle also enables us to locate the identity of the narrator as something produced by that historical moment and spoken within a discourse that moment provides. The best possible case, as I have called it, is the case in which the narrator may be understood as claiming that he is freed, by the transcendent power of love, from the social and economic conditions that the discourse of patronage exists to describe and conceal; that he is freed, therefore, from speaking within the terms of that discourse, and is able either to speak within the terms of another, or to speak a quasi-religious language of love which transcends the limitations that all discourses impose on our utterance. But even that case cannot escape the embrace of the discourse of patronage, precisely because that discourse has its own power, to appropriate for its own purposes the most expansive and the most hyperbolic expressions of authenticity. And even in that case, the claim to an authentic love, which confers on the narrator an authentic, an unconditional identity (or one subject only to the condition that he is truly loved), and which escapes the constraining representation of personal relations as economic relations, can represent that escape only in the terms prescribed for it by the discourse of patronage, which pushes the narrator into behaving as if all that is required to show that one's authentic feelings and identity transcend the constraints of the social, the economic, the historical, is to elude the terms of a particular discourse which in any case refuse to be so eluded.

IV

But I suspect that my main priority should now be to answer the objection that no reader of this poem could conceivably doubt the presence within it of the discourse of patronage, and that I have spent several pages in the laboured statement of the obvious. And any reader of this essay who has consulted Booth's commentary on this sonnet may have found it particularly odd that I should have situated my reading of the poem in the context of a disagreement with his editorial method. For almost all the meanings I have pointed out as belonging within the discourse of patronage are offered by Booth in his glosses on the poem. He does not, it is true, have anything to say about 'love', which is for me the word which suffers most from the parasitic action of the discourse in the later lines of the poem. But for 'more rich in hope' he offers alongside the generalised meaning 'who has more hope, who is richer with respect to hope', a second, 'who is prospectively more wealthy, who has better expectations of wealth', a meaning which certainly attracts attention to the fact that the hope may be for material advancement, if not for the specific kind of material advancement that patronage can offer. The word 'art' is glossed by Booth as '(1) skill; (2) learning; and possibly (3) deviousness' again, a gloss which acknowledges, though it also marginalises, the meaning attributed to the word in the discourse of patronage. 'Scope' is glossed as 'range of ability', but also as 'range of opportunity', the meaning I have foregrounded (180).

But to acknowledge these meanings is not the point, if they are not also recognised as constituting a particular discourse, and thus as inviting us to understand the poem as an utterance made within the terms of that discourse. And Booth's edition does not allow the interpretation I have offered, because though some of the meanings which that discourse attributes to the words in the poem are available in Booth's commentary, they are not available as the constituent parts of a connected discourse in his text of the poem. In that text a different discourse is foregrounded – one which cannot allow the meanings I have pointed out even to appear as some of them do in Booth's commentary, as 'suggestions' or 'overtones' (xi). This different discourse is foregrounded by Booth's repunctuation of the poem, which certainly has the effect of 'modernizing' the poem, though not therefore of enabling a modern reader to 'respond' to it 'very much as a seventeenth-century reader would'.

This is Booth's version:[1]

> When in disgrace with fortune and men's eyes,
> I all alone beweep my outcast state,
> And trouble deaf heav'n with my bootless cries,
> And look upon myself and curse my fate,
> Wishing me like to one more rich in hope,
> Featured like him, like him with friends possessed,
> Desiring this man's art, and that man's scope,
> With what I most enjoy contented least;
> Yet in these thoughts myself almost despising,
> Haply I think on thee, and then my state,
> Like to the lark at break of day arising
> From sullen earth, sings hymns at heaven's gate;
>   For thy sweet love rememb'red such wealth brings,
>   That then I scorn to change my state with kings.

[1] [Stephen Booth, *Shakespeare's Sonnets*, New Haven and London: Yale University Press, 1980.]

My decided preference for the quarto version of this poem means that it would be tendentious for me to produce a paraphrase of this version. But fortunately there is another edition of the sonnets which offers a text for this poem virtually identical with Booth's, and which offers its own paraphrase on the opposite page. It goes like this:

> When down on my luck and with people set against me, all alone I lament my lot as an outsider: but I reproach heaven in vain with my laments, when I look upon myself and curse my fate. I wish myself like one with more hope, like him in looks and surrounded with friends; I find myself envying this man's art and that man's range, least contented with what I most enjoy. In this mood almost despising myself, I happen to think of you: and then, like a lark rising at dawn from sullen earth, I chant hymns to heaven. For thinking of your love brings such wealth to mind that then I would not change my state with kings.

This paraphrase is by A. L. Rowse; and within the limits of what the exercise can do – it can do little more of course than point one way through a poem, privileging those meanings which the paraphraser thinks it most important to draw attention to – within those limits, this seems to me a just representation of the versions of the poem which Rowse and Booth, in their separate editions, have produced; though Booth, as we shall see, would not agree that it is often desirable or even possible to engage in the exercise at all.

Now evidently Rowse is reading a very different poem, and calling attention to very different meanings, from the poem and the meanings I was concerned with. Most particularly, the discourse of patronage seems entirely to have disappeared from the poem; and with it, of course, all those constraints which complicated and, I argued, frustrated the claim to a transcendent love and a transcendent identity which the narrator makes in the last lines of the poem. For if an interpretation sheds, as I would argue this interpretation has done, those meanings in the poem in which is embodied the specific nature of the economic and social constraints which produce, which condition, the narrator's identity, then it will not be hard to represent the narrator as successfully claiming that his identity is unconditional and autonomous. So what is the difference between the two versions, and what accounts for the fact that each seems to move such different meanings into the foreground? There are two kinds of answers available to that question: the first focuses on how this version differs from the first, so as to produce this new (and, I believe, distinctively post-renaissance) meaning; the second focuses on that idea of the nature and function of poetry, of which, I believe, this second version is an expression. Let's look at the first issue first.

In terms of that issue, then, there is a number of possible answers to the question, but only one seems decisive. We could argue, for example, that simply to modernise the poem's spellings is to invite us to believe that we will find modern meanings in the words, or at least will not be invited to speculate on the possible strangeness of those words. We could argue that the changes in punctuation produce in us a similar expectation that the poem's meanings will be immediately available to us, will be, that is, modern meanings. The decisive answer seems to me to be indeed a matter of punctuation, but of one instance of it only: the decision to place a comma in the twelfth line, after 'sullen earth'. Up to that point it is perfectly possible to identify in this poem the discourse of patronage; after that moment it is extremely difficult to persist in the belief that one has identified it, that there are therefore special and strange meanings which are privileged in the poem, or that the conclusion of the poem and the kind of spiritual success it lays claim to are in any way constrained by those meanings.

To place a comma after 'from sullen earth' is to propose, in the first place, a radically different meaning for the word 'state' from the one I proposed. The argument for inserting the comma turns on the fact that line 12 requires that the poet's 'state' be in two places at once: on 'sullen earth' and also at 'heaven's gate'. This will seem – at least if we don't consider the double meaning for 'at' which I proposed earlier ('baying at the moon') – a perfectly reasonable objection, the more persuasive in that if we remove the end stop from the previous line and place it after 'earth', all ambiguity is removed, and the 'state', and the lark with which it is compared, become more neatly congruent in their actions: both start from sullen earth, both rise to heaven's gate. Booth's version of this argument is that the punctuation in the quarto:

> can mislead a modern reader into assuming that he should understand
> *lark* as the only riser, *state* as the only singer, and *From sullen earth* as
> designating only the place from which *state sings*. Actually, the general
> context (downcast spirits and low status), on the other hand, and both
> common knowledge of birds and the inevitable unity of the standard
> phrase 'arising from,' on the other, make any punctuation powerless to
> deny that *state* and *lark* are both singers and risers. However, both the Q
> [quarto] punctuation and the line end pause between *arising* and *From*
> carry a syntactically blurred image of the speaker('s state) sending hymns
> aloft from the earth, sending up hymns to heaven: 'then my state from
> sullen earth sings hymns ... like to the lark arising at daybreak' (181).

There are arguments against this, of course. There is an argument from euphony, that in terms of rhythm and pitch, the triumphant assertion that is made or attempted in these lines is far more convincing if we read:

> and then my state
> (Like to the Larke at breake of daye arising)
> From sullen earth sings himns at Heavens gate ...

than if we read

> and then my state,
> Like to the lark at break of day arising
> From sullen earth, sings hymns at heaven's gate.

The second reading obliges us to descend, both in terms of the pitch and of the ideational content of the lines, back to the low level which the narrator (by the argument of the second paraphrase) has successfully left behind him. But euphony may count for little against what seems to be the logic of the emendation. There is another argument, based on my own paraphrase: I have claimed that much of the pathos of the poem derives from the narrator's simultaneous desire and inability to escape from the limiting conditions of earth and perhaps of discourse; and if the narrator's state can do all that the lark can do, that source of meaning and pathos is abolished. But that argument has no status, as we shall see, in relation to a text in which the meanings it presupposes have been at best concealed, at worst erased.

And it is by this change of punctuation that they are concealed. For if both lark and state arise from sullen earth to heaven's gate, we have to find a meaning for 'state' which is compatible with the notion that it can be successfully elevated above the earth, that it can change its position as the narrator's mood, or the content of his mind, changes. And there is of course such a meaning available, by which 'state' would mean not social condition, which must be changed by social action; not economic condition, which must be changed by material means – not in short something akin to 'estate', but 'state of mind'. We can be in a low state, a low state of mind, and then something can happen which puts us in a better state, which moves us from depression to elation. In Booth's notes, which 'attempt to indicate not only what words mean but when they mean it' (x), 'state', in lines 2, 10, and 14, is glossed as '(1) condition (social, economic, mental, emotional, or spiritual); (2) status, rank' (180). The second of these meanings coincides with my reading of 'state' as 'estate', as do some, but not all, of the meanings Booth lists under (1). I entirely agree that in line 2, when the presence of the discourse of patronage is yet to be established in the poem, 'state' can mean 'mental, emotional, or spiritual state' – say, 'state of mind'. But once the discourse is established, then when the word re-occurs in line 10 of the quarto text, those meanings are pushed aside, and the meanings 'social and economic state', 'status or rank', become the primary meanings available to us. In Booth's edition, the reverse happens: all the meanings of 'state' that define the word as part of the discourse of patronage become at most 'suggestions' or 'overtones', and we are left with 'state of mind' as the primary meaning.

Once the meaning 'state of mind' has thus been selected and foregrounded, it has the effect of attracting all those terms, which, I argued, were attracted by each other into the discourse of patronage in the first poem, back out of that discourse again, and towards those meanings which seem most easily compatible with 'state' as 'state of mind'. The 'outcast state' bewept in line 2 seems to become also primarily a state of mind, a *sense* of oneself as an outsider, rather than a condition of social exclusion. 'In disgrace with Fortune' can quite properly be glossed as, simply, 'down on my luck', and whether that luck operates in relation to one's economic success or, say, one's personal relationships, conceived of as purely personal, becomes immaterial. Indeed, the whole vocabulary of the poem becomes immaterial, for the poem becomes a narrative about a state of mind whose position is determined not by material factors but by *itself*. 'Bootless' comes to mean, simply, 'unavailing'. 'More rich in hope' means 'more generally optimistic'. 'Friends' become personal friends, the kind who help you through a bad patch, by listening to your troubles (lots of black coffee), not by securing you a better social and economic status. 'Art' and 'scope' become, primarily, the technical accomplishment and imaginative range of another poet, whom the poet envies for these alone, and not for his better success in attracting patronage. The boast in the last couplet, that the narrator would not change his state with kings, becomes simply a banal declaration that he would not change his cheerful frame of mind with the frame of mind that kings possess – with the covert assumption, of course that money can't buy you love – and not that he would not swap his lowly economic and social status with the highest earthly 'estate' he can imagine. And finally, even love itself is disinfected by that one comma, which purifies the emotion of all those taints of the material and the self-seeking that the narrator of the first poem, I argued, was powerless to wash away.

Now with the probable exception of the word 'scope', though I have called the meanings thus attributed to the poem in the second version 'modern meanings', I do not mean to imply that they are not meanings which we can believe were present in the poem for its original readers. Indeed, my account of the first version depends absolutely on the assumption that they were, but that in that version they were present as, if you like, that bright side of each word, of each coin in the purse that is the discourse of patronage, and that their function was to attract our attention to that bright side, to the good meanings, away from the dull reverse side, where friends turned out to be of value for what they did for your pocket, where hope was hope for advancement, and where love was requited according to a fixed scale of charges. By concealing the meanings disclosed by the dull side of the words, however, this text conceals much of the content of that bright side as well, for bright and dull are here relative and binary terms, which require and produce each other. It conceals, in short, all those meanings which have to be recovered by historical enquiry, and announces that all the important meanings of the poem are meanings as available to us in the late twentieth century as they were to those who read the quarto edition of the sonnets when it came out in 1609. It is in this sense that the poem in its second version has developed a 'modern' meaning, and one based on a specifically modern, and a specifically liberal, notion of what it is that poems do and mean.

V

That brings me to the second answer to the question I proposed, what accounts for the difference between the two versions, or between – for we can reduce it to that – the different punctuations of lines 11 and 12? I can rephrase this question by asking what it is that has persuaded most editors of the sonnets in this century to privilege the kinds of meanings that are produced by this emendation and numerous others in editions of the sonnets? I will offer a very brief answer: that such editors have had a predisposition to believe two things: that great poetry must be universal, must speak the same meanings to all people at all times, to an unchanging human nature; and that the place where we are all the same is in our minds, the site of our individual identities, which are imagined to be primarily self-produced – to be fundamentally uninfluenced by, independent of, transcendent over whatever in the world might seem to press limiting conditions on that individual identity. Insofar as we are individuals, paradoxically it may seem, so far we are all the same; we differ only as there are, laid over our individual and true (true because individual) identities, the accretions of our different social and personal histories and situations. To reveal that common ground of individuality, we must scrape away whatever seems to threaten to condition our identity, and our individuality will be revealed as pristine, shining, unchanged. If Shakespeare can be shown to speak in that identity (which he can be, if we suppress those meanings in his poems which threaten to obscure it), then he can speak immediately to us, if we too, as we turn to read his poems, can persuade ourselves to believe that here, in poetry, is a language which, by privileging the individual, scrapes away the accretions also of our own particular histories. This belief not only homogenises individuality to universality, to a common and so allegedly fuller humanity; it also homogenises the different histories that might seem to condition different subjects and subjects in different periods; for all those histories are reduced to the same abstract notion, 'history' – to 'ideational static' (391), white noise, through which, if we listen attentively, we will be reassured to discover that the same tune is playing, was playing, and so (we may presume) always will be.

Now Stephen Booth would certainly object to my attributing this position to him, and would certainly object also to my associating his text with Rowse's paraphrase: his belief that the greatness of the sonnets is partly a function of their 'dizzying complexity' (xiii) leads him to believe also that few of them 'can be paraphrased without brutality' (387). I want now to try to do justice, though the attempt will have to be brief, to Booth's arguments, as well as to my own suspicions of them and to my claim that, in spite of everything, Rowse's paraphrase describes Booth's version of the poem quite fairly, and that the assumptions that produced both text and paraphrase are as I have described them.

Booth believes that poetry in general, but Shakespeare's especially, works in such a way as continually to produce an ideational surplus, a range of suggested meanings which must be present in the poem if they are triggered off in the mind of the reader. As we encounter a word in a poem, a whole range of possible meanings are available to us, and in that sense must be present in our mind until they are disambiguated by their context, and cannot be assumed to be cancelled even after they are thus disambiguated. But if they are present, however briefly, they cannot be treated as extraneous to the poem's meaning, which is – and this is one reason why poetry cannot be paraphrased – the whole experience of reading the poem, of participating in the 'action' which the poem performs (514–15). Similarly, groups of words may seem to make, as we read them, fragments of sense which turn out to be surplus to the requirements of the whole syntactical structure in which they inhere, and which are therefore disambiguated by that structure; but they are not, therefore, cancelled from our consciousness or from our unconsciousness (391) – they become and remain a part of the experience, the meaning, of the poem. Thus, it has to be assumed that there is some kind of primary meaning in the poem, whose function is to disambiguate, and to define what is the ideational surplus. To offer a paraphrase of that meaning, however, is to threaten to abolish the surplus, to behave as though it contributes nothing of importance to our experience of reading the poem.

With much of this I agree wholeheartedly [...]. I take issue with Booth, however, over what conclusion we are to draw from the last sentence of my last paragraph. For to me it does not at all seem to follow that because a paraphrase seems to threaten to abolish meanings which are surplus to the primary meaning we should not paraphrase poems. I would argue that whether we should or not, we do effectively paraphrase them when we identify a primary meaning, and it is just as well to try and spell out that meaning, so that we can recognise and test it. I would also argue that we cannot avoid mentally paraphrasing a poem: that it is of the nature of discourses that in any connected utterance they privilege some meanings of words and obscure (though they cannot therefore entirely cancel) others, and that we cannot arrive at any notion of the primary meaning of an utterance except in the terms of discourse. In relation to this particular poem, I am arguing that Jacobean readers could not have constructed a primary meaning for this poem except in terms of the discourse of patronage, whose determining presence in the poem is repeatedly signalled by the poem's vocabulary. To produce a text which conceals that discourse, treats the meanings it privileges as only 'ideational static', is thus the very opposite of enabling the reader to 'respond' to the poem 'very much as a seventeenth-century reader would'. It is, on the contrary, to go a long way towards denying the difference between what a seventeenth-century reader would have identified as the primary meaning of the poem, and the meaning that is attributed to it by the fact that much of its vocabulary is now primarily incorporated within what are now liberal discourses on personal relationships ('friends', 'love'), on the creative artist ('art', 'scope'), and on individual subjectivity ('state' as 'state of mind'), discourses which are no longer in danger of being contaminated by the discourse of patronage.

For Booth, even to suggest what the primary meaning might be, or might once have been, is to do violence to the whole experience, the whole action that the poem is. Though there is, he believes, 'a clear and effectively straightforward sense' (371) in all but a few of the sonnets, it is usually the case that it must not, indeed it *cannot* be stated; and, as we shall see, it is so clear, so straightforward, that to describe it is anyway unnecessary. But Booth also believes that it is a characteristic of the greatness of the sonnets that they give us the sense of 'effortless control of the uncontrollable' (xiii). The effect of this argument is almost to deny that anything in the sonnets can be described as surplus, for almost everything in them is controlled; so that Booth can write 'in the sonnets Shakespeare *uses* [my emphasis] more of the ideational potential in words than the logic of their exposition needs or can admit'. I take it that since it is impossible to demonstrate that Shakespeare or his sonnets (as opposed to the readers of them) 'use', in this active sense, what is surplus to their straightforward meanings, this part of the argument is true by definition, as it were: such control is constitutive of great poetry; since Shakespeare's poems are self-evidently great poems, he and they must be assumed to control, to use, all surplus meanings within infinitely complex but finally coherent and unified statements. He occupies the central position from which all meaning proceeds, and in which the unity of all meanings can – theoretically at least – be reconstituted.

This control, however, is not always Shakespeare's responsibility: sometimes it is indeed the reader who wears the trousers. 'All this complexity and density', writes Booth, 'is not only mastered by a reader but mastered without conscious effort or awareness' (xvii). I should apologise, I suppose, for trying to get some cheap mileage out of Booth's choice of verbs here, and his repeated reference to the reader as 'he'. No doubt he has no intention to exclude women from the circle of readers, and no doubt I have been guilty in my own writings of a similarly casual sexism. But [...] it has been a defining characteristic of liberal discourses on language that they attribute control, 'mastery' of language much more readily, if not exclusively, to men, and it would be a pity to pass up an opportunity to remind myself, as well as others, that these casual choices of verb and pronoun are the signs and instruments of a rather less casual oppression.

The reader's 'mastery', then, enables him to disentangle the surplus from the necessary. But he does not therefore discard the surplus, but produces, at the same time, the 'clear and effectively straightforward sense', and an infinitely ambiguous but still controllable sense who nature is that it *cannot* be disentangled from the straightforward sense. I had better acknowledge that I am not sure that I follow Booth's argument here, and may be misrepresenting it; for I do not really understand how the assertion of Shakespeare's control, and/or the reader's mastery, is ever going to become more than simply an assertion and a mystery. But I do think I see the purposes of the assertion, which are to assert the unity of the poem by asserting the unity of those, the author and/or reader, who produce its meanings, to claim that Shakespeare's poetry is at once as infinitely complex and magisterially controlled as great poetry must be, and to insist that it is nevertheless immediately comprehensible to the modern reader, as all great poetry, which is universal in its appeal, must be.

And I can see what follows from these positions, which is that if the reader 'masters' all the infinite complexity of the text; if (as Booth says) the renaissance reader did the same; and if the sonnets have (all but a few of them) a clear and effectively straightforward sense, then whatever meanings the modern reader notices must be co-extensive with all the meanings which a renaissance reader might have noticed. The straightforward sense which the modern reader both does and does not disentangle from the surplus, must be the same sense as seemed straightforward and in that sense primary to the renaissance reader. Both share the same experience of the sonnets, which are universal, therefore, in their meaning, a meaning which in no crucial way depends on any specifically renaissance meanings the poem may contain. For there are, Booth argues, only 'some relatively rare instances in the sonnets where historical changes in idiom invalidate or distort a modern reader's probable response to a line' (xiii). Except in those rare cases – he finds none in this sonnet – the kinds of meanings which I have argued are introduced into this sonnet by the discourse of patronage are relegated to the surplus, are part of what the modern reader supposedly masters, but not part of the straightforward, clear, and universal sense of the poem.

However great the reader's mastery may be, however, he is not omnipotent; for in order to lay bare, Booth believes, that universal sense, it is necessary to re-spell and re-punctuate the text in such a way as will remove – as far as possible – its strangeness, to reveal the clear sense that both renaissance and modern readers experience in reading the poem, a clear sense which is the same to them both. But, as we have seen, that sense can be claimed to be the same to both, only by claiming that the meanings which the modern reader will most readily attach to the poem are universal meanings. Specifically renaissance meanings, few though they allegedly are, must be relegated, by the processes of editing, to what is surplus to the text's straightforward movement towards unity of meaning. And of course if one of the pressures on how the modern reader determines the meaning of a poem is the expectation that great poems speak a universal language, the meanings she or he will seek out will be such as minimise whatever knowledge they happen to have of the discourses of the renaissance and the historically specific meanings embodied in them: these will be treated as surplus, for they are part of what must be scraped away, though not quite discarded, if the miracle of integration that the poem performs is to be appreciated. An insistence on applying such knowledge, or on allowing it to give more than a casual and provisional shading to the words of a poem, will be a failure to respond to the poem's greatness, its universality.

I do not have the space to represent some of Booth's more subtle qualifications of his positions, but they do seem to me to qualify his apparent belief that an attempt to understand the sonnets need not involve an attempt to understand the historically specific discourses they employ, and which, I have been arguing, their narrator can never elude. So I want to end this essay by addressing a question to myself. For it could reasonably be objected that if I insist on arguing that the sonnets speak a strange language whose meanings we must work to recover, and which is the production of a historical moment which is strange to us, I can have no means of experiencing the poems as the modern readers that Booth has in mind experience them, as poems which *move* them. So let me assert that I am much moved by this sonnet, in the quarto version, though not in Booth's. I find it moving by virtue of its *attempt*, and I italicise the word, to assert an ideal of transcendent love, and of a transcendent, autonomous identity, and to grasp at these as the means and the result of an escape from the oppression of the system of patronage and the constraints it imposes on the freedom of the narrator. But it is far from true that I find the poem less moving the more I examine the discourse which is the linguistic representation of those constraints, and attempt to understand how it constrains at once the narrator and the language he uses.

I can put it like this. Booth's text locates the affective power of the poem in its alleged power to transcend the conditions in which it was produced. For me, this does not reveal a universal content in the poem: it empties it of content, diminishes its pathos, and represents all the affective power of the poem as a function of the uncomplicated progress from depression to the elation of its final lines. I have argued (and he would no doubt disagree with me) that Booth's text and commentary represent the meanings in the poem by which its historical specificity is defined merely as white noise. To do this is, by implication, to treat the historically specific meanings and discourses of every 'great' poem simply as a metaphor for whatever it is, at any time, that imposes limits to our ability to assert our independence of the histories and discourses that constrain our freedom of action and speech. It makes all poems tell the same dull story, of how an empty individuality easily escapes from an empty history. For me, the pathos of this poem is, I repeat, inextricably a function of how it represents the specificity of the historical moment it produces and which produced it: a pathos which arises from the narrator's attempt to claim a transcendence he cannot achieve. He cannot achieve it, not simply because all such attempts must of their nature fail, but because the historical moment he seeks to transcend is represented by a discourse whose nature and function is to contaminate the very language by which that assertion of transcendence must try to find expression. For me, the pathos of the poem – I can repeat here my earlier point – is that the narrator can find no words to assert the transcendent power of true love, which cannot be interpreted as making a request for a couple of quid.

(From John Barrell (1988) *Poetry, Language and Politics*, Manchester: Manchester University Press, pp.18–43)

Text 10

William Wordsworth and Samuel Taylor Coleridge, critical comment on Shakespeare's Sonnets

The Romantic poets and critics William Wordsworth (1770–1850) and Samuel Taylor Coleridge (1772–1834) were interested in the sonnets because of their intense admiration for Shakespeare, but they were disturbed both by the poems' literary qualities and by their sexual content. Coleridge in particular goes to elaborate lengths to persuade his infant son Hartley (to whom this note is addressed on the occasion of his Christening) of Shakespeare's moral purity.

[Wordsworth]

These sonnets beginning at [127] to his mistress, are worse than a puzzle-peg. They are abominably harsh, obscure, and worthless. The others are for the most part much better, have many fine lines[,] very fine lines and passages. They are also in many places warm with passion. Their chief faults – and heavy ones they are – are sameness, tediousness, quaintness, and elaborate obscurity.

[Coleridge]

I can by no means subscribe to the above pencil mark of W. Wordsworth; which, however, it is my wish should never be erased. It is *his*: and grievously am I mistaken, and deplorably will Englishmen have degenerated if the being *his* will not in times to come give it a value, as of a little reverential relic – the rude mark of his hand left by the sweat of haste in a St Veronica handkerchief! ... My sweet Hartley! if thou livest, thou wilt not part with this book without sad necessity and a pang at heart. Oh, be never weary of reperusing the first four volumes of this collection, my eldest born! ... These sonnets thou, I trust, if God preserve thy life, Hartley! thou wilt read with a deep interest, having learnt to love the plays of Shakespeare, co-ordinate with Milton, and subordinate only to thy Bible. To thee, I trust, they will help to explain the mind of Shakespeare, and if thou wouldst understand these sonnets, thou must read the chapter in Potter's *Antiquities* on the Greek lovers – of whom were that Theban band of brothers over whom Philip, their victor, stood weeping; and surveying their dead bodies, each with his shield over the body of his friend, all dead in the place where they fought, solemnly cursed those whose base, fleshly, and most calumnious fancies had suspected their love of desires against nature. This pure love Shakespeare appears to have felt – to have been in no way ashamed of or even to have suspected that others could have suspected it. Yet at the same time he knew that so strong a love would have been made more completely a thing of permanence and reality, and have been blessed more by nature and taken under her more especial protection, if this object of his love had been at the same time a possible object of desire – for nature is not soul only. In this feeling he must have written the twentieth sonnet; but its possibility seems never to have entered even his imagination. It is noticeable that not even an allusion to that very worst of all possible vices (for it is wise to think of the disposition, as a *vice*, not of the absurd and despicable act, as a *crime*) not even any allusion to it [occurs] in all his numerous plays – whereas Jonson, Beaumont and Fletcher, and Massinger are full of them. O my son! I pray fervently that thou may'st know inwardly how impossible it was for a Shakespeare not to have been in his heart's heart chaste. I see no elaborate obscurity and very little quaintness – nor do I know any sonnets that will bear such frequent reperusal: so rich in metre, so full of thought and *exquisitest* diction. S. T. Coleridge, Greta Hall, Keswick, Wed. morning, half past three, Nov. 2, 1803.

(From Peter Jones (ed.) (1977) *Shakespeare: The Sonnets – A Casebook*, Basingstoke: Macmillan, pp.41–2)

Text 11

G.K. Hunter, 'The dramatic technique of Shakespeare's sonnets'

G.K. Hunter's essay (1953) advances the idea that the sonnets are best understood as the work of a practising dramatist.

Though most modern critics would accept the fact that Shakespeare's sonnet-sequence has a pervasive poetry with an excellence recognizably Shakespearean, the peculiar quality of this excellence remains undefined. This may be because criticism of the sonnets has been overshadowed by biographical speculation. There have been few aesthetic critics and these have confined themselves to *minutiae*, and have disregarded or noticed only with condemnation the reactions of their biographically-minded fellows. No one seems to have attempted to explain by what means Shakespeare presents traditional materials so that an overwhelmingly biographical reaction is set up in the reader. Neither the accepted categories of lyric or narrative nor the contemporary verse-fashions – Petrarchan, Anti-Petrarchan, Metaphysical, etc. – will account for this unique flavour in the sequence as a whole and for the concentratedly 'Shakespearean' effect of such sonnets as [15, 18, 30, 129]. It is not perhaps a coincidence that the critics who accept these categories tend to find Shakespeare's sonnet-technique in some way misdirected, from Keats with his 'full of fine things said unintentionally – in the intensity of working out conceits' to John Crowe Ransom, 'Shakespeare had no University discipline and developed poetically along lines of least resistance'.

I wish to suggest here that it is rather the approach to the Sonnets as lyric, narrative, or metaphysical exercises that is misdirected. Critics who ignore the biographical approach miss a valuable clue to the bias of Shakespeare's technique – bias which twists the normal Petrarchan line towards the characteristically Shakespearean flavour of

> When not to be receives reproach of being ...
> Oh that our nights of woe might have remembered ...
> Never believe that in my nature reigneth ...

I contend that when Shakespeare writes like this he is not misdirecting his talent, not being a quaint and elaborate lyrist, a failed and soured Petrarchan, a Metaphysical *manqué*, or a passionate autobiographical poet whose confessions are cut short by his conceits, so much as – what one would expect – a *dramatist*.

Let us consider in this light two sonnets which, without being masterpieces, seem to me to sound the authentic Shakespearean note:

> Say that thou didst forsake me for some fault,
> And I will comment upon that offence:
> Speak of my lameness, and I straight will halt,
> Against thy reasons making no defence.
> Thou canst not, love, disgrace me half so ill,
> To set a form upon desired change,
> As I'll myself disgrace; knowing thy will,
> I will acquaintance strangle and look strange;
> Be absent from thy walks; and in my tongue
> Thy sweet beloved name no more shall dwell,
> Lest I, too much profane, should do it wrong,
> And haply of our old acquaintance tell.
> > For thee, against myself I'll vow debate,
> > For I must ne'er love him whom thou dost hate.

[89]

> Was it the proud full sail of his great verse,
> Bound for the prize of all too precious you,
> That did my ripe thoughts in my brain inhearse,
> Making their tomb the womb wherein they grew?
> Was it his spirit, by spirits taught to write
> Above a mortal pitch, that struck me dead?

No, neither he, nor his compeers by night
Giving him aid, my verse astonished. [etc.]

[86]

The power of these poems does not reside in lyrical utterance; the vision they present is an individual's and to that extent like lyric, but in them the reader is not concerned with solitary imaginings presented as of universal significance (as in the Odes of Keats and Shelley), but with the relation of one human heart to others. By setting up a system of tensions between forces presented as persons Shakespeare's sonnets engage the reader's interest in a manner akin to the dramatic. Sonnet [89] is presented as a 'still' from a love-drama, a picture in which the gestures not only make up a present harmony, but hint (with subtle economy of means, which reveals the dramatist) at a psychological background, so that a powerful reaction is built up, as if to a history of love. In Sonnet [86] the number of characters involved is greater, but the technique is the same. An emotional state (estrangement) is expressed by means of a pattern of human figures; as a result of the hints of characterization we become involved as if with personalities, and so experience the dramatic impact. The reaction of the commentator who finds in the 'lameness' of [89] proof of a physical defect in the author is an indication of the force of this impact, and the number of 'keys' to the 'sonnet-story' would seem to show that it is fairly constant throughout the sequence.

At this point the reader might object that the dramatic vividness in Shakespeare's sonnets is only a heightened form of a commonplace Elizabethan quality and that the biographical reaction is not produced by technique so much as by natural curiosity about the greatest and most enigmatic of our poets. Comparisons with other Elizabethan poets show, however, that the Sonnets are not only supreme in dramatic effectiveness, but almost unique in the methods by which this effect is obtained. Many of the sonneteers in Sir Sidney Lee's collection are good dramatic 'plotters' i.e. they can organize a set scene so that the figures contrast effectively and carry well the emotional charge that the author has imparted to them. For example:

Oft with true sighs, oft with uncalled tears,
Now with slow words, now with dumb eloquence;
I Stella's eyes assailed, invade her ears:
But this, at last, is her sweet breathed defence.
 'That who indeed infelt affection bears,
So captivates to his saint both soul and sense;
That wholly hers, all selfish he forbears: [etc.]

(Sidney, *Astrophel and Stella*, [61])

But such scenes are set at a middle-distance from the reader; the effect that is almost unique in Shakespeare is that of immediate contact with the suffering mind. We learn what it felt like to be the lover in such-and-such a situation, and the figures are arranged to increase the poignant immediacy of our apprehension – so that if the beloved is young the lover is represented as old, if the lover is poor the beloved must be high-born, etc. The briliance of the language makes the context of these emotions so vivid that the reader naturally supplies from his imagination a complete dramatic situation.

Shakespeare's 'plots' differ from those of contemporary sonneteers in that we are seldom given visual descriptions of the persons involved. The difference does not involve him in a modern 'psychological' presentation: when the lover appears before the reader there is no self-dramatization in the sense that he is presented as a significant and interesting individual. When we hear of him

Beated and chopped with tanned antiquity   [62]

Desiring this man's art and that man's scope   [29]

As an unperfect actor on the stage   [23]

we are no nearer any conception of his personality. The dramatic power of conveying personal tensions is achieved by patterning the persons, not by analysing them.

Shakespeare uses the conventions of the sonnet *genre* in such a way that he conjures before us the tone and accent of the traditional personages. Thus like other sonnet-heroes Shakespeare's lover suffers from the tyranny of the beloved while welcoming this slavery as a blessed condition:

Being your slave, what should I do but tend
Upon the hours and times of your desire?
I have no precious time at all to spend,
Nor services to do, till you require.
Nor dare I chide the world-without-end hour
Whilst I, my sovereign, watch the clock for you, [etc.]

[57]

The verse is charged here with that heartfelt simplicity which gives the utterance of Shakespeare's greatest dramatic creations their full force. We fully share the feelings of this slave, seeing the objects described as coloured by his predominating emotion. Sidney, whose treatment of Petrarchan situations can often be compared with Shakespeare's in artistic worth, gives charm to a parallel description:

... now, like slave-born Muscovite,
I call it praise to suffer tyranny:
    And now employ the remnant of my wit
To make myself believe that all is well;
While with a feeling skill, I paint my hell.

[2]

But the effect here is different in kind from Shakespeare's; the intellect is more analytical, and the simile has the objective quality of a rational self-criticism, which Shakespeare's lacks. In Sidney there seems to be a greater distance between speaker and reader and consequently the reader tends to take a less implicated and so less biographical view of the situation.

The tradition in which the Sonnets are written did not always provide material entirely suitable for Shakespeare's dramatic technique; but even in his treatments of the more mechanically ingenious themes something of the same quality of imagination emerges. Sonnet [46] deals with the traditional theme of a war between the heart and eye; a more commonplace treatment of the same theme may be seen in Thomas Watson's *Tears of Fancy*:

My hart accus'd mine eies and was offended,
Vowing the cause was in mine eies aspiring:
Mine eies affirmd my hart might well amend it,

If he at first had banisht loues desiring.
Hart said that loue did enter at the eies,
And from the eies descended to the hart:
Eies said that in the hart did sparkes arise,
Which kindled flame that wrought the inward smart,
Hart said eies tears might soone haue quencht that fl[ame]
Eies said ... [etc.]

[20]

Compare Shakespeare:

Mine eye and heart are at a mortal war,
How to divide the conquest of thy sight;
Mine eye my heart thy picture's sight would bar,
My heart mine eye the freedom of that right.
My heart doth plead that thou in him dost lie,
A closet never pierced with crystal eyes,
But the defendant doth that plea deny,
And says in him thy fair appearance lies.
To 'cide this title is impanneled
A quest of thoughts, all tenants to the heart;
And by their verdict is determined
The clear eye's moiety and the dear heart's part:
  As thus; mine eye's due is thine outward part,
  And my heart's right thine inward love of heart.

[46]

Shakespeare's poem is not simply a better example of a conceited sonnet, it is a more affecting poem, and this is because he makes the conceit serve a felt human situation. Watson concentrates on the antithetical litigants to such an extent that he loses sight of the human 'I' and 'thou'. Shakespeare, in spite of the frigidity of many of the images ('conquest', 'picture', 'closet'), manages to animate the legal imagery with a sense of the lover's craving. He never forgets that the poem is a lover's confession, and accordingly it is directed throughout towards the figure of the beloved.

The same pressure of desire in the speaking voice shapes Shakespeare's treatment of another stock theme – the vision of the beloved in a dream – in such a way that the conceits employed are subordinated to the expression of personal emotion:

When most I wink, then do mine eyes best see,
For all the day they view things unrespected;
But when I sleep, in dreams they look on thee,
And, darkly bright, are bright in dark directed.
Then thou, whose shadow shadows doth make bright,
How would thy shadow's form form happy show
To the clear day with thy much clearer light,
When to unseeing eyes thy shade shines so! [etc.]

[43]

Here 'darkly bright, are bright in dark directed' is not merely a piece of wordplay but also a triumphant dance of words expressing the lover's delight. The emphatic 'thee' in line three and 'thou' in line five impress on us the fact that the poem, for all its conceits, is a love poem directed towards a beloved object. The contrasts between the radiance of the dream and the drabness of reality, the brightness of the beloved and the brightness of the sun, remain expressive of an emotional situation. Shakespeare does not pursue the paradox into areas where it is liberated from this dramatic use and acquires the 'metaphysical' interest of seeming to comment on the nature of experience in general. This is the effect of Sidney's treatment of the same theme:

> I start! look! hark! but what in closed up sense
> Was held, in open sense it flies away;
> Leaving me nought but wailing eloquence.
> I, seeing better sights in sight's decay;
> Called it anew, and wooed sleep again:
> But him her host, that unkind guest had slain.

> [38]

Here the subsidiary antitheses between closed sleep and open sight, between sight and eloquence, between sleep and Stella as host and guest seem concerned to pursue the mystery in the experience rather than to convey the emotional tension involved. The last line has a degree of detachment common in Sidney but rare in Shakespeare. Other treatments of this theme further sharpen our sense of Shakespeare's individual bias. Linche's version (*Diella*, [24]) and Griffin's (*Fidessa*, [14]) are dramatically 'plotted', but raise no emotion. These poets are content to bombast out their fourteen lines with vapid repetitions, whereas Shakespeare's words are for ever creating in the mind of the reader *new* relationships.

At the same time he avoids the enlargement of intellectual interest, the refinement of perception, which accompanies the elaboration of similar material in the poems of Donne. Some critics have claimed that 'the ... sonnets as a performance represent Shakespeare seeking such effects as John Donne ... was achieving'. I think this is an error. Donne's poem 'The Dreame' (though not Petrarchan and not a sonnet) obviously springs from the convention we have discussed above. Here however we find not the stock contrast between the cruelty of the real lady and the kindness of the phantom, but a more philosophical distinction: the phantom is banished by the coming of the real mistress, but her going again makes the lover question the nature of that reality (in a way not found in any of the previous treatments). The subsidiary antitheses reason/phantasy, fable/history, etc., show us that Donne is not concerned to build up a poignant image of a loving mind; the figure of the beloved in Donne is not the goal of the whole poem, but rather a symbol for the deeper mystery of the things that lovers experience:

> Coming and staying show'd thee, thee,
> But rising makes me doubt, that now,
>   Thou art not thou.

It is the whole problem of identity that is raised by lines like these.

The bias of Shakespeare's style is no less evident in his handling of details of technique than in the general effect of his treatment of stock themes. He uses the rhetorical tricks which were the common property of the sonneteers but in a way which is mainly expressive of an individual's emotion. For example, the paradoxes in the Sonnets are used less to present the piquantly paradoxical quality of the objective Petrarchan situation and more to communicate a paradoxical quality in the lover's emotion. Of course, lines like 'Still losing when I saw myself to win' [119] can easily be paralleled from other sonneteers – e.g. Drayton's 'Where most I lost, there most of all I wan' (*Idea*, 62). But where Drayton and others tend to use such paradoxes to pattern a situation, Shakespeare's are usually expressive – we feel what it is to endure such situations:

> Thou blind fool, Love, what dost thou to mine eyes,
> That they behold, and see not what they see?
> They know what beauty is, see where it lies,
> Yet what the best is take the worst to be.

> [137]

> My love is as a fever, longing still
> For that which longer nurseth the disease;
> Feeding on that which doth preserve the ill,
> The uncertain sickly appetite to please.

> [147]

> O, from what power hast thou this powerful might
> With insufficiency my heart to sway?
> To make me give the lie to my true sight,
> And swear that brightness doth not grace the day?

> [150]

In such cases it is not the situation that is paradoxical; it is the condition of the lover's being.

Again, this does not mean that the figure has become 'Metaphysical' in Shakespeare, i.e. that it has become a speculative comment on the human condition. When Donne says

> I must confesse, it could not chuse but bee
> Prophane, to think thee any thing but thee.

> (*The Dreame*)

or

> Since thou and I sigh one anothers breath,
> Who e'r sighes most, is cruellest, and hastes the others death.

> (*A Valediction: of Weeping*)

he uses paradoxical playfulness to indicate a state of loving but detached emotion; any difficulty in understanding the meaning seems to mirror the intellectual effort of the poet to bring into focus (and almost within comprehension) a truly human but hitherto undescribed situation. Donne's analysis of the state of loving enlarges our appreciation of human richness by its bizarre re-association of elements plucked out of their normal contexts; here, we feel, is a mind thinking its way through an emotional situation; Shakespeare's world is still recognizably a world of 'normal contexts'; the vision is unhackneyed only because he records the intense immediacy of individuals caught in the stock situation:

> Only my plague this far I count my gain,
> That she that makes me sin awards me pain.

> [141]

Here, as in the dramas, the individual voice transcends and transforms the convention Shakespeare accepted.

In simile, as in paradox, Shakespeare's bias is towards expressiveness. In most of the Sonnets in Sir Sidney Lee's collection the simile is a device either to describe the physical charms of the beloved or to indicate general conditions in the Petrarchan situation:

> Like as a ship, that through the ocean wide,
> By conduct of some star, doth make her way ...
> So I, whose star, that wont with her bright ray
> Me to direct, with clouds is over-cast,
> Do wander now, in darkness and dismay ...

> (Spenser, [34])

> As in some countries, far remote from hence,
> The wretched creature destined to die;
> Having the judgment due to his offence
> By Surgeons begged, their Art on him to try ...
> Even so my Mistress works upon my ill ...

> (Drayton, 50)

These (and the many like them) give clarity and force to the poems they adorn, but do not impart that sense of immediate emotional contact which a majority of Shakespeare's similes, drawn from the familiar experience of similar humanity, do give:

> Lo, as a careful housewife runs to catch
> One of her feather'd creatures broke away,
> Sets down her babe, and makes all swift dispatch ...
> So runn'st thou after that which flies from thee,
> Whilst I thy babe chase thee afar behind ...

> [143]

> So am I as the rich, whose blessed key
> Can bring him to his sweet up-locked treasure ...

> [52]

In [143] the emotional relationships are defined and made immediate by the simile; in [52] it is the human emotion implicit in the comparison which makes the chief effect.

Treatments of the same theme – absence – in poems of merit which use simile as the main feature of their construction may be compared, to show in an extended fashion Shakespeare's individual use of this figure.

> How like a winter hath my absence been
> From thee, the pleasure of the fleeting year!
> What freezings have I felt, what dark days seen!
> What old December's bareness every where!
> And yet this time removed was summer's time;
> The teeming autumn, big with rich increase,

Bearing the wanton burthen of the prime,
Like widowed wombs after their lords' decease:
Yet this abundant issue seem'd to me
But hope of orphans and unfather'd fruit;
For summer and his pleasures wait on thee,
And, thou away, the very birds are mute;
   Or, if they sing, 'tis with so dull a cheer
   That leaves look pale, dreading the winter's near.

[97]

Like as the Culver, on the bared bough,
Sits mourning for the absence of her mate;
And, in her songs, sends many a wishful vow
For his return that seems to linger late:
So I alone, now left disconsolate,
Mourn to myself the absence of my love;
And, wandering here and there all desolate,
Seek with my plaints to match that mournful dove.
No joy of aught that under heaven doth hove
Can comfort me, but her own joyous sight:
Whose sweet aspect both God and man can move,
In her unspotted pleasance to delight.
   Dark is my day, while her fair light I miss,
   And dead my life that wants such lively bliss.

(Spenser, [88])

Spenser's simile is a graceful one and conveys the gentle melancholy of the poem, but it does not make the lover's feelings vivid by conveying them in images universally charged with these emotions. Shakespeare's 'December's bareness' and 'dark days' are stripped back to their bare function as objective correlative of the emotion between lover and beloved; they do not intrude at all between the reader and this emotion. Spenser's culver on the other hand is intruded deliberately as a symbol to indicate the mood of the poem (rather than the mood of the persons in the poem). Accordingly, Spenser's image has the charm of an idyll; Shakespeare's generates in the reader a reaction more proper to drama.

Further details of Shakespeare's subject-matter and style could be analysed, but enough has no doubt been said to show how far from the fashions of which they were born Shakespeare's sonnets are taken by his dramatically expressive way of writing. The subject-matter and the rhetoric may be that of the Petrarchan tradition, the effect may sometimes seem Metaphysical, but the uniquely Shakespearean quality of the sequence is not to be explained by either of these labels. We have here what we might expect: a dramatist describes a series of emotional situations between persons (real or fictitious) in a series of separate short poems; the Petrarchan instruments turn in his hands into a means of expressing and concentrating the great human emotions, desire, jealousy, fear, hope and despair, and of raising in the reader the dramatic reactions of pity and terror by his implication in the lives and fates of the persons depicted.

(From Peter Jones (ed.) (1977) *Shakespeare: The Sonnets – A Casebook*, Basingstoke: Macmillan, pp.120–32)

Text 12

Heather Dubrow, 'The sonnets' from Captive Victors: Shakespeare's Narrative Poems and Sonnets

Heather Dubrow counters G.K. Hunter's argument by comparing some of Shakespeare's sonnets with poems by Sidney, Drayton and Petrarch to suggest the noticeably undramatic quality of Shakespeare's poems.

We assume that the nondramatic poetry of a great playwright will in fact be dramatic in many senses of that complex term. And we assume that when a writer who among his manifold gifts is a skilled storyteller chooses to write sonnets, at least some of them will be narrative. Though *Venus and Adonis* and *The Rape of Lucrece* challenge the conventional wisdom about their author in many other ways, they do implicitly support such presuppositions about his sonnets: because he renders the epyllion tradition so dramatic and reinterprets Senecan conventions as a way of characterizing Lucrece, we anticipate a similar approach to the mode of the sonnets. Such expectations help to explain why, despite all the other controversies about these lyrics, certain concepts are so repeatedly and so uncritically brought to bear on interpretations of them. We are regularly informed, for example, that they are "dramas" or "stories", a view reflected in the frequency with which critics of the sonnets include the word "dramatic" in the titles of their studies and then proceed to comment on the "plots" and the "characters" that they find in the sequence. But in literary criticism, as in so many other human activities, we are prone to see what we expect to see, and nothing else. While Shakespeare's sonnets evidently do include certain dramatic and narrative elements, in focusing on that aspect of them we have overlooked a more revealing and more surprising fact: several of the characteristics central to other dramatic and narrative poetry, including other Renaissance sonnet sequences, are signally absent from Shakespeare's contributions to the genre. And, more to our purposes here, it is through that very absence that these poems reveal many of the subtleties of their speaker's temperament.

A comparison of Shakespeare's Sonnet 87 with two other works that also concern a leavetaking demonstrates the mode of his sonnets. The famous lines of Drayton's *Idea* 61 remind us how a poem in what is essentially a lyric mode can in fact become dramatic:

> Since ther's no helpe, Come let us kisse and part.
> Nay, I have done: you get no more of Me,
> And I am glad, yea glad with all my heart,
> That thus so cleanly, I my Selfe can free.
> Shake hands for ever, Cancell all our Vowes,
> And when We meet at any time againe,
> Be it not seene in either of our Browes,
> That We one jot of former Love reteyne;
> Now at the last gaspe, of Loves latest Breath,
> When his Pulse fayling, Passion speechlesse lies,
> When Faith is kneeling by his bed of Death,
> And Innocence is closing up his Eyes.
> Now if thou would'st, when all have given him over,
> From Death to Life, thou might'st him yet recover.

Rather than describing the episode in which the lovers part, Drayton enacts it. We are asked to believe (and thanks to his skill the illusion is persuasive) that we are actually witnessing the speaker bidding farewell to his lady. We are as conscious of her implicit but powerful presence as that speaker is himself. And we are conscious, too, that what the poem claims to enact is a specified and unique moment in time. To be sure, Drayton briefly uses allegory to distance us from that moment – but his main reason for establishing such a distance is to create a foil against which his final appeal to the woman will seem all the more immediate.

Though Petrarch's *Canzonière* 190 is primarily concerned with rendering certain states of mind – the poet's joy at the beauty of Laura and his intense sorrow at her loss – he evokes those states by telling a story:

> Una candida cerva sopra l'erba
> verde m'apparve con duo corna d'oro,
> fra due riviere all'ombra d'un alloro,
> levando 'l sole, a la stagione acerba.
>
> Era sua vista sì dolce superba
> ch'i'lasciai per seguirla ogni lavoro,
> come l'avaro che 'n cercar tesoro
> con diletto l'affanno disacerba.
>
> "Nessun me tocchi," al bel collo d'intorno
> scritto avea di diamanti e di topazi.
> "Libera farmi al mio Cesare parve."
>
> Et era'l sol già vòlto al mezzo giorno,
> gli occhi miei stanchi di mirar, non sazi,
> quand'io caddi ne l'acqua et ella sparve.

> A white doe on the green grass appeared to me, with two golden horns, between two rivers, in the shade of a laurel, when the sun was rising in the unripe season.

> Her look was so sweet and proud that to follow her I left every task, like the miser who as he seeks treasure sweetens his trouble with delight.

> "Let no one touch me," she bore written with diamonds and topazes around her lovely neck. "It has pleased my Caesar to make me free."

> And the sun had already turned at midday; my eyes were tired by looking but not sated, when I fell into the water, and she disappeared.

Petrarch's poem may be visionary and mystical, but like other narratives it is firmly anchored in time. It has a clear beginning, middle, and end: at the opening of the poem the speaker sees the deer, then he admires her, and then he loses her.

Shakespeare interprets a leavetaking very differently in Sonnet 87:

> Farewell, thou art too dear for my possessing,
> And like enough thou know'st thy estimate.
> The charter of thy worth gives thee releasing;
> My bonds in thee are all determinate.
> For how do I hold thee but by thy granting,
> And for that riches where is my deserving?
> The cause of this fair gift in me is wanting,

And so my patent back again is swerving.
Thyself thou gav'st, thy own worth then not knowing,
Or me, to whom thou gav'st, else mistaking;
So thy great gift, upon misprision growing,
Comes home again, on better judgment making.
    Thus have I had thee as a dream doth flatter,
    In sleep a king, but waking no such matter.

The opening word, "Farewell" (1), suggests that this sonnet is going to enact a parting in much the same way that Drayton's does; and the third quatrain does in a sense tell a story. Yet Shakespeare's poem is not necessarily a rendition of a particular event that takes place at a particular moment: one cannot tell whether the parting is in the process of happening or has already occurred. His primary concern is not to imitate an incident in which a lover says farewell but rather to evoke the lover's reflections on the process of parting. And Shakespeare's sonnet differs from Drayton's in another and no less significant way: while most of the assertions in Drayton's sonnet are addressed to the beloved, most of those in Shakespeare's are not. In the couplet, for example, Shakespeare's speaker seems to be brooding on his experiences rather than either enacting them or announcing their significance to the person he has loved.

The characteristics of that couplet and of the sonnet in which it figures recur throughout Shakespeare's sonnet sequence. The narrative, dramatic, and lyrical modes are not, of course, necessarily exclusive of each other, either in general or in Shakespeare's sonnets in particular. In his sequence as a whole, and not infrequently within a single sonnet, we do encounter instances of all three modes. Sonnets 153 and 154, for example, are certainly narrative according to virtually any definition of that term; and, as I have already indicated, the entire sequence is indubitably dramatic in the important sense that it bodies forth the speaker himself. Nonetheless, it is not the presence of some narrative and dramatic elements but rather the absence of others that is most striking when we read Shakespeare's sequence and most telling when we compare it with the sonnets composed by other Renaissance poets. And that absence reflects central patterns in his speaker's temperament.

One of the clearest indications that the majority of Shakespeare's sonnets are in certain senses neither narrative nor dramatic is that they do not include a temporal sequence of events, as does, for example, Petrarch's "Una candida cerva sopra l'erba." As we read Shakespeare's sonnets, we witness tortuous shifts in the speaker's emotions and judgments, but very seldom do we encounter a chronological progression of occurrences. Instead, his monologues take place in the kind of eternal present that is usually a mark of lyric poetry. Characteristically, they generalize about an event that recurs frequently rather than focusing on one instance of it: "When I consider everything that grows" (15.1); "When to the sessions of sweet silent thought / I summon up rememberance of things past" (30.1–2). Even a poem like Sonnet 48, which at first appears to be launching a chronological story ("How careful was I, when I took my way, / Each trifle under truest bars to thrust" [1–2]), soon switches to the sort of atemporal generalizations that are in fact more typical of the sequence ("Thee have I not locked up in any chest" [9]).

In another sense, too, the sonnet sequence that so vividly evokes the horrors of time is not itself rooted in time: Shakespeare's poems seldom refer to datable real incidents or even to incidents that occur at a specific, though symbolic, moment. Petrarch alludes to the date of his meeting with the real woman who was transformed into Laura and the date of her death, and his sequence may also have complex symbolic relationships to the calendar. Spenser's sonnets are apparently keyed to the seasons. One of Daniel's refers to a trip to Italy. But in Shakespeare we find very few such references. To be sure, in one poem the speaker does suggest that he met his beloved three years before; but nowhere else does he allude to time in so specific a way. And Shakespeare is no more specific about place. We know that Sidney's Stella takes a ride on the Thames, while Shakespeare's sonnets never mention a particular locale.

The omission of such allusions to place and time is all the more suggestive in the light of Shakespeare's repeated – one is almost tempted to say frenetic – puns on "will." Like Sidney's play on "rich" or his adoption of the pseudonym "Astrophil," these puns are evidently intended to remind us that the poems in question are linked to autobiographical experience. One would presume that the same attitudes that lead a poet to pun on, and hence draw attention to, his own name might well encourage him to refer to specific dates and places. But this Shakespeare chooses not to do.

The lack of a temporal perspective in most of his sonnets reflects the absence of anecdotal sonnets. With only a handful of exceptions, Shakespeare's sequence omits not only the mythological stories that so frequently grace the sequences of other sonnet writers but also nonmythological allegories such as Spenser's *Amoretti* 75 ("One day I wrote her name vpon the strand, / But came the waues and washed it away" [1–2]). Moreover, Shakespeare seldom chooses to narrate an incident that happens to the lovers. Compare, for example, his ninety-first sonnet with *Astrophil and Stella* 41:

91

Some glory in their birth, some in their skill,
Some in their wealth, some in their body's force,
Some in their garments, though new-fangled ill,
Some in their hawks and hounds, some in their horse;
And every humor hath his adjunct pleasure,
Wherein it finds a joy above the rest.
But these particulars are not my measure;
All these I better in one general best.
Thy love is better than high birth to me,
Richer than wealth, prouder than garment's cost,
Of more delight than hawks or horses be;
And having thee, of all men's pride I boast;
    Wretched in this alone, that thou mayst take
    All this away, and me most wretched make.

41

HAVING this day my horse, my hand, my launce
    Guided so well, that I obtain'd the prize,
    Both by the judgement of the English eyes,
And of some sent from that sweet enemie *Fraunce*;

Horsemen my skill in horsemanship advaunce;
   Towne-folkes my strength; a daintier judge applies
   His praise to sleight, which from good use doth rise;
Some luckie wits impute it but to chaunce;
   Others, because of both sides I do take
My bloud from them, who did excell in this,
Thinke Nature me a man of armes did make.
How farre they shoote awrie! the true cause is,
   Stella lookt on, and from her heavenly face
   Sent forth the beames, which made so faire my race.

While both poems play the values of the court against those of love, Sidney does so by telling a story. (It is significant, too, that Shakespeare's speaker is more alienated from that court than Astrophil is; his psychological distance from it parallels the distancing effected by Shakespeare's mode.) Or, to put it another way, it is as uncharacteristic of Shakespeare to begin a sonnet with "One day" as it is characteristic of many other sonneteers to do so.

A sonnet that does not narrate an anecdote may, of course, be anchored in a specific event or situation nonetheless: it can be the outgrowth of an occurrence which, though not recounted systematically, is mentioned frequently and specifically in the course of the poem. Most readers have assumed that the vast majority of Shakespeare's sonnets are "situational" in this sense. But in point of fact comparatively few of them are. In some of Shakespeare's monologues the reflections are inspired not by a particular situation but by a general problem: thus in Sonnet 94 the speaker evokes a certain kind of personality, and Sonnet 129 is an anguished consideration of the nature of lust. Because poems like these rely so heavily on generalizations, critics regularly describe them as interesting exceptions to Shakespeare's approach elsewhere in the sequence. They are, however, merely extreme instances of their author's tendency to detach the speaker's emotions and speculations from an immediate situation.

Similarly, some poems in the sequence suggest that a specific incident lies behind the speaker's reactions but omit any discussion of details. We learn little about the "forsaking" to which Sonnet 89 alludes, for example, or about the reasons for the parting described in the absence sonnets. As we read Sonnet 35 we do not know what the "sensual fault" (9) to which it refers may be or even whether "fault" indicates a particular lapse or a general character trait. While Sonnet 122 is indubitably based on an episode, the gift of a notebook, it specifies no further information about that event; instead the poem turns at once to broader observations about the relationship between giver and receiver, such as "Nor need I tallies thy dear love to score" (10). In contrast, when Sidney describes Stella's journey on the Thames in *Astrophil and Stella* 103, he devotes the poem to details about the episode itself, such as the behaviour of the winds and her own blushes.

In other words, if we try to enumerate the situations on which Shakespeare's sonnets are based, we find that our list is short and the events on it vague. The poet encourages the Friend to marry; there is a period of separation, and there are one or more quarrels; they exchange one or more notebooks; the Friend betrays the speaker with the Dark Lady. In *Astrophil and Stella*, in contrast, a sequence about two-thirds the length of Shakespeare's, the situations include a stolen kiss, Stella's illness, that ride on the Thames, an absence, a quarrel, Astrophil's triumph in a tournament, and many more. As these lists would suggest, the image of a footprint, so potent and so revealing a metaphor in the *Canzonière*, might also serve as an emblem for Shakespeare's approach to the genre: he bases his sonnets on mere traces of events.

If most of Shakespeare's sonnets do not tell stories, neither do they enact dramas in the way that Drayton's *Idea* 61 does. One Shakespearean has observed, "By setting up a system of tensions between forces presented as persons, Shakespeare's sonnets engage the reader's interest in a manner akin to the dramatic," and it is true that some of these works, notably the poems addressed to Time, do operate this way. But most do not: Shakespeare's sonnets embody the tensions of conflicting forces, but those forces are more often internalized within the speaker than dramatized as characters.

Though the Friend and the Dark Lady dominate the speaker's thoughts, in some important respects they do not function as active participants within the sonnets. The problems engendered by their behavior are frighteningly immediate, but the characters themselves are not. Except for the fact that the young man is attractive and the lady is dark, we do not know how they look. Unlike the main characters in most sonnet sequences, they are never assigned names, even fictional ones, even in those poems that refer to them in the third person rather than in the second. The epithets by which they are addressed serve, if anything, to distance us further from them. When, for example, Shakespeare opens Sonnet 56 on the command, "Sweet love, renew your force" (1), he establishes an unresolved ambiguity about whether the poem concerns his beloved or the abstract quality of love or both. When he directs an apostrophe to "Lascivious Grace" (40.13), he initially seems as much to be brooding on the abstraction that the epithet expresses as to be talking to the person who has been reduced (or who has willingly reduced himself) to the state expressed by that oxymoron. Similarly, only once (34.13) in the 154 sonnets does Shakespeare allude to the movements or gestures of the beloved in a way that suggests that he is physically present and actually listening to the speaker. Contrast *Astrophil and Stella* 31, which so unequivocally sets up the fiction that Astrophil is in the presence of the moon, or *Astrophil and Stella* 47, whose "Soft, but here she comes" (13) so effectively signals Stella's arrival.

It is a truth as significant as it is neglected that the Friend and the Dark Lady are not quoted directly within the poems. Despite all his experience in writing plays, Shakespeare chooses not to create the kind of dialogue on which such sonnets as *Astrophil and Stella* 54 or *Idea* 24 or even *Amoretti* 75 are based. On those rare occasions when the words of the beloved are recorded, they are presented in a form that distances us from the statements and their speakers: the poet either uses indirect discourse to report what the beloved has said ("When my love swears that she is made of truth" [138.1]) or predicts what he or she is likely to say rather than what has actually been said ("O then vouchsafe me but this loving thought: / Had my friend's muse grown with this growing age" [32.9–10]).

Similarly, Cupid makes only the briefest of appearances in the sonnets, and when he is present, Shakespeare, unlike most of his contemporaries, does not attempt to render him as a dramatic character. Whereas *Astrophil and Stella* 8, for instance, describes the behavior of the god of love at some length, Shakespeare's Sonnet 137 turns immediately from its brief apostrophe to him ("Thou blind fool love" [1]) to a direct, unallegorical anatomy of the speaker's feelings. It is revealing, moreover, that the kinds of human characters who populate other sequences and create miniature dramas by arguing with the speaker are totally absent from Shakespeare's poems.

The ladies who are Laura's companions, the cynical friend who berates Drayton, the court nymphs who criticize Astrophil – no figures like these appear in Shakespeare's sonnets.

Nor is Shakespeare prone to replace them with internalized characters. Though the morality tradition influences his sequence in other ways, only rarely does he depict the conflicts within his speaker as allegorical personages engaged in a confrontation. Many of his sonnets concern a debate between opposing forces such as reason and passion; but very few evoke that debate through allegorical characters like those that figure so prominently in *Astrophil and Stella.*

Most of Shakespeare's sonnets are not narrative, then, in the sense that the speaker is not recounting a story to the reader or to any other implied audience. And they are not dramatic in the sense that we are not witnessing a confrontation that occurs at a specific place and time between a speaker and a particular listener or even between two clearly distinguished personages within the speaker. Instead, the lyric mode predominates. Some of the poems resemble an internalized meditation, others a letter, others a monologue that the beloved hears but apparently does not respond to. The soliloquy immediately presents itself as a parallel to and an inspiration for Shakespeare's unusual approach to the sonnet, and in certain respects the comparison is illuminating. The speaker in Shakespeare's sonnets often seems to be thinking aloud, to be at once speaking audibly and meditating. But, as the passages that I have cited suggest, in one crucial way the sonnets differ from the soliloquies that are so frequently embedded in their author's plays: the soliloquy normally takes place at a unique moment and is often provoked by a clearly defined event that has preceded it, whereas most of the sonnets are signally lacking in those types of particularization.

(From Heather Dubrow (1987) *Captive Victors: Shakespeare's Narrative Poems and Sonnets*, Ithaca: Cornell University Press, pp.171–82)

Text 13

Bruce Smith, 'The secret sharer' from Homosexual Desire in Shakespeare's England: A Cultural Poetics

Bruce Smith's work represents the growing critical interest in the representation of homosexual desire in early modern literature.

Shakespeare's early sonnets are an attempt to impose his vision simultaneously on time and on the friend.

Then comes sonnet 20:

> A Woman's face with natures own hand painted,
> Haste thou the Master Mistris of my passion,
> A womans gentle hart but not acquainted
> With shifting change as is false womens fashion,
> An eye more bright than theirs, lesse false in rowling:
> Gilding the object where-upon it gazeth,
> A man in hew all *Hews* in his controwling,
> Which steales mens eyes and womens soules amaseth.
> And for a woman were thou first created,

Till nature as she wrought thee fell a dotinge,
And by addition me of thee defeated,
By adding one thing to my purpose nothing.
   But since she prickt thee out for womens pleasure,
   Mine be thy love and thy loves use their treasure.

With this poem four things change dramatically: the ends to which the poet speaks, the language that he uses, the imaginative setting in which he situates himself, and the self-identity he assumes.

Quite suddenly, hortatory verse starts sounding like amatory verse. A reader who is out for secrets is forced to reconsider what he or she has read already. As Pequigney argues, we can see in the first twenty sonnets a progression in which the poet's sexual feelings for the friend, held carefully in check at first, gradually emerge as the poet's real subject. Homosocial desire changes by degrees into homosexual desire. The word "love" first enters the sonnets very obliquely indeed when the poet appeals to the friend's "selfe love" as a motive for begetting progeny (3.8). In sonnet 5 love is still a property of the friend, though more ambiguously so, when the poet remarks "the lovely gaze where every eye doth dwell" (5.2). The personal significance of that word for the poet becomes increasingly clear – and increasingly physical – as he begs the friend to have a child, to create another self "for love of me" (10.13), as he ventures to call him "love" (13.1) and "deare my love" (13.11), as he goes to war with time "for love of you" (15.13), as he defies time to carve wrinkles in "my loves faire brow" (19.9), as he boasts "My love shall in my verse ever live young" (19.14). Is "my love" in this line a name for the friend, or does it refer to the poet's feelings?

"Love" and "my love" emerge after sonnet 13 as the poet's favorite epithets for the young man. Speaking to him and speaking about him, the poet refers to the young man by that title more than twenty times. Only seven times does the poet refer to him as his "friend." "Love," "lover," and "lovely," as Booth points out, were ambiguous if not ambivalent in sixteenth- and seventeenth-century usage. They might or might not suggest sexual desire, depending on the context. The context in Shakespeare's sonnets is, to say the least, equivocal. "Love," on equal terms with "mistress," is likewise how the poet speaks to and about the woman who is the subject of the 27 sonnets printed toward the end in Thorpe's edition. Only once does he call her his "friend." We have, then, two people – and three terms for talking about them. At one extreme is "mistress," with its explicitly sexual reference. At the other extreme is "friend," with its largely nonsexual reference. In between is "love," which can be sexual, or nonsexual, or both. "Two loves I have," declares the poet in sonnet 144,

of comfort and dispaire,
Which like two spirits do sugiest me still,
The better angell is a man right faire:
The worser spirit a woman collour'd il.

(144.1–4)

We do no more than respect an ambiguity in early modern English if we follow Shakespeare's example and refer to the young man, not as the poet's "friend," but as his "love."

Questions about love reach a crisis – for the poet, for his readers, and presumably for the young man – in sonnet 20. The issue here is easy enough to state but not so easy to decide: is sonnet 20 a *denial* of sexual desire, or is it an *avowal*? The *literal sense* of what the poet says certainly indicates denial. "Love" versus "love's use": the terms the poet/speaker uses to draw his distinctions derive from Aristotle's *Nicomachean Ethics*. *Philia*, the highest of human bonds, is premised on the *equality* of men as one another's peer; *eros*, a lesser bond, thrives on *inequality*, on needs that each partner fulfils for the other. All of the preceding sonnets, we see in retrospect, have been arguments in an implicit debate. In effect, Shakespeare has been addressing the great question in classical ethics that is posed so often in Shakespeare's comedies about courtship: which has the greater claim on a man, friendship with other men or sexual ties with women? The procreational images of the first nineteen sonnets would seem to place the poet/speaker of the first nineteen sonnets squarely with Daphnaeus, the spokesman in Plutarch's dialogue "Of Love" who urges Bacchon to marry. When Daphnaeus says of marriage that there is "no knot or link in the world more sacred and holy," Protogenes, the critic of women and praiser of pederasty, counters with the "higher" values of male friendship:

> This bond in trueth of wedlocke ... as it is necessry for generation is by
> good right praised by Politicians and law-givers, who recommend the
> same highly unto the people and common multitude: but to speake of
> true love indeed, there is no jot or part thereof in the societie and
> felowship of women ... For amitie is an honest, civill and laudable thing:
> but fleshly pleasure, base, vile, and illiberal.

Here is just the distinction between "love" and "love's use" that Shakespeare draws in sonnet 20. In Plutarch's dialogue, Bacchon's marriage transpires during the very time the debaters are having their argument, making their conclusion – or rather their lack of one – a moot point.

In sonnet 20 the issue is likewise left unresolved. *What* Shakespeare's speaker says is above reproach; *how* he says it has left many readers since George Steevens uneasy, whatever Edmund Malone may have said to reassure them. There is something playfully salacious about those puns on "thing" and "prick" that distinctly recalls Richard Barnfield's poems. Indeed, the whole conceit of sonnet 20, casting a male in the role most sonnets would assign to a female, recalls Barnfield's sonnet 11 ("Sighing, and sadly sitting by my Love, / He ask't the cause of my hearts sorrowing"). In Shakespeare's sonnet 20, as so often in Barnfield, sexual innuendo seems to be working at cross purposes to moral innocence. To lament that the friend has "one thing to my purpose no-thing" might seem to imply that friendship and sexual passion, "love" and "love's use," are two separate things. The tone, however, makes one wonder just what the persona's "purpose" is. Does he find other parts of the beloved's anatomy more commodious? If Shakespeare is citing Plutarch, he calls him to witness on both sides of the case.

Shakespeare's speaker may side with Plutarch's Daphnaeus on the issue of "love" versus "love's use," but he echoes Protogenes, Plutarch's homosexual apologist, when it comes to which kind of beauty is superior, male or female. The diptych that sonnet 20 forms with sonnet 21 is hinged on a contrast between the young man's fresh face "with natures own hand painted" (20.1) and the "painted beauty" (21.2) that inspires the muses of most other poets. The implied contrast *within* both poems is between male and female, as it may be also *between* them. Male beauty is superior to female, according to Plutarch's Protogenes, for just the reasons Shakespeare's speaker cites: "it is not besmered with sweet ointments, nor tricked up and trimmed, but plaine and simply alwaies a man shall see it, without any intising allurements" (fol. 1133). Whatever suspicions a reader may have about the sonnet's tone are encouraged by the capitalizations and italics in Thorpe's edition. "Woman," "Master Mistris," and *"Hews"* are all tricked out as possible code words, as possible keys to a closely guarded secret that has been hinted at since "beauties *Rose*" in sonnet 1. [...] In its social, narrative, and rhetorical contexts, sonnet 20 comes across as an extremely sophisticated version of "Come live with me and be my love."

There is a sense, then, in which the early sonnets are gestures of power not just toward time and toward the friend but toward the poet's own self: they are attempts to convince not only the friend but the persona himself that the cosmic heterosexuality exemplified in Spenser's Epithalamion has highest claims on erotic desire. They argue Elizabethan orthodoxy. For the friend, the early sonnets are poems of persuasion; for the persona, they are poems of renunciation. The whole scenario here seems uncannily similar to Barnfield's eclogues. We encounter the same pair of characters, the same implied setting, the same double sense of time, the same tension between conventional and unconventional sexualities. Like Barnfield's Daphnis toward the end of the eclogues, Shakespeare's persona in the first nineteen sonnets speaks as an older man to a younger, as experience to innocence, as disciplined desire to overpowering beauty. Both speakers counsel marriage. Implicit, perhaps, in Shakespeare's luxuriant images of flowers and trees is the pastoral landscape in which Barnfield plays out his erotic fantasies to their ultimately chaste end. There is the same sharply divided attitude toward time: both poets celebrate the pleasures of morning, of spring, of "this thy golden time," but both are just as keenly conscious of time's destructive power. Finally, both sets of poems turn on the same conflict between male–male attachments and heterosexual passion. That is to say, Shakespeare's early sonnets, like Barnfield's eclogues and sonnets, enact the rites of wooing that make up the Myth of the Passionate Shepherd.

Sonnet 20 may be a poem of courtship, but Shakespeare does not stop there. Like Horace, but unlike most Renaissance poets who write about love, Shakespeare goes on to write about what happens when emotional desire becomes physical act. John Donne's love poems, infamous as they may be in this regard, are all about the before ("Come, Madame, come, ... / Off with that girdle") and the after ("Busie old foole, / unruly Sunne, / Why dost thou thus, / Through windowes, and through curtaines call on us?"). They *imply* the physical and emotional realities of lovemaking, but they do not talk about them directly. Those emotional and physical realities are Shakespeare's very subject in the poems that succeed sonnet 20. Quite in keeping with all the other ways in which the sonnets play off experience itself against the words that would inscribe it, sexual experience in the sonnets resides largely in puns. Many of the puns that Stephen Booth has caught and cataloged occur not just once, in individual sonnets, but are sustained through the whole sequence: "have" (52.14, 87.13, 110.9–2, 129.6), "use" (2.9, 4.7, 6.5, 20.14, 40.6, 48.3, 78.3, 134.10), "will" (for male and female sexual organs as well as for sexual desire: 57.13, 112.3, 134.2, 135.passim, 136.passim, 143.13, 154.9), "pride" (for penis: 64.2, 52.12, 151.9–11), and "all" (for penis, likely by analogy with "awl": 26.8, 75.9–14, 109.13–14). As heard by Booth, the couplet to sonnet 109 embodies something more substantial than sentiment:

> For nothing this wide Universe I call,
> Save thou my Rose, in it thou art my all.

(109.13–14)

"All" or "no-thing": when it comes to homosexual puns, most academic readers of Shakespeare's sonnets have insisted on the nothing. Booth gallantly tries to have it both ways, noting the possibility of homosexual double entendres but finding a metaphorical excuse for their presence. Of sonnet 98 ("From you have I beene absent in the spring') he says, for example:

> The language of this sonnet and of sonnet 99 ["The forward violet thus did I chide"] is full of unexploited relevance to sexual love .... All these senses remain dormant throughout the poem; they function only to the extent that such a concentration of potentially suggestive terms gives a vague aura of sexuality to the poem and thus ... reinforces the persistent and essential analogy Shakespeare draws between the speaker's relationship with a beloved and the traditional courtly love poet's relationship with a mistress.

Joseph Pequigney will have none of this. The sonnets to the young man trace the course of a sexually consummated love affair, Pequigney argues, and in the sexual puns of the sonnets about the young man, no less than in the sexual puns of the sonnets about the mistress, Shakespeare is talking about the psychological and anatomical realities of sexual love. As a record of a love affair, the sonnets about the young man tell a three-part story, with a beginning (sonnets 1–19, in which the poet falls in love), a middle (sonnets 20–99, in which the poet's passion "finds fruition in sexual acts"), and an end (sonnets 100–126, in which the poet's love wanes).

In this story of wooing, winning, and ruing, the diptych of sonnets 20/21 is the turning point. Sexual puns introduced in the next several sonnets continue through the one hundred twenty-five that follow. The rite of passage from sexual innocence to sexual experience is marked ceremonially in sonnet 22 ("My glass shall not persuade me I am old / So long as youth and thou are of one date"), with its exchange of hearts from one lover's breast to the other's and its echoes of St. Paul's text on man and wife as "one flesh," appointed in the *Book of Common Prayer* to be read during the marriage rite:

> For all that beauty that doth cover thee,
> Is but the seemely rayment of my heart,
> Which in thy brest doth live, as thine in me.
> How can I then be elder then thou art?

(22.5–8)

If the application of the biblical text seems metaphorical here, it persists as the subtext in all the later sonnets that imagine the friend's relations with the poet's mistress in blatantly fleshly terms, as body closing with body and shutting the poet out. The next sonnet in the sequence worries the distinction between figures of speech and things themselves until it becomes hard to say just where words give place to bodies. With its word play on "actor," "part," "fierce thing," "love's strength," and "decay," sonnet 23 makes us see how being (1) an actor in the theater, (2) a player of lovers' word games, (3) a writer of poems, and (4) a performer in bed are all aspects of the same thing:

> As an unperfect actor on the stage,
> Who with his feare is put besides his part,
> Or some fierce thing repleat with too much rage,
> Whose strengths abondance weakens his owne heart;
> So I for fear of trust, forget to say,
> The perfect ceremony of loves right,
> And in mine owne loves strength seeme to decay,
> Ore-charged with burthen of mine owne loves might.

(23.1–8)

The rival poet who later emerges in sonnets 78 to 86 thus poses a threat to the persona on two fronts: sexual as well as rhetorical. The nine poems in this group are packed with sexual puns on "pen," "will," "spirit," and "pride." The rival poet finds it much easier than Shakespeare's speaker/poet/lover both to make love and to make poems out of love. Alerted by sonnet 23, a reader who is looking out for secrets should be ready by the time he gets to sonnet 26 ("Lord of my love, to whome in vassalage / Thy merrit hath my dutie strongly knit") to see the puns for penis that Booth finds in "show my wit" (26.4), "all naked" (26.8), "tottered loving" (26.11), and "show my head" (26.14). In this context, the linked pair formed by sonnets 27 ("Weary with toyle, I haste me to my bed") and 28 ("How can I then returne in happy plight / That am debard the benifit of rest?"), in which the friend's "shadow" (27.10) haunts the poet in his bed and keeps him from sleeping, figures as Shakespeare's version of Horace toiling in his dreams after Ligurinus. What emerges in the sonnets that follow immediately after 20/21 is not so much a narrative context as a rhetorical one: these poems invite us not only to read *between* the lines, to deduce the story that has inspired them, but in a quite particular way to read *within* the lines, to decode puns and so make ourselves privy to secrets – secrets that are specifically sexual.

Along with the shifts in sonnet 20 in purpose and in language comes a shift in the implied world of the poems, in the imagined setting within which the persona and his two loves, male and female, play out their drama of sexual desire. The pastoral images of the first twenty sonnets are replaced by chambers and closets (46), beds (27, 142), chests (48, 52, 65), mirrors (63, 77), and clocks (57). The delights of the *locus amoenus* give way to the confidences of the bedchamber. It is in just such a setting that we often overhear Shakespeare's persona in the confessions that succeed sonnet 20. In sonnet 27 ("Weary with toyle, I haste me to my bed") the love appears to the poet in his bed "like a jewell (hunge in ghastly night)" (27.11). The cabinet of secrets that is implicit in this conjunction of bedchamber, jewel, and the sonnet itself as secrets committed to paper is noted explicitly when the poet returns to the same scene later in the sequence. Once the persona begins to imagine his love betraying him, the love-as-jewel turns into something to be locked up, something that must be protected from theft. Setting out on a journey, the persona tells his love in sonnet 48, he carefully stowed away his valuables. But his love – "thou, to whom my jewels trifles are" [line 5] – cannot be secured so easily:

> Thee have I not lockt up in any chest,
> Save where thou art not though I feel thou art,
> Within the gentle closure of my brest,
> From whence at pleasure thou maist come and part.

(48.9–12)

The image here is like a figure–ground puzzle: it wavers between the figurative idea of the friend's image locked away in the persona's heart and the physical reality of his love enclosed in the persona's embrace. By sonnet 52 images of jewels and chests, of locking things up, have taken on specifically sexual meanings:

> So am I as the rich whose blessed key,
> Can bring him to his sweet up-locked treasure,
> The which he will not ev'ry hour survay,
> For blunting the fine point of seldome pleasure.

(52.1–4)

The jewels here may recall the persona's mental image of his love in sonnets 27 and 48, but the suggestion of appetite in the fourth line, the fear of "blunting the fine point of seldome pleasure," invites us to read the poem in graphically physical terms. The "sweet up-locked treasure" may be not so much an idealized image of his love as a very real part of his love's anatomy.

In the new imaginative space after sonnet 20, questions of public versus private take on an urgency that is absent entirely from the first nineteen poems. As early as sonnet 25 ("Let those who are in favor with their stars, / Of publike honour and proud titles boast") the poet sets up a contrast, often to be repeated, between worldly ostentation and the homely fact of the friends' love for one another. Not always is that separation between public and private felt so happily. Troubled imaginings in sonnet 36 ("Let me confesse that we two must be twaine, / Although our undivided loves are one") of a time when the poet may not "acknowledge" the friend nor the friend show "publike kindness" to the poet seem to have less to do with the young man's possibly higher social station than with "bewailed guilt" on the part of the poet – dark hints of wrongdoing that are sounded again in sonnets 88 ("With mine owne weakenesse being best acquainted, / Upon thy part I can set downe a story / Of faults conceald" [5–7]), 89 ("Say that thou didst forsake mee for some falt, / And I will comment upon that offence"), 90 ("Then hate me when thou wilt, if ever, now, / Now while the world is bent my deeds to crosse"), 112 ("Your love and pittie doth th'impression fill, / Which vulgar scandall stampt upon my brow"), 120 ("That you were once unkind be-friends mee now"), and 121 ("Tis better to be vile then vile esteemed, / When not to be, receives reproach of being").

After the persona's first avowal of sexual desire in sonnet 20, we would expect [...] a moral or legal intervention, on the part of the poet's conscience if not from some other person. Even Barnfield, for all his salacious imaginings, lays aside his illicit desires for the "higher" concerns of epic poetry – and for marriage. In Shakespeare's sonnets no such thing happens. We hear nothing about moral reservations. No thought of the law provokes fear. In the course of his self-confessions after sonnet 20 Shakespeare's speaker struggles with problems of authority, to be sure, but those problems have nothing to do with moral philosophy or the law. They concern instead authority in being the lover of another man and authority in writing about homosexual love.

The familiar, even complacent role the poet enjoys in the first nineteen sonnets ends abruptly after sonnets 20/21: to declare homosexual desire – and to *act* on it – changes everything. Conventional structures of ideology and power explode; the fragile proprieties of the first nineteen poems are shattered. In the early sonnets power is all on the persona's side. His age, his experience, above all his powers as a poet put him in command of the situation at hand. Both the sonnet as a medium and orthodox heterosexuality as the message are firmly under his control. As long as he plays the sage older friend, it is he who is doing the acting; the young friend's role is to react. Admitting his passion changes all that. "I" and "you" no longer have their comfortable separate identity. The poet who doubts his own abilities in sonnet 23 ("As an unperfect actor on the stage") is quite another person from the poet who confidently went to war with time in sonnet 15 ("When I consider every thing that growes, / Holds in perfection but a little moment"). Critics customarily speak of the young man as the poet's "friend," but the perplexed relationship described in the sonnets after 20/21 is anything but Aristotle's *philia*, with its easy mutuality between men who are equals.

Different from the first nineteen poems in the relationship they imply between speaker and listener, the love sonnets to the young man differ just as much from the sonnets about the mistress. The frustrated idealism of sonnets 20 through 126 stands in the sharpest possible contrast to the resigned cynicism of the sonnets addressed to the so-called "dark lady." Many of the latter have, indeed, something of Horace's genial urbanity about them. "Therefore I lye with her, and she with me, / And in our faults by lyes we flattered be" (138.12–14): for all their cynicism, sonnets 127 to 154 communicate a mutuality, a sensual understanding between speaker and listener, that so often is painfully not the case in sonnets 20 through 126. Shakespeare devotes 126 highly varied sonnets to the young man and only 28 alternately affable and sarcastic sonnets to the mistress for the same reason that the fourth- and fifth-century Greeks devoted so much more attention in their philosophical writings to the love between men and boys than to the love between men and women: in each case it was the bond between male and male that seemed the more complicated and problematic. Once Shakespeare's poet has declared his passion, the rhetoric of friendship no longer seems adequate. Rapture, jealousy, self-advertisement, self-denigration: the shifting moods and shifting roles of sonnets 20 through 126 run absolutely counter to Renaissance ideas of friendship. Apologists for the sonnets as testimonials to friendship have not read their Aristotle, Cicero, and Montaigne.

(From Bruce R. Smith (1994) *Homosexual Desire in Shakespeare's England: A Cultural Poetics*, Chicago: University of Chicago Press, pp.248–57)

Text 14

Helen Vendler, 'Sonnet 20' from The Art of 'Shakespeare's Sonnets'

Helen Vendler is a leading critic of poetry, who has also published studies of the work of John Keats, Wallace Stevens and Seamus Heaney. In her criticism of Shakespeare's poetry, she presents an exhaustive commentary of each sonnet in an attempt to isolate their poetic distinctiveness. Her argument also entails a broader attack on historicist criticism on the grounds that lyric poetry is primarily engaged with aesthetic rather than political concerns.

This little myth of origin arises, probably, from the idea (in sonnets 11 and 19) that Nature, as sculptor or artist, conceives a mental pattern from which she then prints or models her creatures. The charming notion that between the moment of pattern-conceiving and the moment of its fleshed accomplishment Nature could change her mind is the idea generating the sestet of the sonnet, which is offered as an explanatory myth to account for the young man's startling simultaneous possession of a man's penis and a woman's face. To the speaker, it is inconceivable that anyone could fail to fall in love with that face, even if the beholder were of the same sex as the face. "If I, a man, could fall in love with that face, even though it belongs to one of my own sex, so could Nature (a woman) also fall in love with it, even though in the original pattern it were a woman's face." By this back-formation of myth, Nature, astonished by her own success in pattern-making, conceives a same-sex attachment, so to speak; but *she* (ah, fortunate Goddess) has the power to make the body attached to the face she falls in love with of the right sex for heterosexual intercourse. "I have fallen a-doting," says Nature, "and must have this creature for my pleasure"; and so she adds, in finishing the embodiment of her best pattern in flesh, a prick for her own use. The speaker who has fallen a-doting on a face of his own sex has, alas, no such divine transformative powers.

The poem is a *jeu d'esprit*, as all such myths of origin are (how the rose became red, etc.), and its lack of inhibition is partly due to its (eventual) lightness of expression in the sestet. However, before its resolution in fancifulness, the poem vents a good deal of aggression.

The *untainted* pattern of sonnet 19 may have provoked the pure (with Nature's own hand *painted*) pattern of the master/mistress. But the octave of this poem is first a denigration of ordinary women, saying that they are, for the most part, false. The *true* pattern of woman can be discerned in the woman's face and woman's gentle heart present in the master/mistress. A hierarchy of aesthetic and moral value is established by the comparatives – *more bright* (outward), *less false* (inward).

There are some difficulties of language, notably the climactic emphasis on *hues* (line 7) and the odd *–eth* endings on verbs (*gaze, amaze*) that could apparently have ended as well in *–es*. Bizarre as it may appear, the poem seems to have been created in such a way as to have the individual letters of the word *h-e-w-s* (the Quarto spelling) or *h-u-e-s* in as many lines as possible (I have not checked all the *Sonnets*, but the random checking of a few has not turned up another sonnet of which a comparable assertion could be made). The list of available letters (not words) in each of the fourteen lines (Quarto spelling) is as follows: hews, hues, hews, hews, hews, hew[z], hews, hews, hews, hews, he[ ], hues, hews, hues (with a phonetic pun on *use*). The *h* needed for *hews* is contributed in line 8 by *amazeth*, thereby perhaps explaining the *–eth* endings. *Hew* is climactic in line 7 because it is the word by which the master/mistress controls almost all the other lines. The high proportion (2.7 percent) of *w*'s in the total of letters in this sonnet is also explicable by the necessity of making *hew* as often as possible. Though neither *hew* nor *hue* can be found complete in line 11, which contains only an *h* and an *e*, there are of course two *hew*'s in line 7, preserving the proportion of one *hew* per line, all *in his controlling*. If this anagrammatic play is in fact intended, the sonnet becomes even more fantastic than its theme suggests.

The speaker's sterile play of the master/mistress against the putative falsity of women can be explained by his anger at women for not being the young man, at the young man for not being a (sexually available) woman. Frustration summons the fantasy of not having to be frustrated, of wielding a power as strong as Nature's – and so the little myth of original tampering by Nature is fantasized into being. Though Galen thought all embryos were originally female [...], it is Shakespeare who creates the causal myth that the change to maleness in this case arises from Nature's falling in love with the projected female, and *therefore* rendering her male. Under all the play, one is only sure that the speaker, too, has fallen a-doting; and the rather bitter wit – on *acquainted* [cunt], *"one* thing"/"*no*-thing," and *prick* (Nature's joke on the speaker) – is the last flicker of the helplessness of one who cannot play fast and loose, as he would like to, with a physical body. The couplet's defiant final scission of love from intercourse will determine a good deal in the later Young Man sonnets. Once one has separated love from the act of sex, love can – indeed must – eventually stand alone, hugely politic, inhabiting the realm of the Forms. It certainly no longer inhabits the realm of the flesh, though it pervades the emotional and erotic *imaginative* life entirely.

The feminine rhymes throughout the sonnet – a unique case – have often been remarked. The Quarto spellings *rowling* and *controwling* help contribute the necessary *w*'s for *hews*.

(From Helen Vendler (1997) *The Art of 'Shakespeare's Sonnets'*, Cambridge, MA: Harvard University Press, pp.128–9)

Further Reading

The reference lists at the end of the chapters and the texts reprinted in Appendixes 1 and 2 provide a starting-point for further study of *Cymbeline* and *Shakespeare's Sonnets*.

Chapter 1

Of the critical references listed in the chapter, the most useful studies are those by Bergeron (1980), Hamilton (1992), Marcus (1988), Miola (1984), Shapiro (1994), Simonds (1992), Thompson (1991) and Warren (1998).

Further studies with informative chapters on *Cymbeline* include:

Barton, A. (1994) *Essays, Mainly Shakespearean*, Cambridge: Cambridge University Press.

French, M. (1981) *Shakespeare's Division of Experience*, New York: Ballantine Books.

Jordan, C. (1997) *Shakespeare's Monarchies: Ruler and Subject in the Romances*, Ithaca: Cornell University Press.

Palfrey, S. (1997) *Late Shakespeare: A New World of Words*, Oxford: Clarendon Press.

Warren, R. (1989) *'Cymbeline': Shakespeare in Performance*, Manchester: Manchester University Press.

Chapter 2

The best (and cheapest) single volume edition of the sonnets is Kerrigan (1986), which provides a useful introduction alongside excellent notes on each individual poem.

Jones (1977) is a good anthology of earlier sonnets criticism.

More detailed contemporary studies can be found in Dubrow (1987), Smith (1994) and Vendler (1997).

Another consideration of the sexual elements in the sonnets is given by:

De Grazia, M. (1994) 'The scandal of Shakespeare's sonnets', *Shakespeare Survey*, vol.47, pp.35–49.

Acknowledgements

Grateful acknowledgement is made to the following sources for permission to reproduce material in this book:

Appendix 1

Text

Texts 1 and 2: From *Narrative and Dramatic Sources of Shakespeare*, Volume VIII, edited by Geoffrey Bullough. Copyright © 1975 Columbia University Press/Routledge. Reprinted with the permission of the publishers; *Text 3:* Shapiro, M. (1994) *Gender in Play on the Shakespearean Stage: Boy Heroines and Female Pages*, The University of Michigan Press. Copyright © by the University of Michigan 1994; *Text 5:* Shaw, G.B. (1974) *The Bodley Head Bernard Shaw Collected Plays with their Prefaces*, Volume VII, by permission of The Society of Authors, on behalf of the Bernard Shaw Estate; *Text 6:* Copyright © 1992. From *Suffocating Mothers* by Janet Adelman. Reproduced by permission of Taylor & Francis/Routledge, Inc.; *Text 7:* Mikalachki, J. (1995) 'The masculine romance of Roman Britain: *Cymbeline* and early modern English nationalism', *Shakespeare Quarterly*, Volume 46, No. 3, Mowat, B.A. (ed.) Folger Shakespeare Library.

Appendix 2

Text

Text 3: Reprinted by permission of the publisher from *Petrarch's Lyric Poems*, translated and edited by Robert Durling, Cambridge, Mass.: Harvard University Press. Copyright © 1976 by Robert M. Durling; *Text 9:* Barrell, J. (1988) *Poetry, Language and Politics*, Manchester University Press. Copyright © 1988 Professor John Barrell; *Texts 10 and 11:* Jones, P. (ed.) *Shakespeare: The Sonnets – A Casebook*, Macmillan Press Ltd; *Text 12:* Reprinted from Heather Dubrow, *Captive Victors: Shakespeare's Narrative Poems and Sonnets*. Copyright © 1987 Cornell University Press. Used by permission of the publisher, Cornell University Press; *Text 13:* Smith, B.R. (1994) *Homosexual Desire in Shakespeare's England: A Cultural Poetics*, University of Chicago Press. Copyright © 1991, 1994 by The University of Chicago Press; *Text 14:* Reprinted by permission of the publisher from *The Art of 'Shakespeare's Sonnets'*, Helen Vendler, Cambridge, Mass.: The Belknap Press of Harvard University Press. Copyright © 1997 by the President and Fellows of Harvard College.

Index